PENGUIN BOOKS

PARENTING PLUS

ale Medical
niversity of
twelve years
er two chil-

Peggy Tinson, M.D., graduated from New York School and trained in psychiatry at the University of Pennsylvania. She practiced her specialty for twelve years before taking time off to be at home with her children. She lives with her family in Arizona.

Parenting

+PLUS+

Raising Children with
Special Health Needs

PEGGY FINSTON, M.D.

PENGUIN BOOKS

PENGUIN BOOKS
Published by the Penguin Group
Viking Penguin, a division of Penguin Books USA Inc.,
375 Hudson Street, New York, New York 10014, U.S.A.
Penguin Books Ltd, 27 Wrights Lane, London W8 5TZ, England
Penguin Books Australia Ltd, Ringwood, Victoria, Australia
Penguin Books Canada Ltd, 10 Alcorn Avenue, Suite 300,
Toronto, Ontario, Canada M4V 3B2
Penguin Books (N.Z.) Ltd, 182–190 Wairau Road,
Auckland 10, New Zealand

Penguin Books Ltd, Registered Offices:
Harmondsworth, Middlesex, England

First published in the United States of America by
Dutton, an imprint of New American Library, a division of Penguin
Books USA Inc., 1990
Published in Penguin Books 1992

1   3   5   7   9   10   8   6   4   2

THE LIBRARY OF CONGRESS HAS CATALOGUED THE HARDCOVER AS FOLLOWS:
Finston, Peggy.
Parenting plus: raising children with special health needs/
Peggy Finston. — 1st ed.
p.   cm.
Includes bibliographical references.
ISBN 0-525-24885-4 (hc.)
ISBN 0 14 01.6837 0 (pbk.)
1. Parents of handicapped children — United States.   2. Chronically ill children.
I. Title.
HQ759.913.F56   1990
649'.151—dc20   89–28527

Printed in the United States of America
Set in Garamond No. 3
Designed by Liney Li

To Mike, Danny, and Amy

Contents

Acknowledgments

Many, many families who wish to remain anonymous have freely shared their experiences and wisdom in the writing of this book. I should like to thank them. I'd also like to thank those who have made their struggles public in order to help others, including the Diffines, McGlynns, Duffys, and Jackie Cottrell. In addition, numerous people have welcomed me into their support groups and summer camps, including the Hemophilia Association, Cystic Fibrosis Association, Arthritis Foundation, and Parent Asthma Network. Organizations, including the Association of the Care of Children's Health, Pilot Partnerships of Arizona, SKIP (Sick Kids Need Involved People), Delta Society, and Phoenix Children's and St. Joseph's hospitals, have been more than generous with their resources and time. Many professionals, including James Mick, M.D., James McCarver, M.D., James Smidt, M.D., Jane Frost, R.N., Barbara McGinn, Carol Clark, Carlene Hicks, Gayla Remp, and Dody Brandt, have been similarly generous.

Also, I'd like to thank Robert Flaherty, editor of the *Over-the-Counter Review,* who has rare interest in nurturing and encouraging writers, like myself.

Preface

Half-filled cups and silver linings fell out of fashion with Pollyanna and polyester. Today we have become too sophisticated to let any undesirable event escape our attention. Television shows depicting despicable crimes entertain us while figurines and cards of grotesque characters captivate our children. For some peculiar reason, we have come to believe that we are not confronting the *big* picture unless we wallow in cynicism.

But those of us who are raising children with special health needs cannot afford to embrace the negative. We have youngsters who need us. They know they are different. They need us to show them how *not* to hate themselves for being "defective" and how *not* to hate the world for sometimes treating them this way.

Some of our children have potentially fatal conditions, such as leukemia or cystic fibrosis; others will move through life in wheelchairs from cerebral palsy or juvenile arthritis; and still others will take pills, eat special foods, administer insulin or factor VIII, and so on. Despite this diversity, we and our children all face key emotional issues together.

We parents need to get past our guilt so as not to

undermine our strength. We must also learn and teach our children how to live with being different in a world that cherishes sameness. Putting aside our sorry feelings is the first step in helping our youngsters discover what they can do for themselves. Eventually, most of them should become competent in taking care of their own health.

Regardless of our children's condition, almost all of us will have ongoing contact with professionals: doctors, nurses, and teachers. Too often these relationships degenerate into adversary proceedings. Yet we desperately need allies, not opponents. What can we do to help make the professional our partner?

And once our children leave infancy, how can we help them find friends? Prepare them for teasing? Let them take more control of their lives during adolescence?

Many professionals have observed that the disabilities and/or illnesses may not be nearly as limiting as *how* youngsters and their families handle them. Yet little has been written about the "how-tos." Instead, too much of the literature stereotypes parents or reduces their successes to statistics. What we all need to know is, How can we help our youngsters make the most of their circumstances?

We are all improvising as we go along. The reason I wrote this book was that I wanted to give myself a guide, too, along with other parents. I quickly realized that there are no ready answers for the onslaught of questions that inevitably come up. All there is, is "best bets" and hunches. Just to identify these questions during the rush of daily life is a feat in itself; yet how we handle them can make or break our children's spirit. And so many times we struggle with ourselves and our loved ones as we are yanked about by irrational feelings that we assume should have dissipated long ago. We need our goals set in front of us to navigate this rough and elusive path.

Parenting
+PLUS+

This book is about these goals and how to pursue them. What qualities do we want to foster in our children? How can we do this? And how do we nurture our family life and marriage at the same time? What I have written is intended to raise the relevant issues that affect most of us. My own experience, both personal and professional, has provided the skeleton for this work. But many parents and professionals have generously shared their victories and defeats to explain further what we all deal with and what our options can be. They gave this book flesh.

We must remember that our children are our best teachers. Their comments and behaviors will let us know what they need and what has been useful. Our challenge will be to keep our hearts and minds open.

Also, although we have a super job ahead, most of us are not super people, just people. We need to tolerate our failings rather than straitjacket ourselves into some Rock of Gibraltar role. There will be moments when we fall far short of saintly. From time to time, most of us will be burned out about putting out. Shame over these moments is useless; it will only foster our retreat. If we can accept our limitations with the same charity we accept our children's, we can go on and be there for them.

And we have to be the ones. Professionals come and go, but families stay. We all can use input from experts. But only we can figure out, over time, what makes sense for our loved ones. Please read this book, too, in that spirit.

Prologue

Years of medical education had consumed our lives, and Mike and I were more than ready for the "next step." The two of us squeezed under that taut biological wire to get in on humanity's mainstream experience: starting a family. Yet our training in psychiatry could hardly prepare us for the questions and feelings we faced.

Our first child, Danny, stopped babbling when he was a little over a year old. This is hindsight. I didn't confront the fact that there was something seriously wrong with him until six or seven months later. Also, in hindsight, my husband had his concerns much earlier.

Why does he always look away? That was what Mike would ask when he held up our infant, this floppy bundle wrapped in a receiving blanket. He'd gaze at Danny—at first gently and then, later, with a searching intensity—and watch him turn his face toward the wall. My husband would look on anxiously at the soft slope of his neck and that silky mat of brown hair.

Sometimes, Mike would try to outsmart him. He shifted his body so that he faced Danny again. Our son would manage to turn his head even farther away from us. Am I too close? Mike would wonder out loud.

Nothing could be wrong. That had been my automatic response. His questions assailed my postpartum bliss. Danny was nursing well and sleeping comfortably. What more could you expect from a three-month-old? Unfortunately, I didn't know, and I didn't know that I didn't know.

Mike was especially worried because he had witnessed my cesarean section. While I was floating away from the anesthetic vapors, our firstborn came out smoky blue with an Apgar of 3, indicating a serious lack of oxygen. This increased only to 5 after five minutes. The Apgar is a measure of neonatal health; a score between 8 and 10 is considered good.

I hadn't planned to be "out" for his birth. We had wanted a spinal. But the anesthesiologist—a bald, moon-faced man—was losing his patience. He had repeatedly plunged the needle into my back, each time more frantically. He claimed I was too heavy to get it positioned correctly. There were fifty extra pounds of me. Big deal, I thought, as he pushed the black rubber mask against my nose and mouth. I can skip this part and let them do the work.

Of course, later, I cursed myself and my unrestrained gluttony. If I had been thinner, the anesthesiologist could have inserted that needle. When I thought about it, which I tried not to do, I felt I had failed to provide my baby with a safe entry into this life.

But Danny was beautiful. For three years, we had tried to have a child and finally succeeded. I was ready to give him a universe of nurturing, with no questions asked. Everything had to be fine, or some other term intended to quell those unseen anxieties.

Mike told me his concern: infants born with low Apgars are at risk for neurological damage. I couldn't listen. Now I realize that I felt too guilty. A silent battle began between us—Mike's perplexed looks and my all-too-ready explanations.

But no one can run away from this kind of truth for too long.

First, there was the play group that took place in a neighbor's basement. Three chirping toddlers would be falling over toys and each other. Occasionally, they would tramp off, but quickly return to the comforting gaze of their mothers. Not my son. Danny would crawl with a frightening fury completely out of sight—up the stairs or into closets. I would dash out of the room every few minutes and search. Was I doing something "wrong" to cause my son to behave in this way? No, I would tell myself, he's just independent, that's all.

And more painful comparisons. Like many parents, I initially found reasons to obliterate these from my vision. I routinely used to go to a park and meet a certain mother. Like me, she had cut down to a part-time career to spend those first few years at home. We were also both on the other side of thirty-five and our children were only three months apart. But they were different.

I would watch her daughter point and gesture to my friend about what seemed like every conceivable decision. Should she go on the slide, across the sandbox, or over to the swing? Meanwhile, Danny would be running about in a frenzied silence. I'd follow—trying to catch him and his gaze—and attempt to do something together. Any mutual activity would have done—tossing pebbles or singing "horsie" as he bobbed on one of those spring metal ducks or fishes.

"Susan," my friend would call. The girl would immedi

ately scamper over. But Danny would wander when I called, sometimes off into the street. I'd panic, call louder, but he would keep on going, without a pause to his incessant motion.

Maybe I wasn't being firm enough, a professional friend casually suggested. Maybe he was just too balky, too soon, I thought. But nothing could be wrong with my baby.

My pediatrician confirmed this. "He listens better than my kid," he answered after I mentioned my observation.

But Danny doesn't say any words, and his friends do, I persisted. The doctor replied that Einstein didn't talk until he was five. (I have since learned from my research that if you are concerned about your child being developmentally delayed or worse, you are almost inevitably going to hear about Einstein and his woes.)

Was it significant that Danny's percentile of weight had dropped from 25 percent to 10 percent on the growth chart? Again, my pediatrician did not want me to worry. "It's just that he's such an active fellow, aren't you?" he asked my son whom I now remember writhing in my straitjacket-like arms. I had started holding him like this to keep him from tearing places apart—including the drawers, medical equipment, and other untouchables found in doctors' offices.

In supermarkets, I noticed other toddlers sitting contentedly in shopping-cart seats, often scrutinizing their mothers' faces. The women would effortlessly push their children from the tomatoes to the lettuce, and even leave them momentarily to grab a bag of apples. But Danny couldn't handle that. His body would jerk around in unpredictable rhythms Nothing seemed to calm him. I took to wearing him in the Gerry carrier on my back. But I wasn't ready, yet, to ask myself why this extra measure was necessary. I just did it.

Other things happened that stymied Mike and me and sapped us of energy. We both became ill with a "flu" that didn't go away. I eventually had to give up my practice of psychiatry because of fatigue. Mike barely dragged himself to work each day and would collapse when he returned home.

During the following year of sustained illness, I was reassured by other well-meaning physicians that there was no physical basis for our muscle aches, memory loss, and headaches. My internist said I had postviral "blahs" that should eventually end. Researchers I called at the National Institutes of Health could not add to that. A professor of toxicology Mike contacted at the University of Pennsylvania assured us that if we were being poisoned by something in our environment, everyone on our street would be sick. At this same time, we also saw Danny's face turn pasty white, saw darkening rings encircle his eyes.

Another friend, who was a child psychologist, inquired why Danny had stopped making noises. I don't remember what I said, but it was something that effectively dismissed her concern. I was lucky: She had the courage to say it again a few weeks later. I listened.

We took Danny to a variety of professionals in search of an answer. A psychologist initially thought that he could be autistic. A child analyst told us to give him autonomy. The third professional, part of a nationally known group, said he was developmentally delayed.

That label, like some other medical labels, only describes what is already clinically observable. It doesn't tell you why this is happening, how to correct it, and what the future holds. Even so, the words helped. The chronic debate that had been festering between Mike and me dissolved. The problem was out in the open and we were confronting it together.

All three experts had assured us that we weren't causing Danny's difficulty. We needed to hear that. Mike had imagined that he was somehow scaring this baby. I wondered whether I was capable of giving him what he needed—whatever that was.

The professionals thought that the lack of oxygen might have been the cause. I couldn't accept that, not only because I felt responsible but also because I had not personally witnessed his blueness at birth. There had to be some problem that could be fixed. As if turned out, my denial or persistence, whichever you want to call it, was my ally.

It was one of those Sunday mornings after breakfast. Danny, now almost two and a half, was thrashing about the living room, Mike was propped up on the couch mindlessly turning the pages of one section of the *Philadelphia Enquirer,* and I was sprawled out on the rug, staring blankly at advertisements in the magazine supplement. We were both too sick to read, but kept up this ritual of living until one o'clock nap time arrived.

Then I spotted an article about how pollution can assault the immune system and make people sensitive to substances in their environment, including common organic solvents and foods. These sensitivities can result in skin rashes, joint pains, nausea, diarrhea, mental symptoms, and a host of other maladies that can't be verified by either physical examination or standard laboratory tests. As a result, the illness was not, and still isn't, recognized by most physicians. The adults described in the article sounded like my husband and me. The child could have been Danny.

Once we started talking about our suspicions, we learned that three of our acquaintances (an accountant, a baby-sitter, and a colleague) were also ill with a similar undiagnosed condition. Each of them experienced temporary relief by visiting unindustrialized areas (Florida, Nova Scotia, Greece). We were encouraged by their reports.

It took the following six months to verify that this, in fact, was our problem. Four trips to unpolluted places allowed Mike and me to feel like our old selves again. Danny, for the first time, could make eye contact and stay still. On one trip, he sat contentedly at a table, playing with clay for two solid hours. Relapses shortly after each of our returns convinced us we had to move. But we were elated. The allergies that had interfered with my son's bonding and development could be controlled. My fat belly was not at fault, after all.

That was over five years ago. We have been fortunate. We packed up and left, sold our house, and moved to a clean-air rural community. I found a doctor who put all of us on a rotary diversified diet, in which we eliminate certain foods (dairy products, wheat, corn, sugar, chocolate, and food dyes) and rotate the remaining grains, protein, oils, fruits, and vegetables every four days. My daughter, Amy, born five years ago, has similar sensitivities. She has been with this program since birth and has bypassed some of her brother's developmental problems. And Danny, with the help of some dedicated preschool teachers, has caught up socially. Also, as long as he sticks to his diet, he is normal physically except for monthly earaches.

The end of this story is happy, and yet, in some ways, the challenge has just begun. My control over my children's behavior, including what morsels they put in their mouths, is inevitably waning, as it should be. Now, their shot at "normality" will increasingly depend on *them* and how well *they* accept this diet. How can I foster this acceptance? How can I lessen their embarrassment about their special foods? And how can I undercut their sense of deprivation, which leads to anger and isolation?

Of course, my answers, like those of other parents, keep changing with time and circumstances. And how creative we all must be with our solutions to try and keep them satisfied. But the other day, my son noticed something that made me feel I've been stumbling along on the right path.

Both Danny and Amy will occasionally tell me how they

wish they could have Snickers, ice-cream cones, Red Hots, and all the other nos. Their sweets consist of the wheat-free, milk-free, sugar-free, red dye–free snacks I can make or buy (they do exist). The three of us had been getting some nuts at our local health-food store. Later, my son said that while I was paying for our purchase, he saw a little girl crying. The reason, which both he and Amy thought was "totally awesome," was that her mother said she couldn't have a fruit leather today, one of our snacks. Danny remarked, "She was really crying over a fruit leather. And we can have that all the time."

What happened to us is not unusual. Many mothers and fathers face the reality of an illness at their own tempo. Many go through a number of professionals before they find a correct diagnosis and treatment. And we all have had our moments of desperation and elation. For this reason, I have drawn freely on my experiences and those of other parents to write about raising our children.

1. Don't Ask "What Did I Do Wrong?"

But We Can't Help Ourselves

So many of us embrace the role of mother and father with the idea of being perfect protectors of those we bring into this world. A child's chronic illness or disability dashes away that naïve, but comforting fantasy. It seems only natural to ask ourselves why and how we could have prevented it, which is the same thing as asking what we did wrong.

Once Mike and I understood what had caused our son's problems, we felt compelled to identify how we might have contributed to them. I was the one who fell in love with our house, situated only 500 yards from the city's major artery. The 300,000 cars that sputtered down this superhighway each day produced foul fumes that were intolerable for Danny—and for both of us, too, for that matter. Mike pointed out how he had enthusiastically applied the latest energy conservation methods to our home. Our cozy nest became a "tight building" in which insufficient air exchange was causing nausea, headaches, and fatigue. This overload of pollutants had evidently sensitized all of us to certain foods, too. And it had taken me so long to recognize Danny's difficulties.

Was this too much self-recrimination? I think so. But the guilt that parents feel is often unfair, frequently irrational, and yet particularly compelling. Can you see yourself in any of the following examples?

WE CAUSED IT

Many of us manage to find ways to implicate ourselves for whatever happened. Mothers will scrutinize their pregnancy and subsequent care of their child. One woman believes her infant's kidney tumor was caused by the melanoma she had removed during her pregnancy. Another says that her teenager's crippling arthritis was due to the many antibiotics she allowed her daughter to have when she was younger. These mothers are convinced, despite their doctors' reassurance to the contrary.

Both parents may investigate their family trees. Did they pass on the responsible genes? One father believed that his year-old son's unexplained distress must be his fault: He had a cousin who died from cystic fibrosis and he believed that that must be the problem. "I was finally off the hook when we found out he had epilepsy."

Sometimes the blame does belong to heredity. Don, who has asthma, recalls: "We tried to do everything perfectly—the Lamaze method of birth and then my former wife followed the Adelle Davis diet. When both boys ended up with asthma, we felt we had given them a legacy of allergies." A mother who, like her daughter, has asthma does not blame herself for her daughter's heart defect. "I only drank an occasional wine cooler while pregnant and I did not take my concerns about that seriously. But I feel massive guilt about her asthma because I passed that on to her." These parents are well aware that they do not control their genes, but they still feel responsible for having them.

Self-blame can be especially intense when there is a known genetic transmission and a parent makes an informed choice. "I didn't feel too badly when my first daughter was born with PKU [phenylketonuria]," recalls one mother. "I didn't know I was a carrier and at that time, the diet was advised only for the first six years. Then we had our second child and he turned out to have PKU. The diet is now recommended into adulthood. That hit me much harder."

Also, like Mike and me, many parents believe that certain choices they made may have contributed to the illness or disability. One father of a baby with Down's syndrome was working in a hospital that had poorly controlled ethylene oxide levels. A mother of a child with epilepsy recalls, "We traced the problem to his birth. I had a C-section and he didn't have enough oxygen with the anesthesia. Things might have been different if I had gone to another doctor."

WE DIDN'T CAUSE IT, BUT WE BLAME OURSELVES FOR BEING A PART OF IT

Just being a witness to an unfortunate event lends itself to the soul-searching question: What was my part? Our children's vulnerability and dependence on us intensify this guilt by association. Some parents are quite clear that their youngster's condition did not come about through their inadvertent choices, negligence, or genetic makeup. Yet they feel accountable.

Sherry prided herself on getting the very best diaper service for her two-year-old daughter. One day, the laundry failed to remove a bleach. The chemical reacted with the child's urine to give her third-degree burns necessitating hospitalization. She asks herself, "When your child is lying there helpless, who else is there to blame?"

WE GAVE UP ON HER

Detachment is far from our fantasies of parenthood. And certainly most outsiders could not imagine that either, preferring to think of parents as unrelentingly heroic. Yet enough of us live through these moments of desperation. We can have so much guilt about these wishes that we feel we can't talk about them. But still it's worth trying.

At one parents' meeting, a father described how he felt when he learned his newborn with Down's syndrome also had a heart defect. "I was sure that this baby was going to die. I picked out a plot and asked my wife whether she wanted to bury the body or have it cremated because cremating doesn't cost anything for children under three."

This man's courage in sharing inspired similar admissions. Was he heartless? No. He was trying to deal with the pain of loss by taking a tiny bit of control over it.

Frank Deford describes this process in *Alex: The Life of a Child*. He recalls when he first learned his infant daughter had cystic fibrosis:

> I didn't know Alex yet. She was still so young and, of course, she had always been sick. I guess that was the blessing. What frightened me was that she *would* survive this, and then I would get to know her, and then she would die and hurt me. That scared me more than the possibility that she would die immediately. I remember lying in the bed next to Carol that night, talking about this, about what we would do if Alex

died. That would be God's will. If she lived to die some other time, it would be my distress. I fell off to sleep praying that God's will be done.[1]

WE DIDN'T SEE THE PROBLEM SOONER

In the beginning, many of us discount the "little" signs that threaten to disrupt our trust in our child's future. We cling to the hope that he will outgrow the problem and latch on to this reassurance when it is offered by others. That was a large part of my guilt and of others to whom I have talked. Adelle has a two-year-old boy with agranulocytosis, a rare blood disorder. She says, "I should have listened to my instincts sooner. I was continually asking why my son always had boils on his chin and severe skin rashes and I wasn't getting good answers."

WE DIDN'T OR AREN'T TAKING GOOD ENOUGH CARE OF HIM

"You are never really comfortable. You always worry and ask yourself, Am I doing my best?" says Sally, whose son has a heart defect.

Many of us long to take charge of our child's treatment. It gives us a sense of mastery and reaffirms our role as protectors. But the day-to-day management of a child's illness is fraught with ambiguities. It is a balancing act in which we weigh the importance of several competing interests.

In *Journey,* by Robert and Suzanne Massie, Suzanne Massie describes raising her son, who has hemophilia. "It was not simply enough to say Don't do this and Don't do that, because sometimes, whether he 'did' anything or not, he would bleed. Other times, when he was more active than usual, inexplicably *nothing happened.* One day, walking around the house was enough to cause bleeding; the next day he would fall down a flight of stairs and there would hardly be a bruise. So we often guessed wrong, and when we did there was no one to blame but ourselves."[2]

We seek the least restrictive life that will protect our children, but what is that? For me, the question translates into whether Danny and Amy can "get away with" eating eggs at an Easter Egg hunt at school. The mother of a girl with asthma wonders if her daughter can join her friends outside on a windy day. The father of a boy with hemophilia questions whether he can roughhouse with his son. We want them to participate.

We also want to avoid friction. How much do we need to enforce treatment when that conflicts with what they want? Do we insist that our son with diabetes clean his plate when he insists he's not hungry? Or that our daughter with cystic fibrosis have her treatment even though she is almost out the door to visit her friend? What exactly is worth the struggle of wills and what is worth forgetting?

And then there is money. Karen, a single parent, is striving to support her three sons. One of them has diabetes. "I wonder when I buy the cheaper cuts, is that meat lean enough?" Carmen prematurely put her infant son on whole milk. "I wanted to cut our food bill. Later, we learned he had a milk allergy. I feel if I hadn't been so quick, maybe he wouldn't have that problem."

Every day, we must make decisions about our child's health without the benefit of sufficient information. The fact is that we don't know, and doctors can't tell us about many of these questions. We can only try. Sometimes we make the wrong choice and feel guilty.

WE CAN'T PROTECT HER FROM THE PAIN SHE FEELS

We realize that despite our wishes, we are unable to shield our children from so much. It may be the physical pain of the condition, or the treatment, for that matter. Parents of those who have been hospitalized feel this acutely. They are angry at doctors and nurses for not being more sensitive and angry at the IVs, blood tests, and X rays that are inflicted on their youngsters. And they are also angry at themselves. They have to stand there and let it happen.

Sally's son was operated on for a heart defect when he was two. "I was there for him, but I couldn't prepare him for this. Many times I wanted to pick him up and flee, rather than have him go through another procedure." Martha's four-year-old daughter needed chemotherapy spinal injections for leukemia. "They were torture. I'd see her struggle on the table and in a crazy way I felt glad that she just wasn't taking it, even though I knew she needed the medicine."

Of course, parents may not be as helpless as they think about some issues (see Chapter 6, "Make the Professional Your Partner"). But none of us starts out smart, knowing what's negotiable. Mary Jo, whose son has had multiple hospital admissions for asthma, says, "I had no control when they tried to get an IV in over and over again. It took several times before I asked whether this was really necessary. When you don't know what's going on, it is hard to ask good questions."

Also, our children look to us to keep them safe. When they go through the trials of treatment, they can easily judge us as having failed them. Some of us will not be completely impervious to this verdict. Our guilt will be reinforced.

Younger children will communicate blame indirectly. But their message usually is not lost. Sally recalls that after surgery, her son no longer trusted her or her husband. "For the first few months, he did not want to leave home. If I said, 'Let's go out for ice cream,' he wouldn't believe me. He refused to get in the car and repeated, 'No. Home.'" My own son put in a request for another mother after going through a series of painful allergy tests.

Barry, an adult with hemophilia, recalls, "I blamed my

mom. I knew intellectually it was not her fault, but when you are seven or eight and your knee is five times what it should be and hurting, you don't think. I never talked about it with her and I wish I had."

We also cannot protect our children from the emotional pain that they suffer as a result of the illness or disability. This may be the struggle to maintain friends, fears about dating, and the uncertainty of their adulthood. We will deal with these topics in later chapters.

WE ARE NEGLECTING OUR OTHER CHILDREN

The fact is, often we are, but it's beyond our control. It seems both natural and reasonable for parents to become centered on the child who is ill or disabled. Denise's daughter has severe asthma and a heart defect, and her son has felt the loss. "It's taken lots of energy to keep Erica alive," says Denise. "Certain times I have to be up every two hours around the clock to keep her out of the hospital and then if she's been in the hospital I have to give her those treatments for about a week afterward. It bothers Thomas the most because we used to do so many things together, like go to the park. If we plan something, it always seems that something comes up with my daughter that interferes with that." In Chapter 2, we will talk more about how parents can help their other children.

OTHERS BLAME US TOO

It is a distressing experience: We already feel guilty and then talk to someone who also blames us. This message can come from a relative, a friend, or a stranger. If asked, these guilt stimulators might describe themselves as "trying to be helpful." Nonetheless, their words assault us because we are already so vulnerable.

Inquiries such as, "Why didn't you know something was wrong sooner?" and "Are you sure he's a good doctor?" amply communicate that our competence is being questioned. And then the unsolicited advice. My park "friend" watched how I literally had to catch Danny before he ran into the street and force him to look at me. Then I would tell him as firmly as I could that he must come when I said, "Come here." I even tried to practice this with him. Later, she stopped meeting with me, saying that my "technique" upset her. If her child had that problem, she let me know, she would certainly handle it much better. At the time, I was stung by her reaction because of my guilt; evidently I was using the wrong technique, and had no idea what the right one might be.

Guilt can also be aroused by our contact with professionals, who may unintentionally provoke it. Sometimes, just the questioning during a medical interview can aggravate this feeling, especially before the diagnosis is known. We may indict ourselves with each answer. Once the condition has been identified, we may squirm in response to the doctor's inquiry, worrying whether we are being careful enough with our child's treatment.

Contact with nurses and physical therapists involved with home-based services can also stimulate guilt feelings. Susan Duffy, one of the authors of *Acceptance Is Only the First Battle*, has a daughter with Down's syndrome and gastrointestinal anomalies.[3] She describes how these home-based services teach parents to become their child's best teacher. But there is a potential downside to this role. Parents may blame themselves for their youngster's lack of progress. Even if he is progressing, parents may still feel too culpable to set realistic limits of what they can and can't do. A professional may either help or hinder them in this task by her reaction.

"We were lucky," Duffy says. "We had a home trainer who told us, 'Your kid is doing great. Take a break.' She knew we needed praise for our daughter and we also needed praise for ourselves. On the other hand, my friend's trainer told her, 'Your kid is doing great with these four programs. How about adding a fifth?' You need someone to give you permission to take time off and set priorities about which programs are most important."

But sometimes the guilt imparted by professionals is intentional. It may come from their belief that our child's problem is psychological. In the book *Parents Speak Out,* John Gallagher describes how physicians and nurses implied that he and his wife were responsible for their son's asthma. "We spent many hours being interviewed and questioned with the obvious purpose of seeing if we were, in some fashion, precipitating the attacks of our child through our own anxieties and problems."[4] Not too long ago, mothers who had children with autism were similarly accused of being defective nurturers.

Professionals can also blame from unwarranted personal prejudice. Sherry, whose daughter had been burned from improperly treated diapers, eventually sued the diaper service. "But the lawyers interrogated us about our personal hygiene. That compounded my guilt. The interns and residents stared when they visited my daughter in the hospital and asked me critical questions like, 'Do you keep a clean home?' I felt compelled to let them know that I had not abused her and that we had a dream house."

Professionals may sometimes stimulate guilt when we, the parents, disagree with their recommendation. Although they are experts, they may not necessarily know what's best for *our* child (see Chapter 6). Linda Diffine's thirteen-year-old daughter has a degenerative muscular disease. This mother, who is president of the Arizona chapter of SKIP (Sick Kids Need Involved People), explains, "Professionals lay guilt about some decisions we have to make. Renée has scoliosis and they say she needs back surgery. That would mean hospitalization for many months, and at the end, she would lose all her muscle tone. She will have a short life anyway and taking a year out for that would be a big piece. Renée agrees. The problem is that some professionals feel that we are compromising her."

WE FEEL SHAME

Shame is different from guilt. Shame is not that we caused the problem, but that we are defective for having created it. The result is that we want to hide. In an age in which good health is considered a virtue, lack of it in ourselves or our offspring can almost be a disgrace.

Becky found out that she was a carrier for fragile X, which results in mental retardation. Her discovery came after their fourth child. "We both have master's degrees and we had everything going for us, and look what happened. Our middle child is incredibly bright and my husband is so intelligent. Now look what he has to live with."

Shame can also be stimulated through our contact with others. A father says he delayed taking his daughter to the emergency room for her frequent asthma attacks. "You don't want to be identified as 'Here they come again' and you wonder whether you did the right thing because you were afraid of a little embarrassment."

Guilt Has Many Teachers

We sense guilt, we buckle under its weight, and yet its boundaries and substance elude us. This is because we absorb guilt from so many different sources. And while some of these guilts dominate our awareness, others lurk in our unconscious. Nonetheless, all these themes can resonate with one another, like the background strings of an orchestra, to make us feel like unworthy parents.

OUR SEXUAL STEREOTYPES

These gender prescriptions surround us, despite the cultural upheaval of the past twenty years. Mothers are supposed to be all there, all the time. But we can't be. Nobody can. Yet the question nags at us, "Shouldn't we at least try?" Look through the back issues of most women's magazines and you'll find some survey proving that the kids of working moms do just as well as those of the stay-at-homes. We are still trying to dismantle the earth-mother ideal that accuses us.

Mothers of children with special health needs can feel this dictum to be there, all the time, even more intensely. There are so many more instances in which we can't provide that mythical total nurturance. We can't kiss it and make it better.

Other gender stereotypes assault fathers. So much of their role is tied up with asserting control at home and at work. They can't succeed, either, but the expectation is still there. The macho heroes who stalk movie screens are defining, even if caricatured, what we want from a "real" man. But many a real father has told me how guilty he felt for "allowing" some tragedy to happen to his child. Grant Oyler's son had AIDS. Oyler said to his wife, "I get so scared. And so mad. Because Ben's dying and there's not one single thing I can do about it. Do you know what that does to my insides? My whole life my dad did everything for us. No matter what went wrong, he'd fix it. And when my son really needs me, I can't do anything."[5]

Although these roles may be unfulfillable, they can still wield sufficient power to generate guilt.

OUR MORAL/RELIGIOUS VALUES

While some moral guilt inspires us to be better people, too much can undermine our confidence and self-esteem. Our judgment about ourselves may spring from the rigid, simplistic teachings of childhood, unmodified by adult thinking. For example, parents may sometimes take a youngster's condition as a sign of punishment: I must have been bad for this to have happened. A mother who gave birth to a son with cerebral palsy said, "For the first six months, I was convinced I must have done something terrible. I even went back to my teenage years when I was promiscuous, thinking that was the reason."

The corollary to this is: If you are good, only good things will happen. This thinking exasperates Dorothy, who is a nurse and a devout Baptist. She also has had disfiguring rheumatoid arthritis since her late teens. "I find it grating when religious people link health with the spirit. Yes, there are some verses that suggest that if you are a good person you will be prosperous and healthy. But I think that is taking a portion of the Scriptures and jumping on it."

Instead of drawing strength from religious beliefs, we may sometimes unwittingly use them to drag ourselves down. None of us can afford to do this.

OUR FAMILY STANDARDS

We may also absorb guilt from our upbringing. The stereotype Jewish mother or father knows no ethnic or racial boundaries. Certain folks just can't be satisfied; and as parents, their children are left with a legacy of guilt and anger for not pleasing them. As grown-ups, they generally see themselves as failures. They have not measured up to their parents' standards, whatever they are: beauty, intelligence, wealth, and so on. If they then go on to have their own children who have medical problems, these youngsters become another sign of failure. They have produced a less-than-perfect offspring.

Parents may collect guilt by falling short of cultural, religious, and family standards. We have not fulfilled certain ideals of earth mother and powerful protector. Our child's problems are a sign that God has abandoned us. And, as a measure of our personal inadequacy, we have created a "damaged" human being. While this thinking is upsetting, it usually does lie within our awareness. It is unfair, but we can talk about it.

But there are other guilts that are far more insidious, because they hide from us.

OUR HIDDEN ANGER, ESPECIALLY TOWARD A CHILD WITH PROBLEMS

Psychoanalytic theory explains how repressed anger hurts us. Basically, people have hostility that they can't admit, usually because they would judge themselves as less worthy for having felt it. Although it is unexpressed, the feeling does not go away. The bearer of unconscious wrath senses he has tucked it away somewhere and punishes himself accordingly. The anger is transformed into guilt that can lead to an unending penance.

Parents of children with special health needs are subject to this kind of guilt. The anger that we cannot face may be the anger we feel toward our child. Helen Featherstone, in *A Difference in the Family*, deals with this issue:

Certain kinds of anger can be exceedingly upsetting. Rereading a draft of this chapter, I realized with a shock that I had not even mentioned the fact that parents may feel angry at their own disabled child. Experience has taught me that such omissions usually mean something. But what? . . . I realize that, often

as I scold my able-bodied daughters, I am rarely vo-
cally or consciously angry with my severely disabled
son. Rationally this makes sense. . . . Nevertheless, he
can be a pain in the neck. . . . Turning from my own
responses to the writings of others, I find a similar
void.[6]

What kind of parent feels anger toward a child who already
has problems? Certainly not the parent we want to be. Our
hostility, if we dare recognize it, can be felt as a further mark
of our inadequacy. And even if we know we feel it, who
would be able to listen to our confession without judging?
Not many.

I discovered the extent of my own anger five years after
the fact. Like most toddlers, Danny used to fall and cry. But
when I tried to comfort him, he would push me away. It
didn't matter what I said or did. Always the little hands would
press against my chest and face. My guts told me to go on
hugging. I later learned that my instincts had been right. But
at the time, I felt deficient as a mother and, yes, I must have
been angry with him for making me feel that way. I buried
this. After all, he couldn't help what he was doing.

Then, in 1987, long after Danny's social recovery, I was
giving a talk at the annual Arizona SKIP Meeting. The topic
was "Coping with Childhood Illness," and I had breezed
through some of the misguided clichés about coping, how
we can help our kids to cope, and was now into what parents
can do for themselves. I mentioned what seemed like a
straightforward statement: what was most painful for me. I
recalled the frustration I felt toward Danny for something
totally beyond his control. I started to cry up there on the
podium. I didn't know how angry I felt until then or how
long I had carried the guilt about that with me.

What should be comforting for us to realize is that this

anger generally springs not from hating our child, but from hating the consequences of her illness or disability. It may be the sense of vulnerability her condition arouses in us, the profound change in life-style, or her limitations, for that matter. And sometimes we may have an awareness of some negative feelings. Jill, a family counselor, adopted a girl with Down's. She acknowledges that she feels most guilty when she is impatient. "There are times, like going out the front door, that I'd like to see my daughter do things faster even though I know she can't."

Anger can also come from our sense of helplessness. Another mother's infant daughter was mostly inconsolable because of epilepsy. "We tried everything we could to comfort this baby who screamed all night. I was so exhausted I felt like strangling her. But what kind of a monster could be mad at a kid who's sick?"

The power of this anger and the guilt it induces lie in the fact that it is hidden. We run from the anger because we secretly fear that we are unable to love our child. This is not true for most of us.

But there is another kind of guilt to which parents are subject. It is even more unfair and also more irrational. For this reason, we find it difficult to articulate to ourselves and feel foolish admitting it to others. It knows no culture, age, or sex, and assaults our self-esteem. This is the guilt that springs from our latent feelings of omnipotence.

OUR MISGUIDED SENSE OF POWER

As children, we use what is called egocentric or magical thinking. We see ourselves at the center of the universe and our parents and significant others as revolving around *us*. But this exalted position brings with it impossible responsibilities. Everything that happens, both good and bad, lands on our shoulders.

Luckily, the hard knocks on the playground, and life for that matter, chip away at this self-centeredness. This process starts when we are four or five and continues in a more refined manner well into adulthood. On the downside, we learn that we are not omnipotent and cannot effect as many changes as we would like. Some call this mid-life blues or the "Big Chill," after the movie. But there's a plus, too, to this enlightenment. We learn that we are not responsible for most of the calamities around us. And that's good to know.

Crisis changes that. Our adult thinking slips away or regresses, usually without our awareness. We return to that self-centered spot where we are supposed to be able to control everything. Our inevitable failure can bring a tragic kind of guilt.

I use the word *tragic* because this particular guilt pervades the thinking of victims, the people who least need it. Concentration camp survivors, women who have been raped, and those who have lost a loved one through death are just a few examples. These people are often plagued by an irrational sense that there was something they could have done differently to prevent whatever happened. Joseph Wambaugh's nonfiction book *The Onion Field* chronicles a police officer's guilt and emotional deterioration after he helplessly watches the execution of his partner.[7]

Parents can also tread in a swamp of undeserved blame. How many of us, in recounting stories about our children, also share our collection of "What-if-I-didn'ts?" Behind these observations sneaks the wish, "Had I done this differently, I could have avoided what happened."

Unfortunately, society—that is, those with whom we come in contact—can reinforce this irrational guilt. "Couldn't they fight back?" is a common enough complaint lodged against those who finished their lives at Auschwitz and other such death camps. And rape? We're still in the dark ages of empathy. A recent survey presented mock rape scenarios to college students and found that nearly two-thirds believed that the victim was at least in part to blame. Eugenia Gerdes, the Bucknell psychology professor who designed this study, explained, "Just the fact that they are willing to suggest things the woman might have done to provoke the rape, even when the defendant was clearly guilty, shows that people still fail to understand rape as a violent crime."[8] The police officer in *The Onion Field* was shunned and shamed by his peers for not preventing his partner's death. And I have already mentioned how we parents may come in contact with guilt-stimulating friends, relatives, and professionals. But the question here is *why?* Why do people readily assume this irrational guilt? Why do we continue to believe that we could have prevented whatever happened? And for that matter, why are others so eager to reinforce this?

The answer is simple, and yet binding. Guilt restores our sense of order and, therefore, is a reassurance in a senseless world. This feeling provides us with a reason for the event— a clear cause and effect—and this makes us feel less vulnerable. If we are ultimately responsible, we can be masters of our fate in the future, if not the present. When we find something wrong that we did last time, we can keep it from happening again. Likewise, those who know of our misfortune can instruct themselves on how to avoid it for themselves.

For example, Martha told me that she was convinced that her daughter contracted leukemia because she and her husband had taken a one-month missionary trip the year that the diagnosis was made. "It was difficult leaving the kids, but I felt we needed it for our marriage. Heather was only two and not old enough to understand. She must have thought that we died. I think this stress caused her cancer. Now, I sometimes think of separating from my husband, but I won't because I'm afraid my daughter will get sick again."

The impulse to explain is irresistible and often defies fact.

Few physicians would agree with Martha's explanation. But now this mother feels she has a way to keep her daughter healthy. And she is in good company. A recent study of parents whose children had leukemia showed these kinds of private, nonscientific theories to be quite common.[9]

Guilt that gives the illusion of control is powerful among parents. After all, it reduces our anxiety. But, of course, the drawback is that this feeling accuses us and is a terrible burden. Laura's daughter was in her first year of college when she was discovered to have a brain tumor. The mother recalls, "Everyone told me not to feel guilty, but it plagued me for the next year and a half. Finally, I realized that if I believed I caused it, I could do something to make it go away. My guilt gave me a sense of control and that's why I couldn't let go of it. But I wish someone could have told me why."

Guilt Has Staying Power

The guilt that most of us feel is complicated, but generally has little to do with the reality of our child's condition. The feeling usually does not spring from the facts of what we did or did not do. As a result, our discovery of other facts probably will not exonerate us.

For the same reason, others' telling us "It's not your fault" is often ineffective. But when we fail to shake our self-accusations after some well-intentioned advice, we may begin to feel guilty about feeling guilty. This becomes another sign of failure.

We can spare ourselves some agony by realizing that this guilt is *not* readily dismissed. It's not something anyone can be talked out of. And even when the feeling leaves, it frequently returns, especially when our child's condition is worsening.

Uncovering Hidden Guilt

The most harmful guilt is that which is hidden. We can bury this feeling underground, far away from the light of fairness and reason. When we do this, we never have the opportunity to evaluate it ourselves or subject it to the scrutiny of others. Denying guilt thrusts us that much more into the grip of it.

People turn away from their guilt generally because they see it as an additional failure. They believe that they should be above it. One father insisted that he didn't blame himself for his daughter's diabetes. He knew better because he had worked in health care for twenty years. Later, he added, "I searched our family tree for who might have given it to her and it didn't come from my side."

Here are some signs of hidden guilt.

Continuing to look for explanations when there are none. We may do this to exonerate ourselves. A mother has a child with a genetic metabolic defect. She admits in a parents' group, "I didn't do anything wrong in my pregnancy so I don't feel responsible. But I keep asking why and searching for something that might have been in our environment."

Unnecessarily apologizing for or explaining our child. A mother of a small boy with developmental delays says, "I feel I have to explain to everyone who comes across Jason what is wrong. If they say he's bright, then I feel compelled to correct them and let them know he's probably older than they think. This doesn't make any sense."

Overprotecting our child. This cliché is frequently applied to parents of children with special health needs. Most of the people I talked to overprotect, if you want to call it that, out of anxiety. Their youngsters have life-threatening conditions. But there are a few parents whose guilt leads them to do far too much. One mother has a teenager with diabetes and is still preparing all her foods. "I wanted to make her happy and so I did it all for her. Now she won't let me stop." (See Chapter 3.)

Depriving ourselves. Balancing an ill child's greater need for us with our own needs for "time out" is difficult. It is even more difficult when we are blaming ourselves and don't know it. After the birth of her third child, who had cerebral palsy, Margaret Stanzler writes, "I punished myself mercilessly. I gave up my job. I manipulated my baby's legs for hours each day in physical therapy. I took him to many different doctors." While she felt this was initially beneficial for both of them, she realized that she needed to foster some healthy separation.

Stanzler describes a discussion group in which mothers protested that they would not consider taking a break from their children with disabilities. Their reasons—that they couldn't trust anyone, sometimes not even their spouse—didn't seem realistic. There was a respite care facility in the area staffed by therapists and nurses, available on a sliding scale. "The problem for many parents was not so much in finding adequate care for their disabled kids as it was in overcoming their feelings of guilt." Her own solution: "I am careful about the sitters I hire, but now I can see that my son can benefit from a different caretaker part of the time. I feel like a person, not a slave."[10]

The Anger of "Why Me?"

The anger: "Why me?" is really the flip side of guilt: "What did I do wrong?" While infrequently parents legitimately *should* be blaming themselves or someone else, when someone really was at fault, this is usually not the case. Most often, the anger and blame have little basis in reality; instead they derive their staying power from our profound need to find reasons for what has happened.

Nancy's daughter had spinal meningitis when she was three days old and now, at fourteen, she has intractable epilepsy. "I don't have guilt, but I'm still angry and there's no miracle cure for that." After her daughter was born with a heart defect, Ann felt furious when she saw other mothers with normal babies. Becky's son was born with fragile X. "I'm angry about the unfairness. I still remember that there was another girl in the labor room next to me. She had three cardiologists hovering over her, and they left me in a room by myself. At 11:02 P.M. she delivered a normal baby. Three minutes later my son was born and needed to be resuscitated. He had hyaline membrane disease and a cleft palate and was in the hospital for the next two months."

Angry parents may be less tortured than guilty ones because their fury is directed at someone other than themselves. Even so, there is a downside. Unrestrained anger tends to make parents view their children as victims and this undermines everyone's optimism. In addition, those who approach the family to help may sense this blame and turn away.

Some of the strategies I suggest later for managing guilt also apply to anger. Harold Kushner has some advice on the subject of anger in *When Bad Things Happen to Good People*. He says:

> The goal, if we can achieve it, would be to *be angry at the situation*, rather than ourselves, or those who

might have prevented it or are close to us trying to help us, or at God who let it happen. Getting angry at ourselves makes us depressed. Being angry at other people scares them away and makes it harder for them to help us. Being angry at God erects a barrier between us and all the sustaining, comforting resources of religion that are there to help us in such times. But being angry at the situation, recognizing it as something rotten, unfair, and totally undeserved, shouting about it, denouncing it, crying over it, permits us to discharge the anger which is a part of being hurt, without making it harder for us to be helped.[11]

Managing Our Guilt

Although guilt is often enmeshed with loving feelings—with our profound wish for things to be different—it can do real harm. Once we accept this verdict, we carry it over into our future. It can be an ongoing judgment that accuses our daily acts and decisions. We become incompetent and unworthy in our own eyes. Our children sense this and feel responsible for our misery. At the very least, we need to try to manage our guilt for them. Here are some suggestions.

EMBRACE YOUR GUILT

Confession is a time-tested method of exorcising our emotional demons. We need the opportunity to talk about how we think we caused the problem. Many parents confess to their religious leaders, relatives, friends, and support groups. And we need to do it over and over again. Some even write articles and books about their guilt, like myself.

The point is not to silence yourself with "shoulds." Don't let anyone stop you with logic about how your child's problem is not your fault. After enough talking, the feeling may begin to fade. One mother whose teenage daughter is wheelchair-bound from arthritis says, "I finally came to a place where I realized that there was nothing I could do, no matter how I blamed myself. She was going to have to live with this."

LET A HIGHER POWER OR "BIG PICTURE" HELP YOU, IF YOU CAN

Some parents derive strength from religious convictions. One mother said of her daughter's illness, a form of lupus, "We rely on God and our church." Others do not find comfort here. Regardless, it is useful to develop some "big picture" concept that can transport us away from our self-accusations to a larger view of life. This view is an acknowledgment of our powerlessness. Many events are beyond anyone's control.

PUT GUILT IN ITS PLACE: IT IS SERIOUS, BUT DON'T TAKE IT SERIOUSLY

Even though we feel our guilt, we don't have to listen to it. There is a choice. We don't have to take these feelings as valid judgments about ourselves.

Alice has a son with epilepsy and a daughter with diabetes. "It's no fun to go to a restaurant and have to jump up and give an insulin shot. But I think it's okay for me to be fed up once in a while. It doesn't mean I don't empathize with my children. I also see my guilt as an involuntary reflex and I am not mad at myself for feeling this way. My husband and I are not superpeople."

EMBRACE THE FACTS

Knowledge can be the path away from our day-to-day struggles with the problem. What we find out may help unburden us. Cindy, who has a teenage son with autism, recalls, "It took a while, but once the information was put in front of me, I could absorb that this was not my fault. It also took a while to find the right doctors who could tell me this."

Likewise, we may blame ourselves for not seeing our child's problem sooner. Yet many conditions don't announce themselves with dramatic trouble. Rather, they emerge slowly, subtly disrupting everyone's sense of ease. If these are the facts of your child's illness, believe them. We are not seers. And sometimes things have to become really bad before we can locate the appropriate professional to help us. It's true, hindsight is always 20/20.

LOOK AT THE FACTS DIFFERENTLY

Although a child's relapse can generate guilt, it doesn't have to. Mary Jo's son has asthma. "I used to think I must have let him do something he shouldn't when he had to be hospitalized. But I've changed. Now, I feel I learn something new about what restrictions are absolutely necessary. He can't keep up with our schedule, and wind and grass are horrendous. But he's doing a lot more because I am willing to give it a try."

Three years ago, Danny's preschool teacher informed me that he was "high" again. I was upset. Just when I thought I had the foods figured out, he was reacting to something. The culprit turned out to be grape juice. But rather than blame myself for not diluting it, I decided to congratulate myself for my vigilance in tracking it down. After all, it's likely that many children will suffer some relapse. What seems to matter is how on top of it we are.

REALIZE THAT YOU CAN GIVE
YOUR CHILD WHAT NO OTHER PERSON CAN

We're "only" parents, but how important that is. Only we have the passionate attachment to our children to see them through these crises on a day-to-day basis. And we have the power to feed their self-esteem through our love.

Sherry felt helpless when her daughter was hospitalized for the chemical burns produced by the diaper. "But once I got home, and introduced my own methods of parenting, I could see that being with my child was going to be good for her. For example, I could feed her what she liked when she was hungry. That made a big difference because she was refusing food in the hospital. And when I saw her develop normally, that really relieved my guilt."

ASK YOURSELF "WHAT ARE YOU DOING RIGHT?"

Some of us nurse our children through incredible odds, burdened by the most dire predictions. When our child finally makes it—in one way or another—it's something to mark in our memories. Mary Lou's wheelchair-bound child with cerebral palsy will "walk" to a regular school with his friends. Denise's daughter with asthma and a heart defect missed seventy-five days of developmental kindergarten last year. "She was behind and I was even told that she was retarded. Now she's in extended-day kindergarten, going every day, making friends, and loving the program. That helped my guilt." Susan Duffy's seven-and-a-half-year-old child with Down's had a tracheostomy for the first six years of her life. She will be attending first grade next year and is reading at a second-grade level. We can't make it better, but we have forged some significant victories along the way. Let's relish them when we can.

2. Identify the Problem and Learn How to Live with It

Our youngster's illness or disability expels us from the land where only good things are supposed to happen. Most of us will have little idea of what to expect from her, ourselves, or her condition, for that matter. We peer into the future at the range of possibilities. Some of us will cringe at the worst-case scenarios, which vary enormously, depending on the problem. Cancer threatens life; arthritis damages the body; and allergies, while not visible, may silently ravage development and self-esteem. Despite these profound differences, parents grapple with similar tasks in trying to live as realistically as possible.

The Difficult-to-Diagnose Problem

An attending physician in medical school once told me that "patients need a diagnosis. A label, even if it tells them very little, will reduce anxiety." It was only when Danny became ill that I understood the truth of that statement. *Developmental delay* merely summarized what we were already observing and yet the two words vacuumed up our scattered fears and emptied them into one neat basket.

But this experience has also taught me that a label does something else that you can't take for granted. It signifies that parent and professional have agreed that a problem exists. And getting that agreement can be a project in itself. This is especially true if a child has a relatively rare or atypical medical condition.

THE RIGHT PROFESSIONAL

It's nothing and will go away. You're overreacting. It's a stage. These are the common reassurances that mothers and fathers hear from professionals. Physicians are probably correct to say these words in many instances but *not all the time.* They will not be satisfactory answers for parents who have a child with a difficult-to-diagnose problem. I've talked to some who have scoured the country to find out what is wrong with their son or daughter.

Kathy McGlynn wrote about "Becoming a Detective in the Medical Community" in the book *Acceptance Is Only the First Battle.*[1] This mother describes her middle child, Sean, who was born with a sleep disturbance. By the time he was eighteen months, Sean's violent, nightly screaming had created what she terms a life-threatening situation. She didn't know which would come first, her death through exhaustion or her son's through her deteriorating abilities to care for him. Her pediatrician advised sophisticated EEG testing, which was available only out of state. Results were normal. The conclusion: Sean had a psychological problem. Yet the two psychologists Kathy later consulted suggested that this was a neurological difficulty. Anticonvulsants proved effective. When Sean was five, the family visited the Mayo Clinic in the hope of settling the issue. He was then thought to have night terrors. The anticonvulsants were stopped and he was put on sedatives. The screaming returned. Kathy eventually did a library search at a university and found an article on unusual nocturnal problems in the first decade of life. She wrote to the senior author, who subsequently diagnosed Sean's nocturnal epilepsy by mail.

Kathy told me that her son, now thirteen, finally had an abnormal EEG this past summer. She was relieved because the diagnosis was unquestionably established. "We'd felt like we were still floundering without that rubber stamp of approval."

Some parents will need stamina, patience, and unusual resources to find out what is wrong with their child. That label may not come easily, but if parents don't pursue it, most likely no one else will.

WAITING FOR THE ILLNESS/DISABILITY TO EMERGE

Some parents have had to endure years of ambiguity before obtaining a correct diagnosis. Despite everyone's best efforts, there may be no way around this delay. Linda's daughter, Renée, was born "floppy." "I knew from the start that something was wrong, but I couldn't convince my pediatrician." Renée had physical therapy for muscle weakness when she was two, but didn't start to deteriorate until she was six. "By that time, we knew we had a myopathy. The diagnosis was made of nemaline myopathy, a muscular degenerative disease. There have only been about a hundred other cases."

GETTING THE BEST TREATMENT

Once we have the diagnosis, we may need to consult with experts to find out the state-of-the-art treatment for unusual conditions. Adelle was told by her hematologist that her one-year-old son would die within the year from agranulocytosis, a rare blood disorder. "But the doctor was repeating to us what was in the textbooks," recalls Adelle. "We wanted to find out what was the most recent knowledge. My husband took a week off and phoned everyone he ever met who might have a lead on a medical problem. We found out there were two doctors treating this illness and only thirty cases had been reported in the United States. My husband flew to Michigan and interviewed one of them about his treatment with bacterin. He recorded this conversation and played it for our hematologist." Since then, the couple has learned through this contact of another experimental drug that may be effective.

Parents have been creative in tracking down elusive medical conditions. But first you need to define the condition as precisely as possible from your observations and possibly those of friends, teachers, and others. Modern technology can help too. (Mike and I made home videotapes of Danny that we showed to every professional we consulted.) Written records will allow you to make comparisons over time which you can show to physicians.

As Kathy and other parents have discovered, second, third, and many more medical opinions may be necessary to get that diagnosis. Stay in touch with the doctors you respect. Science keeps progressing, and questions that can't be answered today may be tomorrow. One girl has had behavior problems and a learning disability since two years of age. Gary confided in a parent discussion group, "We could never figure out what was really the matter. Now she is fifteen and will be going for specialized EEG testing. The technology has improved enough that they can record in new areas deeper in the brain."

Speak to nonprofessionals, too. You never know who has been through what or who knows who until you start talking. Kathy worked with a woman whose son was a paramedic. He asked the neurologist he worked with about Sean. The doctor correctly identified the problem as nocturnal epilepsy.

Do your own research. Kathy used an on-line computer search at a university library. I called up the author of a book about allergies, who then referred me to an Arizona specialist. This physician made the diagnosis as Danny launched a fleet of Magic Markers across his Oriental carpet.

Getting the right diagnosis may tell you much more than how to treat your child's condition. You find out what it isn't, and that can be a relief. Without knowledge, fantasies can run ominously rampant. Kathy was afraid Sean might have had cystic fibrosis. "Epilepsy was a piece of cake after that." Annie feared her toddler was retarded but learned that she was hypothyroid and hearing impaired. At first we did not know what caused Danny's developmental delay, how to treat it, or what to expect, but we did learn that he wasn't autistic.

Also, the diagnosis may mean a lot to your child if he is old enough to appreciate that he is ill. If our fears mushroom in ignorance, imagine how unbridled our child's fears must be. A ten-year-old boy breathed a sigh of relief after he was told his blackouts meant he had epilepsy: "I was scared I had a brain tumor."

In addition, the diagnosis may help you accommodate your parenting. For example, there are specific techniques to help children who have hearing and visual impairment and developmental delays. Annie says, "Once I learned my daughter couldn't hear me, I stopped asking her what she wanted for breakfast when my head was stuck in the refrigerator." Pam's son has attention difficulties from Williams syndrome, a genetic defect in calcium metabolism. She makes sure she bends down to his eye level and gives simple, one-sentence requests. Kay takes the time for smelling and touching with her visually impaired son.

But, unfortunately, a diagnosis does not necessarily forecast how severe the illness or disability will be. Rose learned her daughter, Jennifer, had rheumatoid arthritis when she was eleven. Two years later, the girl is wheelchair-bound and enrolled in a home-teaching program. "I never thought she would deteriorate like this." And sometimes the disease is not nearly so disabling as we anticipate. One mother was horrified to learn her son had hemophilia. "We thought what everyone thinks, that he'll bleed to death with the first cut. That hasn't happened at all." Another reported, "I was told when my son was born, 'He has PKU, but don't worry, he won't be retarded.' Of course, I worried until I made it to my first genetics clinic and saw children with PKU who looked healthy."

Facing Her Illness or Disability

While some of us resist absorbing a painful reality, others soak it up, like a sponge, into our every pore. Both approaches may be useful in moderation and harmful in excess.

In the first approach—denial—we put our anguish aside so that we can carry on some semblance of our daily lives. One mother "forgets" that her two-year-old son had a kidney tumor removed. "That was eleven months ago and I only think about it now when he has a checkup." We deal with the reality a little bit at a time. When Rose was told that her daughter had arthritis, she remembers saying initially, "The doctors may be wrong." Dorothy, the nurse with arthritis, recalls that as a teenager she used to pray to God to take the illness away.

Each of these individuals has played a pretend game:

either that the illness hasn't happened or that it might stop happening. This is usually a short-term measure to manage overwhelming anxiety. What counts is that their denial has not interfered with taking care of themselves or their children.

But denial can be harmful, too, in that it prevents parents from getting needed help. Newspapers routinely run stories about mothers and fathers who fail to get lifesaving treatments for their children because of certain religious beliefs.

This turning away from reality can also lead to psychological abuse. It can keep parents from accepting their children way they are, with their limitations. Sharon had been a polio victim before the Salk vaccine was available. She recalls, "My mother couldn't stand anything wrong. I always walked slowly with my feet flopping. We'd be crossing the street and she would clench her teeth and say, 'Can't you walk any better?' as if my legs were normal."

The chances are that if you are reading this book, you are not shutting your eyes to the facts of your child's condition. Yet the line between these facts and denial can become surprisingly blurred under certain circumstances. And since denial is *not* under our control—we do not say to ourselves, "Today I will not accept this"—it is hard for us to see when we have crossed that border into unreality.

Martha argued with the specialist about whether her daughter should continue for follow-up in the leukemia clinic. "We had words, but he gave me every indication that Heather would be fine. There's only a ten percent chance of relapse after the first year off chemotherapy. I want her to be past cancer and done with this phase of her life."

Jack has a son who is allergic to many foods; he is working overtime to cover the expense of the boy's special diet. This parent does not believe that his son's allergies may be causing behavioral problems in second grade. "There's nothing wrong with my kid. I think it's the teacher. She has it in for Tommy because I'm a mechanic."

Are these parents denying or are they heroically resisting the pressures of third parties? How do we recognize this difference in ourselves? Most parents have had misguided advice thrust upon them at one time or another. Yet we can't afford to close our minds to what may be painful to hear. Despite our best intentions, we may occasionally slip into some unreality about our situation. We do this because we are anxious about the future and/or frustrated with the present.

The best way to thwart this tendency in ourselves is to seriously consider the informed opinions that don't agree with our own. Martha continues to discuss with her husband the decision not to go for follow-up appointments with the oncologist. Jack transferred his son to a new school and a new teacher. Perhaps if this father gets similar feedback there, he will hear it differently this time.

While some of us deny, others of us become "possessed." Like a tornado, the reality of the new medical condition whirls through our existence and sucks up all our other concerns. It dominates our thoughts, directs our conversations with friends, and orchestrates our family time together. We pour all our energies into this enemy, the disease, hoping to control it, or better yet, defeat it. This was my experience.

After we learned of our food allergies, I joined La Leche League and an organic food cooperative. Many hours were spent recounting our experiences to those who would listen, trading recipes, and learning how to bake "from scratch." Apparently, I was sufficiently ardent that even long-standing members of these groups were impressed with my zeal. Although it was not my intention, my "regular" friends who fed their kids junk food felt a little sheepish in my presence.

While this initial outpouring may seem excessive, it can

be a useful way to mobilize ourselves and our family. Don't fight it, if you have it. Go with it. It takes a tremendous effort for a family to accommodate itself to an illness or disability and establish new routines. And it is the family who adjusts, not just the child. But usually this does happen and eventually most of us wind down from our crusades.

One year after Alice learned about her then six-year-old son's epilepsy, her eight-year-old daughter was diagnosed as having diabetes. "Initially, I felt consumed by the situation. I was critically aware of how little I knew and that made me insecure. I needed three tries to draw up the insulin correctly and then the injection seemed like it took forever. Now I do it in the middle of cooking dinner or when the phone rings. It's so automatic I don't think about it."

But sometimes our involvement can be excessive, to everyone's detriment. We end up not helping our child or family and depleting ourselves, too. Often, this excess stems from another kind of denial—not that the disease exists, but that we can't fix it. Our wish is that with our total dedication, we can stave off death or relapse. This may be unrealistic.

Denise's daughter, Erica, was born with chronic asthma and a ventricular septal defect. Her heart was repaired when she was two and a half. Over the next two years, she was hospitalized twenty-five times.

I was cautious. From the time she was two, I would follow her with a stethoscope and listen to her chest every time she exerted herself. There was a note on our door that if you had a fever in the past twenty-four hours, please don't come in. We only went out to the doctor's office and the grocery store.

Everybody said I was doing great, but I was going nuts. I had to change for my sanity. Now I'll do the

best I can, but I won't kill myself or take it as a failure
if she has to be hospitalized.

We are helpless about some things, and recognizing this can
free us to direct our energies elsewhere, where we might
make a difference.

Changing Our Life-Style

There are no ready answers for what adjustments parents
must make when their youngster has a chronic illness or
disability, and no book, including this one, can possibly provide that. All of us need to discover what accommodations
are necessary for our situations. We are all inventing the
wheel, but it's a different wheel. Yet there are some common
themes.

It takes time to figure out what we can and can't do. Alice's
description reflects many of our experiences. "It was an ev-
olutionary process. We slowly came to realize that a lot of
what we talked about before our kids were born was not
going to happen, but we started to appreciate what we could
do."

Mothers decide to stay at home or work part-time to keep
on top of what's happening with their children. Alice recalls,
"I was career-oriented—a computer systems analyst at a bank.
With two kids ill that's just not practical now."

And many parents will have to scramble to meet expenses.
There are numerous obvious and hidden health-care costs.
Fathers may continue to stay at the same job for the insurance
benefits. Some mothers seek employment. Mary Jo's son has
asthma and she works four days a week as a legal secretary.
"It's a hardship. You think you get back on your feet and he
goes into the hospital. That takes away from the little vaca-

tions—the $600 you need to go to Disney." Other mothers find ways to work at home. One of Hannah's three children has a heart defect. "It was driving me crazy dropping off the kids at different baby-sitters. I looked at the finances and the money I would save not having child care." This woman is now licensed by the state as a respite care giver for children with handicaps. Rose has started a preschool in her home to stay with her teenage daughter who is wheelchair-bound with arthritis.

Despite these different accommodations, the goal is to live as normally as possible, whatever that turns out to be. Unfortunately, this has become a cliché and, like many, it trivializes the experience. After all, many parents live with abnormal situations. Yet, as one mother wrote, "To decide on any other route, to admit that having a disabled child makes us disabled persons, to say no to the ordinary requirements of daily living is to meet the second enemy—loneliness."[2] It takes a tremendous energy for some of us to live what has been called a regular life. But try, we must.

Living with Ourselves

Do we, personally, have what it takes? We will need staying power to encourage our child when she feels defeated, assertiveness for encounters with professionals, and sheer physical stamina to run a family when one child is in the hospital or homebound. Of course, we don't have a choice and, perhaps, this is one reason some of us manage as well as we do. But we also must reach within ourselves and nurture some special quality that will help get us through.

Denise was dominated by the uncertainty of her daughter's hospitalizations. She has learned the capacity for healthy objectivity. "We can be miserable all the time, or enjoy life when it's quiet and deal with the crises when they come along."

Many of us have had to put aside our private beliefs to do what is best for our children. Martha is an advocate of holistic health. "Here I am against antibiotics and when Heather had leukemia, I had to say yes to chemotherapy drugs which are essentially poisons."

We have had to steel ourselves and inflict pain on our children for their own good. Sherry gave her two-year-old daughter daily whirlpool baths for her third-degree burns. Then she scrubbed off the loose skin with Betadine. "I needed another adult there to help me, otherwise I felt like I was abusing her. When they look at you with their big eyes, what they perceive is that Mom is hurting me."

Parents have also had to let go of pride. Suzanne Massie writes, in *Journey,* "I became a beggar—me, a Swiss, proud and independent, accustomed to relying only on myself and my energy. Hemophilia turned me into a beggar. We needed things all the time. I would have to ask over and over to leave Susy with neighbors while I went to the hospital. I was begging for companionship for Bobby. I was begging for blood."[3]

In addition, we've had to cope with a loss of power over our lives. Our unavoidable reliance on strangers and their goodwill carries with it a unique stress. And although advocacy groups and careful selection of professionals are, of course, essential, they do not erase our ultimate dependence on others. Suzanne Massie describes what she felt like getting blood for her son with hemophilia. "Resentful and proud, I had created my own walls. . . . Locked in my solitary bitterness, I was no longer noticing that if there were all those people who did not give, there were also many others who, for no reason at all, without even being asked, did, quietly and without fanfare."[4]

Managing our vulnerability may be our most critical personal challenge. We can't allow disappointments resulting from this continuing vulnerability to coalesce into one angry ache against the world.

Living with a Difference

Living with a difference is a family affair. This section is concerned with the effects on our child with special health needs, while later, the "Make Your Other Kids Count" section (p. 60) and Chapter 8 deal with other family members.

Jackie Cottrell, a nineteen-year-old girl with cystic fibrosis, writes, "At this point in my life, I realize that it is much easier living *with* CF than living *as* CF."[5] The social consequences of an illness or disability can be as profound as the condition itself.

How many of you have tried to console your child with, "No one's perfect. None of us is alike, and it would be a boring world if we were." While these statements are true, and I have said these same words to Danny and Amy, they do not relieve the ongoing tension, the feeling of being on the fringe. This is because the difficulties inherent in being different plow deep into human nature and assault youngsters on a variety of levels.

There's no way around it—difference matters. At the very least, it robs our youngsters of privacy. It should be an inalienable right: every child should be able to choose what she reveals to others about herself. An illness or disability takes this choice away. Sometimes the medical condition will identify her as different and sometimes it will be the treatment. As a result, she may experience some shame in others having to know her business. This is a natural response. Most people feel this when they are "exposed" without their consent or control.

Difference also stimulates rejection by others. Human beings habitually band together and demonstrate a profound need for conformity. Tied to this need is an abhorrence and a fear of deviance. Someone who is different generally evokes anxiety, confusion, and even embarrassment in the observer.

How many classic children's stories, movies, and books portray the evil or undesirable person with some kind of infirmity, be it a scar, a limp, or a missing limb. If we happen to be different, we can have a problem. The myriad of new terms for children, such as *special* or *exceptional* instead of *crippled* or *retarded, Down's* instead of *Mongoloid, seizure disorder* instead of *epilepsy,* to name a few, unfortunately, does not erase this stigma.

In ranching, infirm bulls are pushed toward the edge of the herd, easily left behind if they can not keep up. People also tend to push aside, psychologically, those they perceive as weaker than they. Most children with special health needs have experienced this rejection. It can happen with words. A child with a congenital heart defect has blue fingertips from lack of oxygen. Each day, when he goes to school, he is goaded by classmates, "Did you have blueberries again for breakfast?"

Rejection can also be accomplished by silence—that is, lack of acknowledgment. Sharon, a polio victim, walks with a rocking gait and reports that even as an adult she is sometimes treated like a nonperson. "I went shopping with my sister. Instead of dealing with me, the saleslady addressed everything to her as if I were incompetent."

On the other hand, difference can also inspire idealization from others. The first time I heard this was from a counselor. He was at a camp for children with cancer but had never had the disease himself. He told me, "These kids aren't like the others. They don't complain about not getting enough and are always grateful about what they are doing." Although this, in fact, may be true of some youngsters with special health needs, it's unlikely to be true of all of them. In the meantime, this innocent-appearing expectation can burden them with having to be *superkids*. In effect, they have to demonstrate that they are as good as everyone else by being better.

Cheri Register has had cystic liver disease since her late teens. In *Living with Chronic Illness,* she protests, "At last I understood why I have a strong impulse to trip the proverbial one-legged marathon runner every time I hear his virtues extolled. It's just not fair. People who are caught up short by illness should not have to scramble to prove their full human value to their healthy counterparts. What the marathon runner represents is a seldom-questioned assumption that illness is a test of character."[6] Is this necessary? (See also Chapter 8 about others idealizing the family.)

The social consequences of being different come up earlier than most of us would like to think. Parents usually feel the pinch first, when their child is too young or unaware to appreciate it for himself. "We'd be okay if we could just stay at home by ourselves," Pam says about her four-year-old boy with Williams syndrome. "Johnny is normal to me, but when I pick him up at preschool, I can see how he can't wait in line like the others. He's not as quick to catch on. That's when it hits me and I cry."

And some children may surprise us with how soon they appreciate this reality for themselves. If their difference is obvious, they may also have a good idea of its impact on others. Rosemary's son has prune-belly syndrome, a congenital lack of musculature in the abdomen. She recalls, "When he was two, Sam was playing with his bicycle and another kid tried to take it away. His shirt was pulled up in the tussle and the kid shrieked and ran away. The very next day, Sam wanted something from another child and he pulled up his shirt to scare him."

As children get older, they absorb not just how we see them, but how others view them too. They become exquisitely sensitive to this larger judgment and easily grasp that they may be "defective" in the eyes of the world. Some youngsters experience shame with this recognition.

One malignant consequence of this shame is denying the illness or disability to the point of endangering health. Jackie attends a Cystic Fibrosis Support Group and has been a counselor at the C.F. camp for the past two summers. But when she was ten she tried to "escape" her condition.

> Until fourth grade, I was a regular kid. . . . However, that year and those students were different. They focused on my disease and considered me to "be" a disease. One girl went so far as to tell her mother not to let me near her baby sister. . . . Being snubbed was not something I was used to and I didn't like it. By the end of the first month of school, I was "forgetting" to take my pills when I ate, I refused to do therapy (CPT) if there were nonfamily members around, and I would force myself not to cough in school. I didn't realize at the time that not doing these things would affect my health in later life.[7]

Another unfortunate result of shame is social withdrawal. Children and parents occasionally do this to avoid questions, explanations, and comparisons. What's harmful is when this becomes an ongoing adjustment. Sharon's legs lost muscle mass and strength from polio. Her mother was embarrassed, and Sharon learned that her difference was something to be embarrassed about. "I didn't go dancing, roller skating, or bowling—anything that would expose my disability. I refused to enter a home economics fashion show in high school because the dress I made would have revealed my legs."

And it hardly matters that a child is born with an illness or has had it since infancy and, therefore, knows no other way of life. The cliché "She doesn't miss what she has never had" does not hold. It may dawn on her slowly that she is different. However, most chldren will invariably make this observation. All they need to do is look around them.

HELPING YOUR CHILD LIVE WITH HER DIFFERENCE

Living with any abnormality is confusing for us and for our child. We struggle with how to help her accept her defects and how to minimize the resulting shame and apology. How can parents protect a youngster from the reactions of others and prepare her for these reactions at the same time?

Separate Your Pain from That of Your Child

Her concerns may be far different from yours, and you can only help her with hers if you hear them. A girl with a zipper scar from cardiac surgery does not want to wear a scoop-neck leotard at ballet class; her mother worries whether this will be too much activity for her. A visually impaired boy frets that he can't play ball as his friends do; his father, recalling his own adolescence, is alarmed that the boy won't be able to drive a car when he is old enough to date. A few years ago, Danny was embarrassed by his rice cake snacks at preschool; I wondered whether he would be able to enter "regular" kindergarten.

While all these concerns are understandable, our child's may seem far less pressing than our own. But they aren't. After all, it is our youngster who primarily has to live with being different. If she learns how to deal with that in the present, she will have at least a chance of managing it in the future. The mother bought turtlenecks for her daughter to wear under her leotard. The father found a store to buy an oversize bat and ball for his son. And Danny and I figured out snacks that would more closely resemble what his classmates were eating.

Talk to Your Child About His Differences

While you don't want to brand your youngster in his own eyes or instill the expectation that he will be rejected by others, you do need to equip him for what he faces. Parental love can not possibly encapsulate him from either the reality of his body or the response of the rest of the world. Saying nothing leaves him defenseless in both areas.

Start talking to him early, using simple words. How early? Janet's two-and-a-half-year-old son points to his zipper scar and explains, "My heart was fixed." Try to mention this difference matter-of-factly when the consequences of it come up. A doctor's appointment, an injection, a pill are opportunities to begin what should become an ongoing discussion. Your child does not have to grasp your words intellectually to understand that you are there to help him deal with this.

What you want to avoid is his asking you because he has already heard about his condition elsewhere. This experience can be shattering. After all, if children can't count on their parents to tell it like it is, what *can* they expect? And you don't want to communicate through silence that either you or he is too fragile to talk about the truth.

Also, use words he is likely to hear from others. Kay's son, Ted, is an albino and visually impaired. She uses the word *albino* and took her three children to a farm that had white rabbits to enhance their understanding.

Many parents would like to reach for euphemisms when the usual labels have frightening implications. Again, if you don't even mention the words *cancer, cystic fibrosis,* or *epilepsy,* your child may hear them first from someone else. After managing six years with a tracheostomy, Keough is entering "regular" first grade. Her mother, Susan Duffy, says, "We were on a local television show and one of the school aides came up to me the next day and said she didn't know that Keough was a Down's child. My daughter has an animated face and it's not immediately obvious. Now I'm worried that some kid will walk up to her and call her a 'retard.' I wonder about telling her that she is a Down's."

What to do? Inform your child about these labels without using them in daily life. For example, "You have a seizure disorder, but some people call this *epilepsy*." You can soften the impact by explaining how the severity of diseases varies, which is the truth. Some people with cystic fibrosis live much longer than others. Also, tell your child that how he cares for himself will improve his chances for better health. Even when a label is misleading, it's advisable to mention the term so that he doesn't hear it elsewhere first. For example, different cancers are really different diseases. Martha struggled against using the word *cancer* because Heather's grandfather had died from that the year before. Eventually, she told her daughter that leukemia was a cancer, but it was not the kind Grandpa had.

Familiar comparisons may enhance a younger child's understanding. Epilepsy can be like a thunder-and-lightning storm through the brain, a cardiac defect is a pump with an ouch, cancer like a garden with too many weeds. Adelle, whose son lacked a certain white cell, told him that his blood was missing one kind of soldier that fights the germs. Nurses, other parents, and educational pamphlets can be fruitful, like an orchard, if your mind is barren when it comes to these metaphors.

However, expect misunderstandings, even with the most informed and/or colorful explanations. Don't be fooled by the logic of older children, either. They can be reacting irrationally while being able to recite all the "right" facts (see

Chapter 4, pp.105 and 114). Therefore, you need to do more than speak to his intellectual understanding of his medical condition, although this is essential. You also need to reassure him about unrealistic fears that may be either lurking behind what he says or openly expressed.

One fear is that "I have caused it." Six-year-old Charlie explained his illness with: "When you do something bad and your Dad doesn't punish you, God will. That's why I have this kidney tumor." Tell your child that many things that happen have no cause, as we know it. *The illness or disability is no one's fault.*

You can also reinforce this no-fault understanding when this question comes up about other people. My son, after meeting Ted, who has albinism, asked me what was wrong with him. "Why didn't God give him enough color?" I told him that certain things happen for no good reason, just like our food allergies.

A second common worry is that the condition is contagious. Mary Jo's four-year-old son learned that when someone coughs on him he gets a cold, which can often progress to an asthmatic attack. He concluded that when he coughs on someone else, he can also give them asthma. His mother corrected his misunderstanding. She knew it would lead to guilt and isolation.

Another irrational fear is that "I am going to die" or "the worst will happen to me." Alice's nine-year-old daughter had already learned about diabetes from television when she was diagnosed as having the disease. Her immediate concern was that it was going to kill her or she would lose her legs. She said, "What's the good in taking insulin, anyway?"

Children can be quite sophisticated in their information and yet interpret it in an emotional, black-and-white fashion. Alice worked on modifying her daughter's initial misconceptions. This mother pointed out how people with diabetes do much better today because of improved care. "If you make certain sacrifices and are honest about what you eat, you should do well."

Invisible Differences Matter Too

Some conditions are obvious: the hair loss from cancer treatment, the barrel chest of cystic fibrosis, the joint deformities from arthritis, among others. These children must deal with the consequences of this recognition: the staring, the questions, and the avoidance by peers. However, they are relieved of others' expectations that they be normal.

But other diseases—epilepsy, food allergies, or mild hemophilia—are essentially invisible. These children look normal, even though functionally they do things their peers don't do: avoid certain foods, take pills, or get occasional transfusions. These youngsters must choose whether to expose their difference. They also have the additional worry about whether their difference is already known. Pat Covelli looks back to when he was ten and the diagnosis of diabetes was made.

On this particular morning the dread was intense. I was going to school; my classmates would know I was different.

At school, I sat at the polished desk, my head down, my eyes on the childish graffiti in the wood. I could not look the other kids in the face, I could only shoot glances at the blackboard in front of the room. Was everyone staring, or was my shame a product of my imagination?

Doctors often soothe the diabetic by saying that people have no way of knowing he has the disease. Comforting to an adult, perhaps, but to a child, surface

appearances mean nothing. I believed that my classmates could see through me.[8]

In other words, an invisible difference does not grant a child
immunity from feeling defective.

Be Ready for Your Child's
Ambivalent Feelings About His Difference
Reinforce the positive and let him blow off steam about the
negative.

Children may vacillate between feeling special and feeling
defective about their difference. An illness or disability brings
a certain extra attention that, in moderation, is not going to
hurt anyone and, in fact, may help. One mother was devastated when her son was found to be hearing impaired. "But
he was thrilled to be like his dad and get a hearing aid."
Eleven-year-old Jennifer was diagnosed as having rheumatoid
arthritis. Her mother recalls, "All the kids lined up to try her
crutches, and she loved being in the limelight. The teacher
sent one boy to the office and when Jennifer looked out the
window she saw that he was using them to get there." Todd's
friends visited him in the hospital when he was first identified
as having diabetes. The twelve-year-old was proud to demonstrate his bravery during blood tests and insulin shots. The
boys then offered their forearms to test their mettle with the
needle. Some children instinctively admire the courage it
takes to cope with either the medical condition or the treatment. Use these opportunities to point out to your youngster
how his illness or disability is not necessarily a turnoff to
other people.

Of course, this does not take away from the times when
he will feel bad about his difference. The mother of the
hearing-impaired boy reported that her son purposely left
his hearing aid at K Mart and occasionally tries not to use it.

Jennifer's mother accompanied her to school the first day because her daughter was anxious about what her classmates would say. Todd ripped off his first identification bracelet because it meant something was wrong with him.

These are the times when our children need us as listeners, not as advisers. Try to stifle well-meaning reassurances—such as, It won't hurt your life, or, Nobody can see it anyway—that might inadvertently close off conversations. Why would we want to do that? Because much of what our children say may be the simple truth. We are unable to help them about many things, and this is painful to hear.

Be Ready for Your Child's Intolerance of Others Who Are Different

The positive is easy for parents to understand and accept. For example, children with cancer often develop intense friendships through organizations such as Rainbow Kids. They learn they are not alone; and only those who have "been through it" can share the gallows humor about losing hair and limbs.

On the other hand, youngsters can also feel proud when they don't appear to have the disease or disability and can somehow dissociate themselves from this group. A boy at cystic fibrosis camp confides, "I don't look like a C.F.'er so the kids can't figure out if I'm a counselor or someone's brother." In a more negative vein, children may express a subtle disdain for those in worse shape than they are. In asthma camp, those with the steroid moon face will occasionally be derided by others who appear more healthy. The boy at C.F. camp says, "I get frustrated with the kids who *let* themselves look sick when there is something they could do about it." Also, some youngsters may also seek out friends who are "more perfect." The child who had blue fingertips from serious congenital heart disease derived great benefit from his friendship with a child who only had learning disabilities. His father says, "This friend was closer to normal and that was great for my son's self-esteem."

Children, and adults for that matter, make these kinds of unfortunate comparisons to reassure themselves that no matter how bad they feel, they are not that bad off. Difference is a heavy burden for anyone, let alone a youngster. While we shouldn't sanction a child's putting down another who is ill or disabled, we also shouldn't put him down for his feelings. Talk with him about how hard it is having his condition, because that is the basis of his negativism toward others like him.

Help Your Child Interpret the Reactions of Others

People react with a range of emotions, from fear to hostility or just discomfort. Your child is going to notice. Making sense of what she observes will help her deal with it next time. Renée can no longer breathe on her own power due to her degenerative muscle disease. Linda took her shopping with her suction and ventilator equipment. "Renée would say, 'Mom, those kids are staring at me,' and I'd explain that they aren't used to seeing people with tubes. Now we have to allow two hours when we go out because she talks to everyone and you hear the kids say, 'Hey, here's that girl again.'"

Be Mindful of What You Say Within Earshot of Your Child

It could be a phone conversation or a chat with a visiting friend. The topic of *the illness* or *disability* inevitably comes up when our child is "stationed" in the area. That first year, I mentioned Danny's food allergies at almost every La Leche League meeting. My obsession, of course, was fueled by anx-

iety. This obsession can create problems because our youngsters will hear our panic, too.

Your child's "listening in" can be useful, however, if you
can get your anxiety under control. Use it as an opportunity
to role-model being matter-of-fact, and maybe even upbeat,
if appropriate. For example, when others used to comment,
"Oh, that must be horrible not to eat all those things," I
would respond by listing all the new products coming on the
market for people with our allergies (the truth, by the way).
Later, Danny used to tell part of the story of how he, along
with Mike and me, became ill, and what we need to do to
stay healthy.

Let Your Child Decide, Within Limits,
Whether He Wants to Talk About His Difference

In Chapter 5, we will talk about what our youngster can say
to his friends about his medical condition. But there is another issue: when he should say it and how much control we
should exert over this process. Sometimes parents can go too
far in their efforts to have their children be unapologetic
about their condition and accepted for who they are. Sally
was attending "circle time" at Andy's kindergarten class. "The
other children were sharing things about themselves and had
brought in pictures of when they were younger. We didn't
have any pictures so I decided to tell the kids about Andy's
heart surgery when he was two. Andy showed his zipper scar
and immediately a girl with spina bifida pulled up her shirt
to show her zipper scar. I thought this was great for him to
see. But outside, in the parking lot, he told me how angry
he was that I did that. I realized he does not want that exposed
and that's why he wears crew necks."

Sometimes a child wants to talk about his difference, but
it has to be on his terms and in his time. The day before first
grade, my son instructed his teacher not to tell the class about

his food allergies. His reason was that he had been teased in kindergarten. Two months later, I was wondering how he would handle the special cookies he brought in for a class party. His teacher promptly told me, "Oh, he told the kids about that a long time ago."

Of course, there are also times when you feel that it is appropriate to reveal this information and your child does not. One mother wanted to tell the parents of her son's friend that he had epilepsy. Her son, who was planning to spend the night there, objected. When it is a question of a health risk, remember, your peace of mind is important. Don't withhold information from others that you believe *might* endanger your child's health. His anger at your disclosure will be much easier to live with than your guilt over some unfortunate event that you could have prevented.

Help Your Child Normalize Within Reason

The psychology of difference dictates that we do a delicate dance that supports how our child is different in some ways and the same in others. There are many methods that youngsters and their parents use to look or function more like their peers. Those with cystic fibrosis wear extra layers of clothes to hide malnutrition. When her son with hemophilia wore braces, Suzanne Massie combed the stores for normal shoes with strong, thick rubber soles, so he wouldn't have to wear the "funny-looking" high ones.[9] Maria's son has a fat-metabolism defect. She is a full-time lawyer and yet goes to the trouble of making foods that resemble what her son's friends are eating. "If Travis is going to a party, I will borrow the cookie cutter from the mother the night before, to bake him the Darth Vader, or whatever, without oil. Facsimiles take a lot of time, but at least he's staying on the diet."

The more "normal" a child looks or acts, the more choices she has about what she reveals and what she wishes to keep private. This may also ease the discomfort and subsequent stereotyping on the part of those she encounters. That in turn will help your child.

In addition, while your child may benefit from belonging to a disease support group, she may also derive esteem from being a part of mainstream organizations. Church clubs, team sports, scouts, with the associated T-shirts, emblems, and uniforms, will support her feeling of sameness with the rest of the world.

Expose Your Child to Others Who Are Different

How do we behave toward others whom we encounter who are ill, elderly, or of a dissimilar race? Do we avert our eyes, avoid discussion with our child, cringe if she walks up and asks a question? All these instances can be opportunities to show her that difference does not make someone less of a person. We hope she will not just learn tolerance for other people, but also apply it to herself.

This opportunity is even more instructive if our child has an ongoing relationship with someone who is different, such as a friend or neighbor. Hannah, who is a respite sitter for youngsters with disabilities, says her own son's heart defect does not appear to be an issue. "Every kid in my house has something wrong with him."

In addition to books about children with special health needs, many public television programs, such as "Sesame Street," support the message that difference is not shameful. It doesn't hurt to point this out when Linda, who is hearing impaired, is on the air—a significant place to be in the eyes of a child.

Living with Our Child's
Special Health Needs

MAKE YOURSELF AN EXPERT

Becoming well versed in your child's disease will allow you to provide better care, as in managing the diet and insulin injections for those with diabetes. It will also help you to spot when he is having difficulty. Hannah recalls, "The day my son got the diagnosis of atrial septal defect, I was on the phone to the American Heart Association for pamphlets. I was already a pulmonary expert and I was going to make myself a cardiac expert. We were told when we took our son home at three weeks that he did not need surgery. But he was sweating and frantic and we recognized that this was not normal." Many times, doctors will be seeing your youngster only after you have succeeded in identifying that there is some problem.

But there are other reasons why you need to know exactly what's going on. Expertise will build your esteem as parents by enhancing your effectiveness. This is a useful coping strategy. The mother of a daughter with rheumatoid arthritis recalls, "There were no rehabilitation programs in Iowa then. It was just the two of us and I would work her limbs every day. That was good for her, but it was also good for me because it gave me a way to do something for her."

Expertise may also enable you to have more flexibility in what you do. Diane's son has hemophilia. She remembers, "Once we could give him the concentrate at home instead of going to the hospital, we regained control over our lives. We were able to go traveling for a day and take the stuff with us."

Your youngster will be reassured by your authority in this area. Practically, you will be able to answer her questions and begin to teach her how to care for herself (see Chapter 4).

In addition, parents are ambassadors to those who touch their child's life. Doctors can write the note, but you will be the one to ensure that their recommendations are followed. You will often need to negotiate with mothers, teachers, and other adults to work out special accommodations so that your child can participate. Thoroughly knowing what you are talking about will help you in this process. For example, one ten-year-old girl has asthma and can't play soccer. Her mother suggested to the coach that she keep score instead of waiting out the physical education class in the nurse's office. The Duffys' role in instructing other adults was even more critical. After they learned how to suction Keough's tracheostomy and do CPR, they trained the teachers and aides in the preschool so that she would be able to attend. Only parents who understand can serve as a buffer between their child and the rest of the world.

Parents have educated themselves in many ways. Some, like Kathy McGlynn, have used computer searches to find relevant articles about rare illnesses. Doris's son's heart problem was relatively common and she could tap into the resources of a national organization. Susan Duffy relied on the doctors and nurses who cared for her daughter during her surgery. "They knew we were from out of state and from a small town, so they took the time to teach us and were always responsive when we called. Also, our pediatrician was willing to call them when he had a question." Alice learned about epilepsy from a parents' support group led by Sandy, a nurse with twenty years' experience in the field. The articles I wrote about environmental allergies gave me access to experts. Two other mothers attended annual meetings on Williams syndrome and phenylketonuria. There are ways!

You can do library reading, too, to research medications

and other treatments. The challenge here is interpreting the information you find. While the *Physicians' Desk Reference* can be useful, it does not differentiate between a drug's common and less usual—and therefore more worrisome—side effects. Journal articles usually give one report of what may be an ongoing medical controversy. And textbooks are usually out-of-date.

The hard part of becoming an expert is knowing when to quit—and that is an issue. You don't want to become either overly responsible or overly controlling. The first can place unrealistic demands on you. Denise did respiratory treatment on her daughter every two hours to keep her out of the hospital with her asthma and congestive heart failure. "I realized that my self-worth was tied up in taking care of her and when the IVs were finally shut off, I got depressed. That was sick. I had to stop trying to be *Supermom*."

Being overly controlling discourages other family members from mastering the information. When I finally figured out the rotary diversified diet, I became the family authority on what everyone should eat. Mama Eminence had to declare before anyone took a legitimate bite. That got old, real quick. I then made a chart with pictures of our ingestion agenda. While no one looks at my work of art today, my effort inspired my son, then three and a half. He memorized the diet and is now the spokesman much of the time.

MAKE YOUR MARRIAGE WORK FOR YOU

Although divorce is no more common among parents of children with special health needs, certain stresses are. Stress is inherent in the situation. If we can work our way past some of the difficult issues, our relationships may prevail and even solidify.

First, parents need to work toward seeing the problem

the same way. Although we can't agree on everything, we need to come to terms with the nature of the condition and how to handle it. We can't sidestep conflict about this, even if we don't openly discuss these issues. This is because the practical consequences will inevitably surface in our daily life and cause friction.

Both Don and his former wife have asthma; but their ideas about raising their two sons with asthma differed dramatically. "She grew up with antibiotics and was against them for our kids. I never had them and I'd listen to them slurping the way I did as a child and I thought, God, that's got to be uncomfortable." This ripple of dissension spread to other areas. "I'd have higher expectations of what they could do, like cleaning their rooms, and she would tell me to lay off. She'd want them to stay home with a sniffle and I'd say, big deal—better to go and suffer at school with an atomizer than sit in front of the TV."

These basic disagreements can be disastrous for everyone. A mother's and father's clashing expectations will interfere with their youngster's adjustment to his condition. And the marriage will be at risk because of continual friction. These conflicts are not easily settled because they usually spring from the parents' emotional baggage left over from their own childhoods. While this couple eventually divorced, some spouses continue to struggle with how serious the condition is and what they should expect from their youngster. A professional may be the most effective person to help sort out realistic from irrational concerns.

Mothers and fathers also need to learn how to help themselves feel better. One of the expectations of marriage is that we should be able to comfort each other about shared problems. But often, we end up obsessing together more than anything else. As one father says, "When we do find time alone, the focus of our conversation is always on what is going to become of our son. You can't expect your spouse to make you feel better when she is feeling the same thing."

The fact is that when one of us is up, our spouse is just as likely to be down. At these times, we are not going to welcome their latest reasons for pessimism. Frank Deford recalls talking with his wife about their daughter, Alex, who had cystic fibrosis.

> I came to hate it—hate her, I suppose—when Carol would tell me how something else, something new, had gone wrong with Alex, how something worse had been discovered. *Don't tell me,* I was screaming inside. . . . I felt if I downplayed sad new developments it would be better for both of us than if I merely echoed Carol's despair. But why should I be surprised when she got mad at me for that? You see, there were also times when I was the one especially depressed about Alex, and if Carol did not seem properly sorrowful, I would loathe her for her callousness or envy her ability to escape the moment. There was no way to win. Grief was bad company and optimism was no antidote.[10]

At those times, we need to find other ways to comfort ourselves. Some of us like to talk and some like to tune out. Unfortunately, this difference in style can create its own friction. A wife can mistakenly attribute her husband's silence to lack of involvement. A husband can listen to his wife's preoccupations and falsely conclude that the child is all she cares about.

We need to accept how our mate distracts himself or herself. Kathy McGlynn recalls, "We ended up at marriage counseling. We learned that we had our own ways of unwinding. It was okay for him to stare at a football game to relax and for me to go downtown shopping. We had to back off and give each other space."

We Need to Share the Burden
The stereotype of the family of the special-needs child is that the wife is consumed with the medical care and the husband is isolated. Often some of this cannot be avoided. Practically, mothers are usually the ones in the trenches, dealing with different professionals and caring for the child. But what counts is not what each spouse is doing or whether tasks are equally divided, but rather their underlying attitude.

Marriages that work do so because there is a "we-ness": we are in this together. Alice explains, "We have always been a team. My husband gives our daughter her shot in the morning because it's easier. When Loren was in the hospital for his brain surgery, I'd stay with him until three and my husband arranged to get off work early to relieve me and stay with our son until midnight."

Couples have to go that extra mile of communication to achieve "we-ness." It doesn't just happen. Mothers have to make deliberate efforts to include fathers when they are on the periphery of medical treatment. "At first," Mary Jo recalls, "our son's asthma treatment was so complicated that it was impossible to keep my husband apprised. Everything was happening so rapidly. I put a schedule on the refrigerator of his current medicines. Then I started to worry, what if something happened to me—like a car accident. That's when I decided to put the crisis medicines and the daily ones in different places. If I was unavailable, my husband could just scoop them up and take our son to the hospital."

Fathers need to do some of the "hands on" care in order to be involved. The men I've met who give insulin injections, attend parent support groups, and go to doctor's appointments do not feel shut out. They also contribute their own informed and independent input. Two is much better than one when dealing with the ambiguities of chronic illness and disabilities.

Teamwork is worth struggling for. Some parents say they have a better marriage for having managed these burdens together. They have had to put aside the dead-end ways of handling anxiety: blaming others or pretending the problem doesn't exist. When we do that with our mate and reach some viable plan, we have forged a new strength in our relationship.

MAKE YOUR OTHER KIDS COUNT

"It's a real deprivation. There's no way to rationalize it to them," says one father, describing the impact of his son's hemophilia on his other children. Siblings experience profound reactions to their brother's or sister's special health needs, reactions as profound as ours.

Like the child who is ill or disabled, brothers and sisters may also misunderstand the condition. They may think that they caused it, through their wishes or actions. One boy secretly believed that he had brought about his younger sister's congenital heart defect because he had purposely hit his mother with a ball when she was pregnant. He exposed his private theory four years later at a church support group. Siblings may also be afraid that the illness is catching or that death is imminent. All these misconceptions lead to fear and guilt.

Your other children may also feel resentful. These circumstances may have prevented them from feeling like "just kids." In younger children, this can come about when we understandably become consumed by the welfare of the youngster with special health needs. Jane's infant son, Mark, was diagnosed as having Wilms' tumor, a cancer of the kidney, and was not expected to live the year.

We pushed Alan, our other son, aside. I remember he would come and ask me to read him a story or play a game and that was the last thing I wanted to do. He was only three and a half then, but he seemed to be a brave little soldier because he showed no emotion.

Then one year ago, in therapy, he was playing in the sandbox with family figures. He slipped Mark and Alan under the sand and the other figures from the hospital rushed to get Mark out. When the therapist asked, "What about Alan?" he said, "Everyone was so excited about getting out his brother that they forgot about him."

Jane cries when describing this incident. None of us wishes to pass over the needs of our other children. But life-threatening conditions, especially, can make their demands seem relatively unimportant.

Older siblings experience this "missed childhood" because of the extra responsibility placed on them. Maureen has a four-year-old brother with hemophilia. "I've never said anything to my mom. I think it is only fair to help her out. But I get tired after a long day at school and she wants me to play pattycake with him in the car."

Brothers and sisters may also resent having this "difference" thrust upon them. A brother, embarrassed by his sister's arthritis, said she walked like a duck and initially refused to help her in school. His mother says, "It took a while for him to realize that she was not faking it even though there were no outward signs. And, more important, no one caused this or could fix it, either. Overnight, he became helpful."

Siblings also notice when their brother or sister with special health needs gets "better" treatment. Adelle says, "My daughter complains that when my son gets hurt, we jump. When she gets hurt we are matter-of-fact. I'm afraid she's right." They also notice when we aren't as ready with the discipline. A mother recalls, "My older daughter once exploded with 'Ali gets away with everything.' This woke me up and I realized that I was catering too much." Children also closely monitor who gets what presents. Judy remembers when her older son said her daughter, who has arthritis, was lucky to get an expensive stereo. "I got angry. I said, 'Do you think that's lucky? She can't go out and play like you and she's behind in school.'"

Another problem for siblings is guilt. Like parental guilt, it is generally unfair in that it springs from irrational thinking. It is also difficult to talk about, especially when it is fueled by hostility. Julia Ellifritt used to feel that her retarded sister was a "social disease that would not go away." She writes, "Maybe I would have felt better if Bonnie would have fought back—she never said anything to me, she never hit me. What is worse, when I would do something to her, she would stand there crying and say 'I love you anyway.' She was defenseless and I abused her. Now, years later, I cannot go to her and ask for her forgiveness—she would not know what I was talking about—so I have to live with my guilt."[11]

There are a number of ways you can help your other children deal with their feelings. First, explain the illness to them. Reassure them about common irrational fears by answering their questions and emphasizing that no one caused this and it is no one's fault. But what about younger children?

Jane says, "We made a mistake. We thought that because Alan was only three and a half, he was too young to understand what was happening to his younger brother. But he was old enough to see that we were upset. We should have said something." Whatever she could have said would have had to have been simple, like "sick tummy" and "doctor." But the words are not important. What counts is the process of saying. The message in that act is, We still love you and you are a part of our family.

Let your other children participate in the treatment in small ways, if appropriate. Although you don't want to push them into being custodians, a little involvement helps them feel useful and makes the illness or disability less frightening. For example, when playing out in the yard, the sisters of one family would report when their younger brother was having an asthma attack.

Use these opportunities to thank them; let them know their help is appreciated. "Being taken for granted" was a major complaint I heard from teenagers at a sibling support group. Courtesy easily gets pushed aside to meet the demands of the moment, but we still need it for the long haul.

Even younger children can become involved in a way that makes the condition less mysterious. Mary Jo says, "The little one is two and a half and he thinks that whatever big brother does, he has to do. When Chris has his steroids in the morning, he will have his pills—vitamins. Also, when Chris is finished with his treatment machine, the younger one will go over and breathe into his mask for a few seconds."

Also, try to respond to what is important to your other children. You can't equalize your attention, but you may be able to get across that their needs count, too, even if they are not life-threatening. Simple things—reading a book or attending a soccer game together—can communicate your interest. Sally's son had surgery for a heart defect. She remembers when her older daughter needed a tooth extration. "She thought it was wonderful how we were all hovering over her, for a change. She went to great lengths in her description about what happened and I thought, 'Oh my God, is this what it takes in her mind to get a special niche in our life?'" Although this mother had her concerns, at least she was there when needed.

You can also help ease their guilt about their needs. After all, next to those of a brother or sister with a chronic illness or disability, their concerns may seem unworthy to them. Mary Lou's son is wheelchair-bound from cerebral palsy. She bought a cheerleading outfit for her older daughter but she didn't want to take it. "I told her that's just one-tenth of what I spend on John for physical therapy. She said he needs that and I said you need the cheerleading, too."

Special attention from a family friend or relative can supplement what you can't give. Martha recalls that when Heather was receiving treatment, an aunt took her older daughter horseback riding.

Be ready for their negative feelings, too. Of course, most brothers and sisters will feel angry, embarrassed, or jealous, at times, toward their sib. But it becomes exceptionally difficult to express these sentiments if their sib happens to have special health needs. They may wonder how they could feel anything but good things toward someone who has significant problems. Also, many children would rather not burden their parents whom they may perceive as already just coping.

When unexpressed, these feelings persist and mushroom, only to erode their self-esteem. These children may then question whether they are worthwhile for being anything less than accepting. Ellifritt writes, "I now know that there is sibling rivalry in every family—that bad feelings are not uncommon. But as a child, I was told those feelings were evil."[12]

You can help your other children by listening to their less-than-accepting thoughts. This can be difficult because the tendency will be to protect the child who is ill or disabled. For example, Judy's outraged response to her son's complaint that his sister was "lucky" to get a stereo probably only increased his guilt and jealousy. Best, I think, to avoid the "trading places" logic. Better to explain that these special presents help to keep her busy because she is limited in what she can do.

Much of their protest may be based in the reality of the situation. You can acknowledge that: Yes, it is difficult having a brother who looks different; it is difficult being unable to do certain activities; it is hard to live with all the other limitations imposed on a family because of the illness or disability. You can also point out that the problem is the condition—not their brother or sister.

And sometimes their complaints—Jack gets away with everything—may really be asking, "Do you love me as much as Jack?" They need reassurance in the face of the ongoing inequity of our attention. That's when you can agree with them that it is not fair. Although you can't make it fair, this is not a measure of how much you care about them.

Try to give your other children their own "space." Out of misguided attempts to have them accept the one who is ill or disabled, parents may insist that they do things with him. While sometimes this may be useful, it can be carried to extremes. For example, one mother demanded that her healthy daughter take her younger brother with hemophilia to almost every one of her social occasions. Your healthy youngsters need their time and escape from these problems too.

Have them join or start a support group. Sibling needs are just being recognized by professionals. These groups can provide a special time for them where they can vent feelings. The one I attended role-played how to handle teasing from peers, how to talk to parents when they are angry, and other situations.

Despite the difficulties, having a brother or sister with special health needs can lead to greater empathy and social stamina. At an early age, these sibs must forgo the "ideal" of fitting in and being like everyone else. Some of these children become unusually sensitive and courageous. Alice brought in a mounted photo essay to an epilepsy support group meeting. Her nine-year-old daughter with diabetes had taken pictures of her seven-year-old son with epilepsy. He had posed in different activities under her direction for a class project. The pictures demonstrated her brother's seizures (his right hand sticking out), his shaved head, and the scar from his surgery. The last few shots concluded with the caption, "Now he is out of the hospital, he can do everything he could do before—play basketball, ride his scooter—but now he has no seizures." Alice's comment was, "I didn't even know when they did this." And that was what was so heartening. The project was not programmed by the parents but inspired by the trust between the children.

LAUGH WHEN YOU CAN

Children and their families develop odd jokes to deal with illness and disability. When Amy started putting pebbles in her mouth, I'd tell her that was not on our diet. The more serious the condition, the more odd the humor can get.

When three-year-old Heather was growing bald from chemotherapy, Martha used to sing "Fuzzy wuzzy had no hair." "The song made it funny to her when she'd pull it out and it kept us from crying." In Rainbow Camp, a counselor who was a recovered cancer patient used to call the kids without hair "Kojak." His colleague says, "He had been through it so he earned the right to say that." The wife of a now deceased man who had cystic fibrosis recalls, "Everyone thought Brad was a little strange. The last time he was in the hospital the doctor came in upset and said, 'I'm sorry, we can't do anything more for you.' Brad replied, 'I can understand why you're so upset. You have to go through this many times. I only have to go through this once.' "

Humor can range from offbeat to black. Unfortunately, the bizarreness can scare people. If you have the gift of humor, select your audience wisely and use it. Don't miss out on this emotional release.

3. Don't Feel Sorry

Similar to guilt, feeling sorry is almost inevitable and easily triggered by events that signal that we are even less able to help our children than we imagined. This was my reaction following a preschool conference four years ago. Danny's teacher had described his social delays with far more precision than any of the previous professionals had been able to. Although I was grateful for her insights, I was also unhappy. Her telling made his difficulties that much more real and intractable in my mind. Carla, whose nineteen-year-old son has dwarfism, says, "Yes, that happens to me. I think it's a lonely thing he has to deal with because everything is difficult, like climbing out of a car or getting dressed. What's one step for me is three for him." Hannah, the mother of a two-year-old boy with multiple heart defects, says, "When we're doing all we can at home and not cutting it because we know he's going into the hospital again, that's when it hits us."

Our regrets are unavoidable, yet they impinge on us differently. Some parents experience sporadic twinges that will pass with a new day and a new beginning. Other parents are plunged into an ongoing despair. And many of us have traveled to the edge of that, too. But pull back, we must. A parent who continuously pities a child will stunt her emotional growth in the following ways.

WE BABY OUR CHILD

We may be powerless to take her condition away, but we can at least try to compensate for it. Responding to these wishes, in moderation, may help us to be giving parents. But in excess, we become infantilizing. By doing too much, we inadvertently discourage our youngster from doing what she can.

Many parents have difficulty recognizing when they are doing too much. After all, child rearing, in the most enlightened and experienced hands, is still fraught with ambiguities. At what point does a child's angry outburst turn into a tantrum? When do we sympathize and when do we set a limit? When do we avoid an activity that frightens our youngster and when do we help her face it? How do we recognize when we are too close to her frustrations and need to pull back?

Parenting books have enduring popularity precisely because no one has yet come up with *the* answers. So many decisions are a judgment call about what we believe to be our child's intent, her actual behavior, and our gut reaction. This book, also, does not have *the* answers. Yet there are certain signs to help us recognize when we may be babying our children.

We Are Afraid to Frustrate Them
A few years ago, a friend and I visited a park with our kids. Danny was duking it out with another youngster over the

swing. Sharing was not in the cards that day and I had to make him cool off in the "quiet corner." At that point, he turned to me with blazing eyes, shrieking, "I hate you. I hate you." My friend's face collapsed in horror. "How terrible," she said. In her mind, these were words of ultimate rejection.

Indeed, no one contemplates having children with the fantasy that there will be days when they hate you. But, in fact, that seems to be the case. We all can easily embrace the nurturing side of parenting. That's when we meet their needs and we get the hugs and kisses that feel good. But parenting also demands that we sometimes frustrate what they want, and that can precipitate our rapid fall from their grace.

Kids with special health needs are kids, more than anything else. Like their healthy contemporaries, they, too, will have days when they have journeyed far beyond that elusive state of mind called reason. When this happens, we need to be direct about what's acceptable because they don't know it for themselves. Limits—we've all heard about them.

Parents who have difficulty setting limits usually have difficulty tolerating their children's anger. This can happen to any mother or father, from time to time. After all, most of us want to be loved by our youngsters. Anger threatens this. We will have trouble being honest when we can't put these needs aside.

Unable to be direct, parents resort to other strategies to get youngsters to comply with their wishes. There's guilt, communicated by a tight smile and a strained, "Hurry up, honey. Please don't make Mommy late again." Or we may try to cajole them with laughter about misbehavior. Or we may produce an infinite regression of reasons, prompted by our child's seemingly justified questions. (I'm not against explanations, but long-winded ones tend actually to be arguments in disguise.) These methods teach only that limits may be played with.

Although the words *I hate you* will never sit well, they seem to be a part of the child-rearing experience, and, at times, will be a reassurance that we are doing our job. There are instances when we must say no. Realistically, our kids are not going to feel love for us at that moment. If they can tell it to our face, so much the better, and that's what I said to my friend.

We Don't Hold Them to the Same
Standards as Our Other Children

While in some ways we can't hold our children with special health needs to the same standards, in other ways we can. Do we expect them to perform the age-appropriate tasks that encourage their taking responsibility for themselves and sharing in the family work?

"No. We didn't," recalls a father whose son grew up with life-threatening asthma. "Picking up after himself, when he went to bed at night, or clearing the dishes from the table . . . these seem like little things, but they had a profound impact. We made excuses for him. When you're afraid your kid's going to die, the tendency is not to be so harsh."

We Keep Them from the Reality of Their Illness

Overprotection is a judgment against parents that has been overused. Even so, it does exist. In Chapter 2, we talked about how we can sometimes be too zealous with medical restrictions. Often, we need to learn through observation what our children can and can't do.

But there is also a psychological overprotection, which can be far more serious. Sometimes, in our misguided effort to shield our youngsters, we take on the impossible task of insulating them from their illness. Mae Gamble, the mother of a son with muscular dystrophy, writes:

We first learned that Jesse had muscular dystrophy when he was ten years old. It was over two years later before we told him he had the disease. We were being protective of his feelings. He was so young. How could he handle it?

Even after we told him . . . we continued to hide most of the painful facts. We avoided going to any meetings or places where we might meet someone with the disease. We insisted that he stay in the mainstream of the school system. He never went to a party, summer camp, or any event sponsored by the Muscular Dystrophy Association. We even managed to keep the family busy on Labor Day so none of us, especially Jesse, could watch the Jerry Lewis Telethon.[1]

This couple eventually came to the conclusion that they actually had been harming their son. "We were robbing him of experiences which would help him learn to accept the disease and live with it. . . . Just because he has a physical weakness does not mean that he is emotionally weak, unable to control his behavior or unable to make decisions for himself." They found that the more they educated their son about his condition, the less anxious he became. Although distressing, the known was less frightening than the unknown.

We Speak for Them
Of course, most of us start out being the mouthpiece for our youngsters. A simple question such as "How old is he?" is easily answered by parents. Yet, at some point, we need to step aside and give the floor to them, whether or not they choose to respond. Although the age at which we do this will vary, depending on their development, the principle remains:

We must relinquish our role as interpreter. To ignore this is to treat our children as incompetent.

Children with visible differences are particularly likely to be pushed into the role of silent observers of conversations. Strangers and casual friends who are uncomfortable may ask, "How is *he* doing?" when *he* is right there. As parents we need to resist answering these queries and redirect them.

WE STIMULATE SELF-PITY AND UNDERMINE THEIR COURAGE

Betsy, now sixteen, was diagnosed as having rheumatoid arthritis when she was eighteen months old. Her mother, Teresa, described her as a frail little girl who cried out in pain whenever she tried to move. She also developed the physical disfigurements that often go with the illness: swollen deformed hands and feet, and a slow limping walk brought about by involvement of her hip joint.

Over the years, Teresa says, she became overpowered by Betsy's pleas for assistance. "First, they were little things like turning on the bathwater. Then she wanted me to carry her instead of using crutches. She refused to even try using them. I couldn't make myself say no, yet I knew that somehow this was going too far."

In elementary school, Betsy's classmates looked after her as if she were a play doll. But in junior high these "friendships" dissolved when the girls were no longer interested in babying her. Betsy, accustomed to being taken care of, had no other way of relating to peers. She was convinced she was as pathetic as she felt. Her mother became desperate as she watched her daughter's embittered withdrawal. Betsy would routinely return from school, prop her bent little body up on the living-room couch, and vilify the girls who rejected her.

Today Teresa says, "I should have pushed her. She should

have had chores, even if she had to crawl across the kitchen floor to do them. That would have been far more useful than my saying, 'It's too bad you can't walk better.' Maybe she would have tried more."

Instead of facing their situation and making the most of it, pitied children rely on others to make it up to them. Of course, the "world" can't. Their expectations are unfulfillable and leave them feeling disillusioned and abandoned. These individuals are too depleted of courage to try and find out what they can do for themselves. Teresa adds, "It's easy to fall into a pattern. You think you are helping them because they are so helpless, but you are just making yourself feel better. I wish I had had a someone around who could have given me different advice."

WE UNDERMINE OUR FAMILY

Our pity is not private. It can be all-consuming and soak up our attention and energy. Kay describes her life after she gave birth to a son with albinism. "I felt so bad for him that I withdrew into my own little world. No one could reach me there and the stares didn't bother me. After a while, my husband got angry and told me to snap out of it. He said I was not doing Ted any good, or anyone else for that matter. He was right."

Also, our pity can tyrannize those around us. The sister who is jealous or the husband who feels pushed aside are implicitly discouraged from talking about their less worthy emotions. Michael, whose brother grew up with diabetes, says, "In our family, I wasn't supposed to discuss how I felt about him. I was just expected to understand. But I didn't see why he got so many special breaks, even if I couldn't say anything."

ULTIMATELY, OUR CHILDREN MAY NOT THANK US FOR OUR PITY

Pity is seductive. It confers a certain importance, and many in unfortunate circumstances may temporarily seek this from others as an emotional compensation. Despite this attraction, children with special health needs may finally reject this "gift." As young as they are, they also sense the downside: Pity erodes self-esteem.

When Jackie Cottrell was in seventh grade, her cystic fibrosis made her feel isolated from her peers. She became desperate for recognition on any terms:

> I unconsciously realized that I had a built-in attention getter. I had a serious illness and if I was noticeably sick, nobody dared ignore me. . . . Nothing could interrupt class more effectively than someone coughing so hard and persistently that they had to hurry from the room to "go get a drink." What no one realized was that water didn't help in the least and that I could, more or less, stop coughing whenever I wanted to.
>
> The final ace up my sleeve was the "hospital." Being in the hospital was, quite honestly, great. My mouth would say, "I don't like being sick," but the rest of me was saying, "Look at all the attention I am getting." . . . What I refused to acknowledge was that people were not being nice to me because I was an interesting person. Rather, they were being nice because I was a "poor, sick, child who is going to die."
>
> Life went on like this for about two years. . . . I received many gifts and had many visitors and never really allowed myself to get completely well. My entire being was based on the fact that I was a girl who had cystic fibrosis. It was slowly dawning on me, though, that possibly I had more to offer the world.[2]

Pity undermines optimism. This letter was written by an eleven-year-old girl with leukemia, one month before she died:

> I have acute lymphoblastic leukemia. But please don't feel sorry for me. I live a perfectly wonderful life.
>
> I go to parties, play games, swing on swings, and for the most part I am able to do whatever I want. I think that this is an important part of life which some parents of children who have leukemia overlook, and I think they should not. I think that children who have leukemia should be able to play whenever they feel up to it, unless they have a cold or just had a shot that makes them sick.[3]

Of course, many of our children may feel sorry for themselves from time to time, just as we do. As parents, we wield tremendous power in either stimulating this reaction or encouraging the opposite: their courage to cope with their circumstances.

How to Fight Feeling Sorry

As with guilt, parents can take control of their pity so that it does not dominate family life. Here are some suggestions.

BECOME A WATCHDOG OF YOUR BEHAVIOR

We are all aware that feelings give rise to behavior. For example, we feel guilty and we may apologize, silently put ourselves down, or find some way to deprive ourselves, such as not going to the movies. What's less obvious is that these behaviors may also reinforce the original feelings. The penance is intended to erase the crime. Actually, sometimes

just the opposite occurs. The punishment reinforces our belief that we should be blaming ourselves. Our guilt has been
fortified.

Feeling sorry works the same way. This emotion can result
in babying our ill children. Each time we engage in these
behaviors, we feed the original feeling. On the other hand,
we can starve the feeling by changing or ceasing what we are
doing.

The first step involves cultivating restraint. We may need
to sit on our natural reactions. Rhoda's twelve-year-old
daughter has rheumatoid arthritis. "I find I have to bite my
tongue. I see her running after her friends on crutches and
I want to yell at her not to do that. But this way she's part
of the group."

The second step requires that we find new ways to respond to our children. Annie says of her five-year-old daughter with hypothyroidism and hearing and visual impairments,
"We used to let her off the hook too easily. We were making
baby sounds, actually jokes, when she was doing something
she shouldn't. Also, we didn't make her complete tasks. Now,
if she spills something, we sit together with a rag until she
cleans it up."

MAKE SOCIAL COMPETENCE YOUR GOAL

Mary, a pulmonary nurse who cares for those with cystic
fibrosis, advises parents, "We don't know how long your child
will live. There may be a cure. You need to raise him so that
you don't have a thirty-year-old brat running around who
can't fit into society."

Social competence is adaptive and another antidote to our
pity. Being relatively at ease with others will naturally allow
our children to do more with more people. They will lead a
more satisfying life. The Duffys' daughter with Down's and

repaired gastrointestinal anomalies is now in "regular" first grade. Susan recalls, "We did not know how well she would do intellectually, but what might get her through these situations was manners. We were very aware of that from the beginning."

Also, putting a priority on social competence communicates to our children that they, also, have a rightful place in this world. "From day one, I put them and myself in a position to be social," says Audrey, who has two sons with cerebral palsy. "Carl came home on the monitor and I took him out in public, even though heads turned. I keep my kids involved like typical children. Carl plays T-ball in his wheelchair by picking a designated runner."

Teaching social competence to a child with special health needs is really not different from teaching this to any child. Of course, this does not make the process any less mysterious. We all have our own ideas of how to go about this task. And for better and sometimes worse, our own behavior will be far more instructive than any of our words. Here are some generalizations:

For starters, we need to expect good manners at home. While this truth may seem self-evident, it's amazing how bad manners can sneak into the most civilized households, including my own. Interruptions and demands fall into this category. And we can't kid ourselves about a barked "please" and "thank you," which are, in fact, orders.

We are not doing our children any favors by allowing them to "get away" with disrespect, especially toward us. This will only make them feel unlovable. (Even young children sense when their words are abusive.) At the same time, they will lose us as effective parents. (If we can't help them control themselves, what can we do?) Many youngsters naturally want to stretch the limits of good manners and see how "nice" they really have to be. It's up to us to remind them.

We can also show, or *role-model,* friendliness outside the home. Make the most of ongoing casual contacts. Hairdressers, librarians, and cashiers provide opportunities for our child to see us talking with others and to practice their own social skills.

And what are these skills? Making eye contact is a must to get any conversation started. We can teach that by first being sure that we have our child's eye contact when we talk to him. If necessary, bend down to his level so that you know you have his attention.

When we go out, we can show him how to get other people's attention: by looking directly at them and piping up with an "Excuse me," or some variant. Stores are wonderful social gyms for practicing these skills. When our child wants something, we can use these opportunities to have him do the asking. Begin with rehearsing what he should say and then accompany him. Gradually work up to having him approach the store clerk on his own.

If your child has a visible illness or disability, you may find that people stare at him when he is distant and avert their eyes when he is close. This is a disheartening experience. Although this avoidance is hurtful, it is generally not hostile. Physical defects are threatening for people. They scare others in that they serve as a reminder of everyone's vulnerability. They shame others in that they promote an irrational vicarious embarrassment. And they stimulate guilt because observers reflect, "There, but for the grace of God, go I." Most individuals cannot pull themselves out of this emotional swamp. Instead, they do the easiest thing, which is to turn away.

If you want your child to socialize, unfair as it is, you need to show him how to go that extra mile of communication. Explain to him that this avoidance is not his fault. Even some grown-ups are made uneasy by the sight of an illness or disability. That's what Linda did when she took Renée grocery shopping attached to her ventilator. She said,

"They just aren't used to seeing people with tubes." Next, give him plenty of practice in getting people's attention.

The more refined social skills, such as learning to listen and ask appropriate questions, will naturally evolve from how we speak with our children, the ensuing exchange, and their basic temperament.

NURTURE YOUR CHILD'S SELF-ESTEEM

We will feel less sorry for the child who loves himself. Like social competence, fostering self-esteem is a process that all parents struggle with. How can we help our kids to feel good about themselves? Volumes have been written about this subject precisely because there is no one answer. However, there are some generalizations.

Accept Your Child

Unfortunately, this has become a child-rearing cliché and, as a result, has had real meaning squeezed out of it. Yet define it we must, in order to grasp our choices and consequences in this complex process. How we accept our children has a profound impact on how they accept themselves. And the "how" is critical. We need to embrace our child's illness or disability a "realistic" amount, whatever that is, and then see him beyond it, whatever that turns out to be.

Although a child is not his medical condition, the experience has shaped him into the person he is. Indeed, it has shaped us as parents, too. Robert K. Massie, Jr., the son of the couple who authored *Journey,* writes, " 'Having a chronic illness' is an elusive concept because one's illness becomes melded into one's identity. To ask what I would be like without hemophilia is an impossible question to answer, like asking who Abraham Lincoln would have been if he had been a midget. Clearly there is a me distinct from hemophilia, but it is hard to say sometimes where the boundaries to that me are. Who would Helen Keller have been if she had been a sighted and hearing little girl?"[4]

In Chapter 2, I mentioned that we can sometimes deny what Massie describes as this "melded" identity by seriously minimizing the illness. This refusal may spring from our wish to protect, but our efforts are misguided. What the child may end up feeling is not protection but rejection.

Harilyn Rousso's parents did not discuss her cerebral palsy and how it might affect her future. Yet her mother made numerous attempts for her to go to physical therapy so that she could learn to walk more normally. Although as a child she didn't understand her mother's reasons, she vehemently opposed her efforts.

> Now I understand why. My mother's attempt to change my walk, strange as it may seem, felt like an assault on myself, an incomplete acceptance of me, an attempt to make me over. I fought it because I wanted to be appreciated as I was. It is hard to believe that a disability, which seems like a liability, a defect, an eyesore, could be an okay, important part of a child's body and self. It's not that I would choose to be disabled, if one could do such a thing, but rather my disability, like other salient characteristics I was born with, is part of me.[5]

As parents, we can't afford emotionally to flee from the illness/disability side of our child. Yet there is no doubt, at least in my mind, that refusing to accept some limitations may help, too, under certain circumstances. That had been my attitude. Danny was not going to grow up a withdrawn individual, severed from the warmth of other people, and that was all there was to it. And many other mothers and fathers have been fueled by a kind of dug-in stubbornness to lick their problem, whatever it was. They also have been

lucky in that they turned out to be right. The startling functioning of many children with Down's syndrome today is due
to their parents' saying no to institutionalization. But we must
make no mistake. The word is *lucky*. There are many other
parents who have been equally as persistent that have not
been as fortunate.

The issue, then, for each of us is what is a "realistic"
amount of normality to expect from our child? If we expect
too much, we run the risk of rejecting him as he is. If we
expect too little, we will fail to encourage him to do the most
he can with himself. There is no one answer for all of us, or
even for all of us dealing with the same condition. The best
we can do is to realize that this is an ongoing question that
we need to consider.

"Seeing the child beyond the illness or disability" is another expression that has had the meaning wrung out of it
by years of overuse. Even so, there is merit in these words.
The idea is that if we view our youngsters primarily as "sick,"
then "sick" will become their view of themselves. Stereotyping, even sympathetic and understanding stereotyping, can
be destructive.

Actually, all parents can blind themselves to those with
whom they are most tightly bonded. Call it an occupational
hazard. Mothers and fathers run the risk of getting overly
focused on one aspect of their youngster. Familiarity breeds
habits, and this includes habits in perceptions. How many of
us have heard others talk about their normal child as the
"tough guy," "brain," or "princess"?

Sometimes parents will do this when they are anxious
about the trait. The danger is that each time parents equate
their child to this one thing, they are unwittingly reinforcing
that quality, whether they like it or not. Also, they may fail
to react to their child's other characteristics. For example, a
youngster who is seen as a "tough guy" is easily labeled that
when he gets into a scuffle. But he may not get the recognition

he needs when he peacefully plays with a peer. This latter event sadly becomes the anomaly that doesn't fit with the boy's image and is, therefore, easily dismissed. While I don't believe we create our child's temperament, we may have more opportunities than we imagine to influence it by our reactions.

Likewise, parents of children with special health needs can also get stuck in mental sets. The most common one for us is seeing our youngsters as victims, either of the disease or of the society that fails to embrace them. Our biases may have more than a grain of truth to back them up. But if we treat them as victims, we unwittingly reinforce helplessness. We may fail, then, to recognize and nurture other qualities that might serve as the antidote.

Linda could have said what amounted to "poor dear" when Renée was stared at in the grocery store. But this would have only served to isolate her daughter further by communicating that people are callous. Instead, this mother explained the reasons for the behavior and then took her out again on other trips.

What kind of person is your son or daughter? Creative? Friendly? A leader? The more we respond positively to these other qualities, the more we may offset his seeing himself as a victim. The parents I talked to volunteered many different things about their youngsters. Renée is constantly playing practical jokes on the unsuspecting—her nurse's son, friends, and so on. Linda describes her daughter: "This is an outgoing girl. It doesn't mean that she is happy all the time, but she is struggling to deal with it." Mary Lou says of John, who is wheelchair-bound from cerebral palsy, "I admire his patience. I have watched him try small tasks for hours and not call it quits. Also, he is generous in giving of himself. Kids come to him to talk when they have problems."

Of course, dealing with the whole child also means recognizing her less-than-laudatory qualities. How does Alexander, who has hemophilia, feel about chores? His mother answers proudly, "He complains, 'Why do I have to do everything?' You know, just like any kid." "Just like any kid" would be a welcome description for most of us. Indeed, I was both surprised and relieved to see that when Amy turned four, she had acquired much of the same irritating behavior that Danny had had. Not all of our trials had been due to developmental delays secondary to food allergies.

Each of us would be well advised to recognize that our youngsters, too, can engage in the usual pain-in-the-neck carryings-on. Their illness or disability does not transform them into saints. And their condition does not take away their apparently inalienable right occasionally to try and drive their parents nuts.

Make Your Child's Life as Predictable as Possible

Youngsters, especially ones under the age of six or seven, have little understanding of linear time and bounce from moment to moment, mostly in the moment. But with our deliberate guidance, life can assume some predictability. This, in turn, should help them experience the world as more manageable and help make them more secure.

Predictability comes from establishing routines. There are many routines during any week, including playtime, bed, meals, going to church. For example, in our home we do certain things at dinner. My husband stumbles in the front door and is besieged by flying children, he changes his clothes, we all set the table, our kitchen is transformed into a Tower of Babel, and then our kids are excused until dessert, and Mike and I get our chance to talk.

Protecting these routines may sound simple but, in fact, can be a challenge. We all set our priorities, but are we able to stick to them during an onslaught of competing demands? For example, there are a myriad of threats to mealtime. Business phone calls and meetings can all but destroy anyone's dinner hour and with it that special period when we get together and share our triumphs and frustrations of the day.

Of course, you will not be able totally to defend any routine from disruption and I'm not sure that that would be desirable, in any case. But you need to warn your children in advance when you deviate from what they anticipate. The younger they are, the more often they need to be reminded that Daddy won't be home tonight for dinner, Mom's going to be away this afternoon, and a baby-sitter will be here, and so on.

Predictability is even more crucial when the event involves your child's health, such as a doctor's appointment. Again, going over the when—such as, next week after school you are going to get allergy shots—allows your youngster to prepare. This emotional groundwork is even more necessary for medical procedures and hospitalization, if you know in advance. Ask the child-life specialists at your facility to suggest how you can specifically help your child prepare.

Support Your Child's Separation

Actually, child rearing is one big weaning process. The breast is only the first stop in our youngster's continual progression away from us. This is also true for the child with an illness or disability. Educating the care giver (for example, teacher, friend's mother) to meet her health needs is crucial and will be covered in Chapters 5 and 6.

Parents need literally to be there at significant times. Each transition—from home to play group, kindergarten, grade school, junior high—is going to generate a certain anxiety in her, and us, for that matter. But there are ways we can alleviate some of this stress.

For younger children: Stay with your child until she settles into a new situation. Taking favored objects from home (for example, stuffed animals) also helps, along with telling her, in terms she understands, when you will return. Use events, along with numbers, to cue into her sense of time ("I will be here after your lunch, at one o'clock"). Separations that are broken up, even by brief contact with a parent, will be easier on younger ones. For example, one working mother has arranged to have lunch with her child. Another picks hers up at preschool and drives her to day care.

For a child over six or seven: She doesn't need hand-holding so much as our "consultation." What do you think would make her comfortable in this new situation? If she doesn't know, your suggestions may help get her to consider different options. For starters, visiting new schools, meeting teachers before class begins, and talking to others who attend are useful strategies.

Supporting this separation early on should help your child later. Even so, she will naturally need you more during times of illness and hospitalization and when she makes that transition back into "normal" life. Jennifer, who is now fifteen, was frightened to return to school on crutches after the diagnosis of rheumatoid arthritis was made. Her mother recalls, "I made it a point to go with her and stayed until she saw how the kids reacted."

Cultivate His Hope

A child can easily get discouraged about his condition. Hope helps him to keep struggling. One mother of four children with food allergies says, "I tell them it's not a forever thing and that helps them do what they have to today." Todd says of his diabetes, "Someday there will be a cure for it."

How realistic must his hope be? Not very, providing it doesn't set him up for obvious disillusionment or interfere with his taking care of himself. A father whose son died from a heart defect when he was twenty-five remembers, "Kirk had three wishes. He wanted to go to college, get married, and have an operation. I knew that by the time the corrective surgery was perfected he would have too much damage to be able to use it. But he got two out of the three."

Religious convictions can also nurture our youngster's hope. Rabbi Kushner, whose son died from progeria at age fourteen, writes,

> I also believe that sick children should pray. They should pray for the strength to bear what they have to bear. . . . They should pray as a way of talking out their fears without the embarrassment of having to say them out loud, and as a reassurance that they are not alone. God is close to them even late at night in the hospital when their parents have gone and all the doctors have left. . . . Sick children can even pray for a miracle to restore them to good health, as long as they do not feel that God is judging them to decide whether or not they deserve a miracle. They should pray because the alternative would be giving up all hope and marking time until the end comes.[6]

Also, don't minimize how important hope is for you. Many parents can agree with this father whose daughter has uncontrollable epilepsy, "If you don't have hope, why bother?"

Give Her a Choice

Our children may be denied the gratification that comes from the usual forms of mastery. Riding bikes and playing sports may not be options for her. But we can exploit the areas in which she can make her own decisions. And these don't have to be dramatic things—just the routine decisions of her life that we may unnecessarily control. Choice will feed her sense of independence.

Audrey, whose two sons have cerebral palsy, says, "As soon as they could, they told the barber what kind of haircut they should have—like a flat top. It's their heads." My kids have snack and juice drawers where they pull out what they want without having to ask me. Managing allowance money and having their own telephone book with friends' numbers will also give them more control over their daily existence. We need to be on the lookout to see where we can back off and let them take over. This constantly changes and it's easy to get in the habit of deciding more than we should.

Use Praise Wisely

If only the words *wonderful* and *very good,* voiced often enough, could infuse the self-esteem that we wish for our children. But, alas, they don't, not even for youngsters with special health needs. Like many words, the more we use them, the less meaning and impact they have on others. If everything is "wonderful," then nothing really is.

Actually, praise can create problems. It communicates our approval, which is, in essence, our judgment. And when our judgment grows too important to our children, it stifles. Youngsters who need to succeed too much will be afraid to do what they can't do well. And what they do will only assume value when it is approved of, as opposed to being enjoyed. When their accomplishments go unnoticed, they feel scorned.

Also, children with special health needs may even feel "talked down to" if given too many compliments. Excessive praise can be a disguised form of pity. It communicates "I feel so sorry for you that I believe I must constantly bolster you."

Children, like everyone, need to feel valued for who they are, not what they do. Dorothy, a school nurse who has had rheumatoid arthritis since adolescence, is sensitive to this issue. "I help teach the self-esteem program and wonder whether there is too much emphasis on what we can accomplish as a way of feeling good. I wouldn't have noticed this had I not been ill myself. There's a real problem if this is the only way you become acceptable to yourself. After all, we are all going to be doing less as we get older, sick or not. How does this approach prepare us?"

Our praise is a tool of motivation. Like any tool, it can be applied poorly. Try not to overdo it.

Avoid "good," "wonderful," and other generalities by themselves. Overused terms will fail to communicate interest and encouragement. Instead, find words that are specific to the task. For example, if it's a drawing, we can say, "I like the colors, the detail, the subject selected, etc."

Compliment the doing more than what's done. Again, with the picture, you can say, "You really must enjoy drawing. It's wonderful to have something you can do on your own which is fun."

Use praise for small "step" achievements. Children easily get the idea that they ought to be doing something "right," right away. They observe what others have drawn, for example, and have no way of knowing about the practice that went into that activity. They need recognition when they put the first few lines on the paper.

Also, use whatever skill you are developing to reinforce the message that mastery takes time. I was struggling over a piece of piano music for weeks. The kids and I went to the library so I could listen to a recording of it. Initially, I wasn't thrilled about having the three of us on one set of earphones. But then my son said, "You know, Mom, he really plays much better than you do." That made the ordeal worthwhile. I could mention how much we all need to practice to do things the way we'd like to.

Don't be afraid to praise so-called failures. That's when you can step in and support your children's efforts. And frankly, their ability to persist without the reward of immediate mastery will be far more useful to them than will any particular skill. The first year of basketball was discouraging for Danny. He was slow to catch on to which was the correct basket and he was the shortest boy, to boot. His team rarely passed to him. But he practiced. And when he was upset after many of the games, Mike and I praised his stick-to-it attitude.

Finally, have the courage not to praise. Our children can easily get sidetracked into performance. Recently Amy and I were in the pool and a little girl came over and asked her *not* her name or do you want to play, but, "Do you want to watch me swim?" My own kids have also been into "Watch me." While acceding to this request in moderation seems reasonable, it can be destructive in excess. Praise "on demand" will not nurture self-esteem. It only communicates that we believe our children to be too fragile to live without it. A terse, or even a prolonged "very nice" will not satisfy a distorted need for our audience. In fact, our response will only stimulate this need because it reinforces their asking.

We need the courage *not* to say "very nice." That's when our children could use our specific direction on how to get away from their "Watch me"s. "Show me one more time and then go play with your friends. I'm going to talk to mine." This alternative may not be readily embraced by many children. But then again, giving up short-term gratification for long-term strength isn't embraced by adults, either—which doesn't mean we shouldn't do it.

Let Your Child Contribute to Family Life

While we all can't do the same things, we can all contribute to the best of our capabilities. Our children with illnesses or disabilities need these opportunities, too. Expecting less from them may seem humane. It is not. Our doing everything only cultivates their sense of helplessness and false expectation that the world will provide. Finding ways that they can help out, no matter how small, will allow them to show that they can pull their own weight.

The chores you select will naturally depend on your child's age and illness. But if you are committed to the importance of her contribution, you surely can find something she can do. The activity should be something social that she can either do with you or in your presence. Denise's daughter, who has a congenital heart defect and asthma, empties the bathroom trash and feeds the goldfish. Rose's teenager with arthritis loads the dishwasher after dinner. "Some days she can't reach the bottom rack so she just does the upper. It makes her feel good when we tell her it's a great job."

Chores for the child with special health needs may also cut down on the resentment of your other children. They see by your actions that there is no one special who is exempt from the tasks of living.

Let Your Child Live by the Family Rules

If we are a "soft touch," we are not doing our children any favor. We are, in essence, treating them as less responsible for their words and deeds than others who are "normal." This kind of permissiveness undermines their self-respect. That's because permissiveness does not support the development of a child's self-control. They will be denied the sense of mastery that comes with being able to one day set their own limits.

Our kids are like any kids, in that it is always open season for what rules they may try to bend. They readily sense when they can sidestep our wishes and quickly seize on the strategies that work. Mark, who was operated on for Wilms' tumor, tells his mother that he shouldn't have to sit in the corner for misbehavior since he only has one kidney. Robie, a teenager with asthma, says he'd mow the lawn if he didn't have allergies. Carmen's son gets headaches from his allergies when she asks him to do a chore. Mary Jo's son with asthma throws a tantrum when she asks him to pick up in his room.

All these parents were wise to the attempt at manipulation. But it can sometimes be difficult to tell whether our empathy or limits are called for. Our children may say, "I feel bad, or sad," but what do they really want from us? A hug? Reassurance that they will feel better? Or a break from feeding the dog? Sometimes they may not be feeling well enough for the task. Other times, their expression of unhappiness may be directed at putting aside something they'd rather not do. Often we have to go on our gut reaction to tell the difference.

Mary Jo recalls that her son used to throw himself on the floor when she asked him to clean up. "I knew he would have trouble breathing. I'd tell him, 'You can throw your fit now.' After it was over, I would treat the attack and then tell him again to clean up his room. We went through this two or three times until he learned."

This is not to say that setting limits is easy, especially when they involve the risk of our children becoming ill. Mary Jo says, "I'd hear him screech and I'd think, Is this really worth it? Of course it was. I wanted him to know that life goes on, even with his asthma. I'd feel guilty, too, but I knew I would get over this."

Observing or hearing about how our children do with others may help us set limits. We may be surprised to learn that they exhibit far more competence with those who are less conditioned to meet their needs. Carmen reports, "My mother got after me for how I was acting with my son. She thought I was doing too much. I saw for myself he'd be happy until I walked through the door. Then he started to whine."

But living by the family rules involves more than equal

discipline and chores. The general idea is that we shouldn't *unnecessarily* distort family life for one person. Of course, we can't help many things, and parents reading this book are well aware of how much additional attention a child with an illness or disability needs. But there may be situations in which we have a choice.

For example, my family was in a restaurant, and I told the waitress about our food allergies so that she would understand why we omitted the buns, butter, and cheese. My son became angry and said, "Why did you have to tell her about my problem?" But our meal involved all of us and we all have this problem. Going along with his request seemed too much. After his cardiac surgery, Sally and her husband would let her son eat whatever he wanted. "But soon," says Sally, "he wanted the whole family to eat what he ate." She thought that this was excessive.

Usually, only we parents have a fine enough appreciation of everyone's limitations and family routines to decide what's "too much." But decide we must, because punting on this question can make our child too powerful. And, like any child, he will naturally seek this power and feel guilty for having it at the same time. (He does not need extra burdens.) His brothers and sisters are also likely to feel anger at the inequity.

In resisting these manipulations, it helps to realize that the attitude of "anything to make her happy" is a forever journey. No one thing will ever satisfy if a child gets sidetracked from the goal of how to make herself happy to how to control others.

HELP YOUR CHILD WITH WHAT SHE *CAN* DO

The process starts early. Our positive attitude will point our children in the direction of doing the most they can. I was particularly struck with this when I visited Kay. Her house is built on a hill of rocky boulders. I was with my daughter and fearful whether Amy could balance on the inclines. Kay's son Ted, then four, is albino and visually impaired. She told me, "I take in baby-sitting and I tell all the moms, 'My son's blind and he's been climbing these since he was two.'" Indeed, Ted was scampering around the edge of ten-foot drop-offs with his chest bent forward. She explained, "I never say to him you can't see that or you can't do that. I look for ways he can." She taught him how to navigate these rocks by first touching the surfaces on all fours and then raising his body, a little at a time. To be honest, I held my breath as I watched Amy trail after him.

Our flexibility—that is, our ability to see how many ways we can "skin a cat"—can go a long way in supporting our children's self-esteem and socialization. How can we modify a situation so that the child can get at least a taste of the activity? Big Wheels instead of bicycles for those with hemophilia, pretreatments with bronchodilators for athletes with asthma, the opportunity to do arthritis exercises alongside classmates in a gym class—these are some of the solutions parents have discovered. Kirk had heart disease and went to high school in the 1960s. His father recalls, "He could only walk up three or four steps before he became breathless. He took all his classes on the same floor. That meant one semester he had four classes of English and the next he had four classes of science, but he graduated. We also found a college for him. It was all in one building and there was an apartment house next to it. He never could have walked a campus."

Sometimes, our children may also surprise us with their own unique solutions. Rose started a preschool in her home to stay with her daughter who is in a wheelchair because of arthritis. "One day, she called for help to put on her shoes. I couldn't come because I was busy with a preschooler. But Jennifer figured out a way. She rolled up a magazine into a half-tube, pushed it in her shoe, and then slipped her foot in it. She was so excited about her new method that she told her arthritis group."

Make the most of the interests they can pursue. Suzanne Massie describes what she did with her son: "When legs cannot move, it is important that the hands be kept busy. So I taught Bobby to sew buttons and to knit; later he learned to weave. Before he could read, I taught him how to cook. But not as a game . . . as a serious business, to teach him discipline and develop in him a sense of perfection in small tasks. This was important because with little or no challenge from the outside he had to learn in other ways to strive for excellence."[7]

Diane's son who has hemophilia has always been fascinated with drama and the arts. "Every May I'd look at all the school and church schedules and sign him up. I'd volunteer to build the sets and paint. Actually, even if my son had not been ill, I don't think he would have liked sports."

BE *JUDICIOUSLY* BLUNT

Some parents have found it useful to be matter-of-fact about the illness or disability when they sense their children slipping into a sea of self-defeating sorrow. Don's son has asthma. "One morning, he sounded like he was sucking in the bathtub, he was so slurpy. I asked him whether he took his meds and he told me he didn't because he didn't want to be different. That was it. I said, 'You've got asthma and that medicine lets you breathe. I grew up with asthma, too. Someday, it will probably leave you, but right now you've got to take care of yourself.' "

Other parents have been even more blunt. All of Sheila's five children have food allergies. "Sometimes they get into complaining. I tell my children that this is a handicap and most everyone has some handicap. We can kick and scream about it or be grateful that there is some way to help ourselves."

This approach may be useful as long as we remain relatively matter-of-fact. However, if we become angry, we can easily end up asking our children to turn off their feelings. They then become even more isolated. Ellen Ruben writes about her experience growing up with diabetes: "My family's favorite lecture was 'You're so lucky compared to other people. You should be glad you are not so-and-so, or that you don't have such and such a problem. Don't complain. Count your blessings.' If I ever said anything negative about diabetes, I felt like an ungrateful brat."[8]

Telling our child about how other people's problems are worse will not make him feel better about his own. Actually, this kind of suffering tends to escalate because the sufferer knows he has not been heard. What we need to do, first, is make sure we *hear* the message. Many times what someone really wants is only acknowledgment of his pain, not the impossible—that we take it away ("Yes, it must be hard for you to watch what the other kids can do"). After that, we can talk about what he *can* do.

LOOK FOR ROLE MODELS

We are fortunate to be living in an era in which people go public with their medical conditions. In writing to different organizations, I learned: Sylvia Chase (network broadcast journalist), Mary Tyler Moore (actress), Bobby Clark and Curt Fraser (hockey players), to name a few, have diabetes; Bobby Jones (basketball player), Gary Howatt (hockey player), and Tony Coelho (former congressman) have epilepsy. Representative Coelho writes, "For years I hesitated to tell people I had epilepsy but when I entered public life I decided to bring it out in the open. . . . I have tried in many ways to become a public figure who works on behalf of all of us who have epilepsy."[9]

These people can be encouraging examples. If our children see them on TV, the ultimate validator, so much the better. One mother says, "My son did not want anyone to know about his diabetes. But then he saw this rock star on some show who said he had it and how life goes on. That helped." Maria, who has a son with a fat-metabolism defect, says, "My son loves basketball, but he is the shortest in his class. He says, 'As long as I grow as tall as Spud Webb [a five-foot-six-inch basketball player].' "

Books and periodicals can also be useful. Figure skater Elizabeth Kornfield has written, in *Dreams Come True*,[10] about how she won't let epilepsy stop her. Magazines and newsletters geared for those with a specific medical condition often feature profiles on individuals who have successfully struggled with the problem. Sometimes our children may even get the opportunity to meet these people. Diane took her son who has hemophilia to hear Robert K. Massie, Jr., talk to their Phoenix support group. The annual meetings of national organizations often schedule afflicted adults who talk directly to parents and their children about how they are coping. Jack Williams, a stockbroker who has had arthritis since age fourteen, spoke at the 1986 American Juvenile Arthritis Organization Conference. "My goals have taken longer," he explained. "It took me five and a half years to finish college and a few more years to complete my MBA. . . . It used to play havoc on my mind that my friends had graduated and were making money and I was still grinding it out. But then I realized what counts is that I finished too."[11] The message, of course, is that our children may have a chance to do the same.

4. Teach Him How to Care for Himself

Medical treatment is more than the daily ritual, or grind, of doing what the doctor says. The event easily becomes emotionally charged for both us and our children. As parents, we focus on making sure that the treatment happens. A certain anxiety is unavoidable, whether we administer the treatment or count on our youngster to do it. Were the exercises performed correctly? Are the medicines effective? Is the special diet adequate? Despite our apprehensions, we may come to welcome, or at least accept, these regimens as a means to the end: better health. But without our deliberate influence, our youngster may not. He may resent the program, and, from his point of view, for good reasons.

Treatment can be a distressing reminder of his illness, and therefore a villain. Seizure disorder medication, insulin injections, and braces become stigmas—the social symbol of his imperfection. Jackie Cottrell believed that her cystic fibrosis made her an outcast in fourth grade; she wanted to erase the evidence, so she "forgot" to take her enzyme pills, omitted her CPT therapy if there were nonfamily members around, and stifled coughing in class.[1]

Medical remedies can range from inconvenient to downright painful. Most children have difficulty appreciating the long-term benefits of what's impinging on their happiness today. Barry grew up with hemophilia in the early fifties. "My dad was a physician. He believed in stretching the tendons and muscles of the joint after a bleed, instead of immobilizing it. That hurt, and at the time, I resented him. Today most hemophiliacs my age have severe arthritis and envy my flexibility."

On a less rational level, treatment, particularly if it is painful, may feel like a punishment. This makes sense especially for children under the age of seven, who typically view illness as the outcome of some wrongdoing on their part. "They stick me because I been bad," explains a four-year-old girl with diabetes.

Physical therapies, specifically, may reinforce our child's prolonged dependence on us when we do the administering. For example, adolescents with cystic fibrosis may not welcome their parents' regular pounding on their backs to help clear their lungs (CPT treatment). Although it may be necessary, it *feels* infantilizing.

Medical regimens demand discipline and abstinence. The child with diabetes or food allergies at a birthday party, the child with asthma at a windy soccer game, the child with hemophilia at a roller-skating rink all need to marshal their strength to say no. When his diabetes was first diagnosed, Pat Covelli recalls: "It was a life of rules, and I began to hate them. Forbidden fruit: how delicious something looks when you are told you can't have it; how tempting to sneak a bite when no one is watching. . . . Before turning diabetic I did not have much of a sweet tooth, but afterward I became insatiable."[2] Our children did not ask for these diseases. Why should they welcome the deprivations of treatment?

As parents, we are charged with a difficult task. We can't get around many of the negatives. Our child's pain and restrictions are givens beyond our control. His sense of punishment and stigmatization usually will not dissipate through our logic alone, but it may, with time. However, we need to discover, and even manufacture, other positives to help compensate. Our youngster's willingness to comply with treatment and long-term health depends, to some extent, on our early efforts. The fact that most children do comply is a confirmation that these positives exist, not the least of which is *our* approval and *his* comfort. We just need to make certain that we milk these positives for all we can.

Only Parents Can Do This

Our children turn to us for guidance, protection, and love. What we may overlook, in times of stress, is our power to influence their attitude toward treatment. We are the ones who wield the emotional leverage to teach our youngsters how to care for themselves. Not the doctors. And not the nurses. Certainly, these professionals can impart the facts and their authority will communicate the importance of following the medical regimen. But it is parents who are able to motivate their youngsters toward healthy behaviors and help them deal with the emotional consequences of the day-to-day restrictions.

Our assuming this role of educator is really no different from what we do anyway. Daily medical care is just a subset of the daily care that parents routinely teach: what you do to stay well and survive in this world. We are the ones who instruct our children to stay off the streets. Long before they appreciate that cars can kill, they remain on the sidewalk out of their love for us. Likewise, this love can be a powerful stimulant for them to learn about their health and to take control of it when they can.

This education reaches far beyond the particular facts of their illness. Our children need us to help them deal with their reactions. Are they sad? Fearful? Angry? Blaming themselves? Usually it's a parent who will hear these feelings. Here are suggestions about how you can educate your youngster.

BECOME THE WATCHDOG OF YOUR ATTITUDE

We are not saints. Many of us harbor negative attitudes about our child's illness and treatment. And why shouldn't we? Like our youngsters, we didn't ask for this.

Parents can be frightened and react excessively. "When my son was first diagnosed, we would panic," recalls the mother of an eleven-year-old with hemophilia. "He'd see our faces and he'd be afraid to go to the doctor. We realized that we were hurting him. We had to accept it better so that he could."

As we have seen, frightened parents can also do the opposite and deny the illness. Mae Gamble became concerned when her son with muscular dystrophy refused to do his exercises and started hiding from others (see Chapter 3). She and her husband realized that they were encouraging his behavior by keeping facts about the illness from him. Their message was that the disease was something to be dreaded and avoided at all costs.[3]

And we may squirm under the financial burden of his condition. Nancy recalls, "Kevin's wheat allergy was too much for our budget and took a lot of my time. I work and the baking in the evenings was hard on me. I'm afraid my son must have caught on because after a while he stopped eating his special foods." This mother came to understand that she had to be more positive if she wanted her son's asthma controlled.

And parents may resent the profound and inescapable emotional strain. Frank Deford describes the treatment of his daughter with cystic fibrosis.

> Imagine, if you will, that every day of your child's life you forced medicines upon her, although they never seemed to do any good; you required her to participate in uncomfortable regimens, which you supervised; and then, for thirty minutes or more, twice a day you turned her upside down and pounded on her. And this never seemed to help either. I have been told that parents let their self-conscious resentment of the illness surface during the treatments, and I must face the fact that this was sometimes surely true of me, too. In some moments I must have thought that I was also being punished. . . . Two thousand times I had to beat my sick child, make her hurt and cry and plead—"No, not the down ones, Daddy"—and in the end, for what?[4]

Some parents may even feel disgust about the changes in their youngsters. One father from the South criticized his daughter with cystic fibrosis for coughing, stating that this was not "ladylike." A mother had a difficult time bringing herself to suction her son's tracheostomy.

Disgust may be even more pronounced when a child has undergone disfiguring changes in appearance. This reaction may be communicated implicitly through a parent's expression and avoidance or, explicitly, through words. Sara Arneson and June Triplett, two pediatric nurses, write about the following patients and their families.

Sharon, age ten, was rehospitalized for the treatment of a severe blood disease and gained a considerable amount of weight. Her mother teased her, calling her "fatty, fatty, two by four." In response, the girl hid under her sheets and would only draw pictures of flowers, explaining, "I only like to draw pretty things."

Five-year-old Timmy underwent removal of his eye for a malignant tumor. At the time of the surgery, his parents openly voiced their fears about how he would look post-operatively. After discharge, they were not able to bring themselves to change his dressings and the boy could not tolerate removing his patch.[5]

While negative feelings may be understandable, they are destructive if communicated. These authors also write about other children who did not attempt to cover up the alterations in their appearance. Their parents were either more accepting of the changes or more *mindful* of voicing their fears in front of their youngsters.

Sandy runs an epilepsy support group. Her message to parents of the newly diagnosed is, "How your child reacts to this disease depends on how you react, since the kid's unconscious." In her exercise to bring this point home, parents take turns lying down on the floor and role-play having a seizure. They shut their eyes and then look up at the other adults, who have a variety of expressions, including shock and fright. The parents then describe their reactions and get a firsthand feel of what their youngsters must experience.

Most of us could probably use this kind of exercise. How does your child imagine you feel about his condition? While you can't purge your heart of pain, fear, or disgust, you can be deliberate about how and where you express this.

LISTEN FOR AND ENCOURAGE HIS QUESTIONS

Denise observes, "My daughter comes out with stuff when I least expect it. The other day she was swinging in the backyard and yells to me, 'Why do I have asthma?' " Kids ask the "darndest things" and they'll do this on their timetable, not ours. We need to be ever alert to when these "heavy" issues glide into the most carefree moments. This may be our richest opportunity to respond effectively to their concerns.

Their more common concerns are: Why me? Will I get well? What will happen to me? Why must I take medicines when I am feeling well? What should I say to the kids at school?

But questions can be multilayered, like a sheet of stratified rock. Surface meanings may bear little resemblance to underlying inquiries. The question "Why do I have asthma?" may be a request for information, such as hereditary predisposition or a simple explanation of what occurs when inhaling pollen. But, if you have already answered this before, you need to think about why the question is being asked again.

Rehearsal

Illness is an emotional event and almost every illness will have a Story, with a big *S*. These events can assume mythic qualities in a child's mind and become welded into his family's history. A youngster will need to review *with us* to make sure *he* has *his* story straight.

When we first moved to Arizona, Danny demanded to hear many times a simplified version of "how the dirty air made us sick." (Actually, we had become sensitized to many things, including polyester, formaldehyde, auto emissions, and foods.) In reciting what happened, it is helpful to try to end on some positive note. I always finished with how we regained our health with our move to Arizona and our special diet. I also used our story to put in a plug for treatment. Maybe you can too.

Youngsters will also want to rehearse any change in treatment. Two years ago, I tried introducing eggs and Amy developed an immediate facial rash. Over the next year, she liked to put these two pieces together—eggs and rash—and then proudly inform us, "I can't eat eggs."

Reassurance

Sometimes a question like "Why do I have asthma?" is asking "Is there something I did to make this happen?" This becomes a variant of "Why me?" Children, and actually many adults under stress, do not experience misfortunes as random, impersonal events. After all, misfortunes are very personal when they happen to you and your family. As mentioned in Chapter 1, we seek ways that we might have brought them on. Here is where parents can offer comfort by emphasizing, "There was nothing you did to cause this."

Security

Our children are understandably anxious to *know* we will be physically and emotionally there for them and that their lives will return to some kind of normal. In other words, will they get well? Many future-oriented questions, such as, How long will I be in the hospital? or, What will happen when I get home? are asking just this.

Pseudoquestions

Sometimes questions are not that at all, but expressions of grievance. For example, May's thirteen-year-old son said, "Why do I *have* to have asthma?" This child was thinking that his illness is not fair. The issue for parents is whether it will be useful to confirm the complaint or seek ways to undercut it. May chose the latter because she felt her son was getting into a habit of feeling sorry for himself.

In trying to discover what children are *really* thinking, it's sometimes helpful to first inquire, "What do *you* think?" That's usually how we will hear their misconceptions (dealt with later in this chapter). Notice also what is their facial expression and tone of voice. An angry, defeated, or frightened look says it all. But most important, we need to encourage these queries. A simple comment from us such as "I like what you're asking or how you are thinking about this" will serve this purpose. This process does more than teach: It nourishes their trust in us, at any age.

BE READY WITH ANSWERS

What do children really grasp about an illness or a disability? We need to understand their thinking in order to answer their questions. Here are some guidelines.

Children Under the Age of Seven

Young children have an illogical, concrete, self-centered view of the world and themselves. *Illogical* means that they don't properly associate cause and effect. A concurrent event is likely to be improperly implicated as the culprit. (I got arthritis because I fell down the steps.) Also, the disease and the symptoms caused by it are one and the same. (Diabetes is when you feel dizzy.)

   Concrete means that children understand best what they can touch, see, and smell. Those with diabetes *see* the color change in the glucometer. Those with cystic fibrosis *watch* the phlegm come up after their backs have been pounded and *smell* their bowels. Youngsters with hemophilia *feel* the bruise after a collision. However, they do not grasp the invisible physiologic mechanisms *within* their body or the rationale of treatment.

As mentioned in Chapter 1, egocentric or magical thinking means that the child sees himself as the cause of what goes on around him, including the bad stuff. Therefore, if he's ill, it must be the result of his misguided action.

Children Between the Ages of Seven and Ten

Children in this age group begin to associate cause and effect. However, their understanding may be black and white: There is only one cause (I got asthma from my mother) and one cure (I stop it by *not* playing outside on windy days). Also, they begin to grasp that treatment and professionals are not necessarily instruments of torture—but are there to help them.

Children Between the Ages of Ten and Twelve

The reasoning ability of children takes a giant step into abstract logic at this age. Symptoms become differentiated from the medical condition (Diabetes causes my blood sugar to change and that can make me dizzy). Also, an illness can have more than one cause, and the child can control it through his actions (If I take the right amount of insulin, I'll have the right amount of sugar in my blood).

But despite these advances, children still may worry that they might have caused it, for example, by not doing one thing correctly. They may also still retain some mistaken notions that lead to poor compliance. For example, at twelve Denise Bradley had some basic misconceptions about diabetes. She writes:

Even if I had exercised faithfully, I could not have taken off the extra weight, the reason being that I was ignorant of the fact that, simply, fat develops from eating more calories than the body burns. Still, I was constantly hungry and under the delusion that I was not eating *that* much. What I failed to understand was that regardless of the quantity I ate, it was more than my body required to function. Instead, I had convinced myself that my fat appeared for another reason—as a punishment for, not the result of, overeating. Exactly who or what was doing the punishing was not clarified in my mind, but, nonetheless, I believed it to be justly given.[6]

Teenage Years

Our teenaged children will have attained complete abstracting ability. However, this knowledge does not necessarily keep them from engaging in irrational and self-destructive behavior. (The issues of their treatment will be discussed in Chapter 7.)

Remember, these guidelines are only just that. While they may help us fashion our answers, they will not ensure immediate understanding or compliance. Our youngster's eyes may glaze over with our explanations that turn out to be too detailed or abstract. When Danny was three, I had to remove his polyester-stuffed animals and gradually replace them with cotton. After I went over these reasons, he asked, "Is polyester Esther's sister?" Also, his capacity for logic may have diminished with the stress of being sick in the same way that *our* reasoning ability is affected (see Chapter 1).

Fortunately, being "on target" with what we say is not as important as our saying something. As long as the relationship is there, we will have many opportunities to modify our words. The suggestions below are geared to reinforce this relationship as much as our children's comprehension.

Start Soon
Start explaining the treatment as early as you begin talking about differences (see Chapter 2). In other words, early. When my daughter was almost two, she was proud to pick out the correct can of juice for that day of our rotating diet. In the following few months, she launched into her first act of rebellion by deliberately selecting the wrong juice. When Sandy's son was four, he had learned to ask those who offered him red-colored food, "Did it grow that way, or did they make it red?"

Keep It Simple
The younger the child, the fewer words you should use. The danger is in flooding him with too many facts. Instead, let one word or an expression become the "code" for his illness. This information will necessarily be incomplete, but it should never be incorrect. After all, you will be building on his early understanding in the following years.

Maria's son with a fat-metabolism defect was on a special diet and had what he termed his "fat problem." My son "jumped around like a flea" when he ate foods his body did not like. Paula's children were on a wheat-free diet for celiac disease. They had symptoms similar to their father, who also had the disease. Their understanding was, "Something in my tummy makes me sick and Daddy has the same thing."

Visual aids can help get our point across. I made a chart with pictures of the foods we are allowed to eat each day. Mary is a nurse who cares for children with cystic fibrosis. She demonstrates the need for respiratory therapy by showing how slime glops in a test tube. Sherry, whose daughter was hospitalized for third-degree diaper burns when she was two, wanted some way to explain this event to her. "We took photos from the waist up that captured the few moments when she was smiling. I have put these in an album with her bracelet and we take it out once in a while." Over the years, these pictures should help the girl talk about this event and put it into a more realistic perpsective.

Elaborate as They Get Older

Children let us know when our answers no longer satisfy them. Usually, they ask again and again with the insistent "But why?" Of course, this process occurs in many areas: We cannot avoid our youngster's increasing demands for more complex explanations about death, sex, violence, you name it. Nor should we try, unless we want to leave the answers to someone else.

When my son was seven, he asked *why* red dye makes his brain go too fast so that he jumps around like a flea. Paula's children, now nine and eleven, want to know *how* does she know for sure that they have celiac disease and need to be on a wheat-free diet.

There are a number of ways to respond to your children's increasing sophistication. Many of these questions may be effectively answered by relying on educational material (we will discuss this later in the chapter). Also, you can elaborate more on how the body works. For example, I told my son that many chemicals, such as drugs and alcohol, affect the brain, not just red dye. But how does red dye do it? he insisted. At that point, I said I didn't know and I wasn't sure if anyone else did, either. Sometimes even grown-ups can observe certain things to be true, but not fully understand the "whys." (Acknowledging our ignorance should, we hope, make us less omnipotent in our children's eyes and reinforce their trust in our honesty.) In addition, the medical profession may be able to help you with their questions, which may, in fact, need further exploration. Paula eventually took her children for a bowel biopsy. The biopsy was negative and their physician said they no longer needed a wheat-free diet.

By the early teens, our children may be sufficiently savvy to teach us a thing or two. Todd brought in charts, insulin bottles, and syringes as a school project about diabetes. For a science fair, Robert K. Massie, Jr., produced an analysis of his own hemophilia, complete with graphs he had made of his bleedings over several months.[7]

Try to Link Symptoms to the Medical Condition and Treatment

Symptoms can be convincing teachers. Children will be most responsive to what they are able to see, touch, or feel. Shakiness from hypoglycemia, wheezing from asthma, or some other discomfort can be repeatedly interpreted to a child. This is how your body says: You need an extra snack; Don't hug the cat; and so on. Then we can talk about treatment as a way to alleviate these symptoms, using their words (Make the shakiness, breathing hard, or whatever go away).

Painful symptoms may speak far more effectively than we can. Barry, an adult with hemophilia, recalls, "My parents didn't say much. It was my decision if I played tag and got injured. Their philosophy was, You play, you pay. It didn't take me long to figure out what I could and couldn't do."

Life-threatening symptoms fall into this same category. A boy with asthma was routinely hospitalized on an emergency basis because he could not breathe. His father recalls, "He became the perfect patient. He was ready to do anything the doctor wished because he was terrified he would die."

Try to Make Silent Symptoms Speak

What is difficult to explain and manage are the silent symptoms. These are the ones that don't directly impinge on our child's experience. As a result, treatment becomes harder to justify in their eyes. Sometimes our youngsters are simply too young to comprehend the illness and the reasons for restrictions. When Andy was three and a half, he developed bruising from insufficient platelets and his mother had to limit him to bed rest. Sally recalls, "I told him that his blood was sick. But that was difficult for him to understand because he felt fine."

Children will have less motivation to follow treatment when their lack of compliance does not result in immediate discomfort. When Jackie Cottrell, now a young adult with cystic fibrosis, was in junior high, she sometimes skipped her CPT therapy (the pounding of her back to dislodge mucous plugs). She says: "If I don't do a treatment, I won't feel the effect for a day. But had I known five years ago what I know now, I would have been more diligent."[8]

Mental symptoms, such as hyperactivity and irritability, are also difficult for parents to use in educating their youngsters. That's because it's usually the family who suffers. The child may be swinging from chandeliers without an inkling that anything's amiss. Bob's four children all had food allergies. "My older son had asthma so he always had concrete evidence of what would happen if he went off his diet. But the younger one would get attacks of aggression and do things like kick his sister in the stomach. He tended to think this was everyone else's problem."

How can we help make these silent symptoms speak? There are certainly no stock answers and what works at one time will most likely not work forever. Sally was able to coax Andy to go to bed. "We had to be creative. We entertained him with videotapes and carpentry projects that my father thought up."

But the active ingredient here is not the particular project, but the family's *effort* in coming up with it. This communicates to the parents how important bed rest is. The extra effort you are willing to make so that the treatment becomes more agreeable will, one hopes, obligate your child. The implicit contract becomes: You do what you are supposed to and I'll do what I can to make it more fun.

Conditions such as cystic fibrosis are not really *that silent.* The cough, days in bed, tummy aches, and abnormal stools are ongoing discomforts. But some of these symptoms, like smelly bowel movements, may be felt as shameful. Understandably, family members may prefer not to draw attention to them, either.

Parents have the difficult task of making their youngster aware of these bodily changes without stimulating shame. A good relationship with professionals should help (see Chapter 6). For example, Mary, a pulmonary nurse, gives her patients tasks that will both educate them and help them control symptoms. A few days before each office visit, these youngsters use charts to record the color of stools and whether they float or sink. Parents can emphasize the medical reasons for these observations, along with the value of their child's contribution: "You will be the one to tell the doctors if you are getting the right amount of enzymes and whether your body is burning enough of the food you give it."

Where symptoms are mental, parents need to be creative. And, frankly, there are many children who will not be able to grasp that they have them. Fifteen-year-old Patty has had severe behavioral problems since birth that are now thought to be due to long-undiagnosed epilepsy. Her father, a social worker, explains, "Patty is different but she is not really aware of this. She can't handle social situations and that's most of life."

The general strategy with mental symptoms is to help a child compare his normal periods to periods when he is not normal—in other words, to give him feedback. Some parents have used their own responses to their child to accomplish this. Eleanor, whose daughter used to be allergic to red dye, would say, "You know how angry I get when you jump around and get wild. Don't eat this and I won't get angry."

Feedback from others may be more helpful with older children. In this way, they know that your concern is not just your "trip." Objective feedback in which a child may draw his own conclusions may be even more potent. Last Christmas, Jill's twelve-year-old nephew Lewis became "wired" from sugar. "We videotape each holiday. As the day wore on, everyone was sitting around opening presents and Lewis was grabbing cookies and jumping around. We've always had a good relationship, so the next day I showed him the tape and he could see right away how he was out of control."

Correct Any Misunderstandings

It seems to be an inescapable reality of the human condition: We say one thing and the other person hears something else. Our children's *normal* irrational thinking provides even more opportunity for distortion. What they understand may be a curious blend of our facts and their fantasies. This is one reason that teaching him how to care for himself is an ongoing process, really a dialogue, over the years. This is also why we need to stay tuned to their interpretation of their illness.

Helen Reisner writes in *Children with Epilepsy:*

One little boy, at age three and a half, was having lunch with a few friends at a neighbor's house. After lunch he picked up his medication and dramatically announced, "If I don't take this medicine, I die." His friends gasped in astonishment and admiration, but when his mom heard the story she knew it was time for another discussion about epilepsy! Who really knows a child's level of understanding? In this case, we find humor in the story, but the child probably wasn't quite sure if he would die or not. The question of death had come up for this child only a few weeks earlier. Although his mother thought she had convinced him that he would not die, he obviously needed more reassurance.

At age five this same boy was asked about his seizures and why he takes medicine. Without hesitation he responded, "Because I have a bad brain." What he meant or understood about his statement, we do not know; however, we should think about the implications of a small child considering his brain "bad."[9]

We don't need to be alarmed if our children don't have their facts right. Most of them won't. However, we do need to be attentive to misunderstandings that might stimulate their guilt or fearfulness of treatment, or life, for that matter. Only if we are sensitized will we be able to hear what sometimes amounts to just a single word—such as *bad*—and recognize that as something we need to talk more about. These common misunderstandings are:

Something tangible and external caused the illness. Candy gave me diabetes.

Blaming self for the illness. I ate too much candy and that gave me diabetes.

"All-or-none" understanding of the illness and treatment. Candy will kill me.

Incorrectly equating the illness with illnesses of others. My cousin died of diabetes when he was nine. I have diabetes and I will die too. Or, I have asthma and get respiratory treatment. My friend who has cystic fibrosis used to get that same treatment and she died. I am going to die too.

Seeing treatment as a punishment. They give me needles because I was bad.

Seeing treatment and procedures as fatal. There are many variations of this misconception. We need to listen for them because children generally do not express them directly. For example, These blood tests will take away all my blood and I'll have none left.

BE READY TO TALK ABOUT DEATH

Parents generally do not welcome talking about death, even with their healthy children. After all, the word succinctly summarizes what most of us fear about life: our inevitable vulnerability, separation, and end. Yet children do grasp this concept, even if it's in their own limited way. For youngsters two and under, death means separation, which is understandable given their extreme dependence on us. Those from about three to five see it as something special, reversible, and involving a kind of departure. My daughter, Amy, at age four, would casually inquire whether she can have my scarf when I die and later ask whether she can feed me when she grows up and I grow down. By ages six to nine, our children become increasingly aware that people, mostly other people, die. It may be a violent magical event, but it is also tied to biology. My son, at age seven, would notice the cemeteries and ask what happens to the buried bodies and what *really* is the soul. By ages ten to twelve, they understand death as final, inevitable, and universal, even though they may have trouble picturing it for themselves and those close to them. By adolescence, the concept of death has become a part of their worldview.

Preparation for coping with the death of others should ideally come from your child's life. The loss of pets, friends, and relatives are occasions when you need to start talking. Children seek to grasp this concept in the same manner and with the same intensity that they try to understand the other big issues of life. Their questions are the basics everyone struggles with: What is death? What makes us die? What happens when we die? The age of your youngster, your religious beliefs, and your social attitudes will all determine what you say.

However, regardless of these factors, there are some useful Don'ts. The first, of course, is not to pass over the question. A joke or a flip remark because *you* are uncomfortable will discourage further discussion. Earl Grollman, author of *Explaining Death to Children,* also advises the following: Don't relate death to sleep. This may give a child a fear of going to sleep, thinking that sleep will bring his death. Avoid misleading generalizations like someone died because he was sick. You need to be specific so that a child does not conclude that every time he gets sick he is in danger of dying. The same goes for saying a person died because he was old. A child may then get the impression that only old people die and feel deceived when he finds out otherwise. (In fact, you may be able to qualify most deaths with the statement that the condition, whatever it is, does not always kill people.) Also, euphemisms intended to ease a youngster's pain—like "Mother has gone on a long journey," or "God took Daddy away because He wants and loves the good"—will only add to his confusion and interfere with his expression of grief.[10] While this advice is straightforward when our child's life is not threatened and when we are talking about animals and other people, it can seem excruciatingly irrelevant when his own death presents a real possibility. What does he grasp then?

There have been no systematic studies of how a youngster's understanding changes with a potentially fatal illness.

Yet many children seem aware of their condition, regardless of what parents decide to share. Professionals who care for the terminally ill have their own collections of anecdotes. One mother was unable to speak about death with her seven-year-old daughter in the final stages of cystic fibrosis. The child drew pictures of herself in a coffin and her mother crying. Another child with a terminal heart condition could not talk with her parents. She told her nurses that she wanted to die on Christmas Day and she did. These stories suggest that some youngsters appreciate their mortality and also feel a certain protectiveness toward the adults who are caring and mourning for them.

Myra Bluebond-Langner described the behavior of terminally ill youngsters in *The Private Worlds of Dying Children*. Their preoccupation with death, she found, is expressed in their play, art, and lack of concern for the future. "When any such behavior occurs," she says, "the question most often asked, if it has not been already asked, is 'Should I tell the child that he is dying?' Since children discover the prognosis whether adults reveal it or not, perhaps the question should be rephrased, 'Should I acknowledge the prognosis with the child?' "[11] Many of the parents and children she studied opted to engage in a mutual pretense. They did not acknowledge the end, which was sensed by both to be inevitable. Evidently, many parents and their youngsters are afraid to add to the immutable hurt of death even by mentioning it.

Although we don't want to tell a child more than he wants to know, we do want to respond to his questions and concerns. Parents can also share feelings in ways that are constructive. For example, when Martha's daughter was four, she was hospitalized for leukemia. "She asked me about death and I told her that your body is like a house and when you die your soul flies away. I said that I didn't want her to fly away." Her daughter would have sensed her mother's desperation, anyway. The telling gives the girl implicit permission to talk about her fears and also reassures her that her mother is staunchly on her side, against the illness.

But if we elect to say nothing, we need to ask ourselves, Are we truly shielding our child or ourselves from the pain? Many parents have wisely chosen to say less instead of more. Tammy has never brought up the mortality of her daughter's lupus, and for what seem like valid reasons: The disease is in relatively good control and the girl has never asked about it. Yet other parents make futile attempts to flee from the obvious. A father of a seventeen-year-old son has decided to withhold the doctor's diagnosis of leukemia, a strategy that seems doomed to failure: The boy—not really a child—will find out anyway and will lose a parent he can trust.

This is not to say that talking about death in any way alleviates sorrow. Linda, the mother of thirteen-year-old Renée, who has a degenerative muscle disease, explains, "We have always been open about everything, including her shortened life span. The hardest thing to listen to is when Renée says, 'It's tough for me to keep working like this. Sometimes I wish I could go to the mountains and lie down and go to sleep.' I know she is talking about dying."

A mother whose five-year-old boy has AIDS describes her son as saying, " 'Jesus doesn't listen to me. . . . I told Him to come and get me, and He didn't.' It really rips your heart out, but I think in a way he is comforting me by telling me it's all right with him. He was diagnosed three years ago, and it's just a matter of time."[12]

Neither of these parents experienced relief from the openness. Yet they decided and needed to listen. And their children evidently *wanted* to talk. Despite the pain, both must have experienced some benefit. A recent study has found that children with cancer who are able to speak candidly about the disease are better adjusted, regardless of the severity of the disease.[13] This makes sense when we consider that the barriers created by unacknowledged realities can cause far more distress than the truth. That's because mutual pretense isolates. Acknowledging relevant truths—including death— help keep relationships alive. And when you get right down to it, that's all any of us have, anyway.

Our children's awareness of death is not really surprising, considering that they meet others with their condition, may listen to television programs and read books related to it, and, most of all, are able to put two and sometimes two hundred together. In deciding what to say, we need to take their sophistication into account, along with what we think they really *want* to know. While this is not an easy task for any parent, it is a critical one, even when our youngster is not threatened by a fatal illness. After all, our answers set a tone for our relationship in the years to come. Can they really talk to us about what frightens them when that also frightens us?

MAKE SYMPTOMS NO-FAULT

Without any encouragement from us, our children may seek to assume responsibility for their symptoms. For example, I once tried introducing eggs back into our diet. My son then reproached himself, "I got a tummy ache. I ate those eggs too fast." Even older children who are sophisticated enough to comprehend the multiplicity of causes of a medical condition may sneak in one that implicates them. "I got arthritis because there is something wrong with my immunity and I didn't take good enough care of myself."

This irrational guilt is understandable because it allows children to feel in control (see Chapter 1 on guilt and parents). The down and dangerous side of this self-blame is that it sets up unrealistic expectations for these children that they can call the shots about their health. And often, they can't. If they do have a relapse, it becomes their failure and their fault. Better, I think, to talk about symptoms as neutrally as possible. They are the messages from our body or how we learn what you can and can't do. That's what I said to Danny. His tummy ache told us that, for now, he shouldn't eat eggs.

Likewise, in talking about tests, it seems natural to reach for evaluative terminology: for example, "You had a *bad* blood sugar" or "Your test was *good*." These simple words place a moral judgment on matters beyond our child's control. Better to use them to describe his efforts, which are, in fact, up to him.

Misplaced encouragement can also turn symptoms into faults. This can occur if we and the doctors misjudge the course of an illness. Linda recalls the few weeks before Renée needed a tracheostomy. Her muscles were getting weaker and she needed respiratory treatments to ensure adequate ventilation. "Something happened that shouldn't have. We thought we were looking at this procedure way down the road. We'd tell Renée that she had to do her treatments so that she didn't have to have a trach. Then she needed one done on an emergency basis. There was no preparation. She saw it as ugly and her failure. We watched her go into a depression for several weeks."

We can sometimes be supportive in ways that unintentionally make our child responsible. A mother whose son had bone cancer believed she was being positive when she told him, "You can lick it. I know you can." He couldn't.

What about symptoms that are caused by our child's noncompliance with treatment? This is a different story and we will talk about it later in this chapter.

ACCENTUATE THE POSITIVES OF TREATMENT

While we often can't take away the pain or inconvenience of a medical regimen, we can talk about what *good* it is doing. These benefits may not be self-evident to our children. Understandably, they will be focused on the immediate experience of getting injections, saying no to certain foods, wasting valuable play time for respiratory therapy, and so on. Early on, we need to indoctrinate them, and that is the word, about how treatment is in their best interests.

. The benefits of treatment fall into the following categories:

This is a good way for people to take care of themselves. Some medical restrictions may make sense for the general population. Emphasize this fact when it is so. For example, Denise Bradley advises parents to tell their children with diabetes, "With a broken pancreas, you can do some things that can help your body. These are things which all people should do, but most do not. Eating healthy foods, exercising, and getting regular sleep may not seem important, but they can help your body stay as healthy as it is today."[14] A similar statement could be made about skateboards for children with hemophilia, red dye and sugar for those with food allergies, and so on. And most of us could use the daily stretching exercises intended for youngsters with arthritis.

This is how we control your symptoms (digestive enzymes for cystic fibrosis, pills for epilepsy, and so on). Children need to be told what the pills and medicines are for in a positive way. For example, one mother said before every insulin injection, "It's time for your medicine. This keeps you healthy."

This reminder is necessary because sometimes youngsters can seize upon the treatment as the culprit of why they feel bad and temporarily "forget" about their illness. Sheila's adolescent son complained bitterly that his food allergy diet made him abnormal. His wise mother says, "I have to scrape him off the walls after he has a cherry Coke. I tell him the more you fight these rules, the less normal you will be." And many parents can use this rationale: *Your treatment is how you become more normal.*

Sometimes our children will come to that very same conclusion on their own. After years of living with out-of-control diabetes, Pat Covelli writes, "I do know that I feel better when my sugar is under control. That, for me, is reason enough for control."[15]

It must be acknowledged that there will be some youngsters who appreciate this on their own. For example, Robert K. Massie, Jr., writes, "Imagine that in order to live a relatively normal life, to pursue your daily activities, all you had to do was stick yourself with a pin or drop a tiny bit of hot wax on your skin every morning. The alternative is for you to spend several days in great pain, and several more in bed, unable to do anything. The slight pain of the hot wax was all that stood between days of anguish and days of joy. Can't you see how easy it is for me to stick myself, can't you see how I welcome it and am thankful for it?"[16]

Small treatments now will help you avoid more uncomfortable treatments later. Sometimes Janice's sons with hemophilia balk when she puts ice packs on their bruises. She tells them, "If we don't stop it ourselves, we will have to go to the nurse and you know that means a transfusion."

Treatment is an investment in your future. (For example, the long-term consequences of cystic fibrosis, diabetes, and so on may be less severe with careful daily management.) The key word here is *investment,* and money can be used as a metaphor. Parents need to be quite deliberate and consistent in teaching about saving. After all, children generally live from moment to moment. In the process of this education, we all witness our offspring blow their allowance for one small toy and also see them put away their dollars in a bank account for a better one. Youngsters can do this when they are able to put off the immediate pleasure of possession for a more valued item.

Our good health is also a kind of bank account. If we continually deplete it for our present wishes (such as going out to play instead of doing respiratory treatments), we will have little left for our future. Unfortunately, life is full of individuals who run through their health bank accounts—those who are smokers, those who are overweight, for example. Without being moralistic, we can point out how *all* of us have only so much good health to spend and we need to cherish and not waste it.

After treatment you will be able to.... Here is where we can be creative in linking medical regimens with something pleasurable, such as an activity. We can use this strategy for daily issues, much like that time-tested "You can have your dessert after you eat your dinner." Mary, a nurse, says to her undernourished cystic fibrosis patients, "You have to have your protein in order to get your carbohydrate snack." Variations would be "You can play outside after you take your afternoon pills," and so on.

We may also use this strategy to motivate our children through ordeals. For example, four-year-old Heather was afraid of the spinal injections for her leukemia. Martha says, "We used these injections as a road mark of her return to health. We would tell her only three left until you go to kindergarten. She would look forward to them, even though they were unpleasant."

What happens when you can't be totally positive? In other words, if you don't do this, such and such will happen to you. One of the difficult dilemmas for parents is *how* to say the *what* that happens. While we can't avoid speaking about consequences, we want to be as matter-of-fact as possible. We want to avoid scare tactics. Usually we resort to them when we ourselves are frightened. Our motivations may be understandable; for example, we may be concerned because our child is skipping medication. But scare tactics may do more to turn our youngster off to *us* than turn him on to treatment. Jackie, now a young adult with cystic fibrosis, says to parents, "It doesn't help to say, You are really sick and you are going to die. Be positive: You have this and we are going to help you with it."

MAKE TREATMENT A PART OF DAILY LIFE

Ideally, children should see their medical regimen as one of their many routine activities, like getting dressed and brushing teeth. Taking pills or doing exercises should be a given, not an issue. Here are some suggestions on how to foster this attitude:

Set aside a special time and place for the treatment. This should blend in with the family routine. For example, insulin shots should be done at a specific time each day that doesn't interfere with dinner.

Make treatment social, if you can. Parents have done this in a variety of ways. Mary, a pulmonary nurse, has a daughter with asthma. "We all take one kind of a pill or another, so we do it together at the breakfast table. This way, my daughter sometimes gets to remind me." Rona does her stretching exercises for arthritis every afternoon. Her mother joins her and she gets her workout, too.

Use special compensations. These let your child know how pleased you are that she is following the treatment. For example, I give my children five natural-colored, nonsugar suckers each week, which they eat when they want. Denise Bradley's mother had set aside a special shelf in the bathroom for her diabetes paraphernalia. This gesture impressed the author because four other family members shared that room![17] Every Friday, Cindy takes her son with diabetes to Baskin-Robbins. "He's allowed a dish of ice cream, but without the cone or toppings."

However, *don't bribe.* There can be an elusive line between a special compensation and a bribe. The difference is in *our* underlying attitude. While the former shows our appreciation for something we already expect, the latter communicates a payoff for something we don't expect. We will be able to tell which it is by our children's response. They are not dummies. They will seek to make the terms more favorable to them. Carmen was desperate to have her son get his allergy injections. "I was buying him G.I. Joes for the shots and it got ridiculous because he would demand them before anything happened. I knew it was getting to be a bribe so I stopped it. I told him he was doing this to get healthy, not to get presents."

We wouldn't buy off a child for taking out the garbage even though we are happy that he shares in the household chores. Likewise, we shouldn't bribe him to take care of himself. That should *always* be his primary motivation and we need to stimulate that.

Be consistent. There will be times when we deviate from treatment. Vacations, illnesses, and other unplanned events will interfere with routines. That is life. However, it is important to give children a careful explanation for the change. Otherwise, they may get the impression that their medical regimen is less than sacred. For example, we make it a rule on vacations that the kids can have their favorite soy products every day (normally they rotate them every four days). The reason this is okay is that they will not grow allergic to soy if they have it daily for a short period of time.

Although these explanations may seem simple, they are important because they give children a needed rationale. Without this, they will not know what to think. Margaret's son followed a strict diet for milk allergy. One night, this mother had learned from a support group that sometimes children develop a tolerance and are able to occasionally eat the offending food. She enthusiastically suggested this to her son the following morning without further explanation. He then asked, "What's the matter? Don't you care about me anymore?"

One of the trickiest situations is when the treatment (such as a diet) becomes less stringent. What happens if the child subsequently has to return to the old, more restrictive regimen? (How you gonna keep 'em down on the farm after they've seen Paree?) Carmen's son's asthma improved tremendously once she moved away from the polluted city. "He was feeling great and it was confusing to him why he had to be off dairy. His diet went to pot. It was only years later that it became obvious that instead of asthma, he now had behavioral symptoms."

Best to leave both you and your child a way out when treatment takes a turn for the better. In other words, make sure he knows that this change may just be temporary: We may need to go back to the old way if the following happens *and* it will be no one's fault.

MAKE YOUR CHILD A PARTICIPANT IN THE TREATMENT

Ellen Ruben's diabetes was diagnosed when she was eleven. She recalls:

> For the next two years, diabetes presented no more major traumas or concerns. Why should it? My mother virtually took over the illness for me. She calculated my diet, prepared my food separately, gave me daily insulin injections, and made sure that I regularly checked my urine for sugar. . . . But my mother's fear of complications from poor control tended to make her overzealous in her management of my diabetes. While she fretted and worried, I contented myself with letting her carry many of my responsibilities. . . . As I grew older and became a teenager, I was expected to assume more responsibility for my own diabetes management. I was supposed to be mature, but I often felt like I was 13 going on 90. . . . I wanted to be spontaneous—no regulated special diet, no confining schedules for shots and urine testing.[18]

We need to put our child in as much control of his medical regimen as possible and as early as possible. In this way, treatment will feel less like rules imposed *on* him and more like what he is *able* to do for himself. Here is how to make your child a participant:

Instead of Telling Him, Ask Questions

Start off with your observation and then pose the question. If your child has asthma and is wheezing, you can say, "You seem to be tight. Do you think you need a treatment?" Sheila's children react to organic solvents. When they were younger, she'd say, "You are acting weird. Did you smell anything bad, like floor polish or Magic Markers?"

Likewise, we can also help older children anticipate with questions. A youngster with diabetes can be asked, "You are going to soccer practice this afternoon. Do you think you could use an extra snack?" For someone with asthma: "Do you think you could use a pretreatment in the nurse's office?"

Give Him Choices

While treatment is not a choice, there are many steps in treatment that can be. Let the child be the one to decide. For example, children can mix chemotherapy medicine in applesauce, chocolate syrup, and so on. Those with diabetes can choose in what room to have their injection and in what part of their body. Even children with restricted diets will have some options about meat, juice, vegetables.

Let Them Do Some of the Treatment

Although our children will certainly not be competent to do it all until they are teenagers, even preschoolers can do something. Young children who are diabetic can cleanse the injection site with alcohol wipes, pinch their skin for the shot, and learn the color and number changes on the glucometer. Those who have food allergies can help shop and bake what's on their diets. Kitchen drawers or shelves can be arranged so that they can get some foods by themselves, without having to ask. Young children with asthma can help hold the nebulizer in front of their mouths. Even the simple act of giving pills can be done in a way that either encourages or undermines the possibility of our youngsters eventually taking charge. For example, one mother of a girl with asthma opens a locked cabinet every morning. Her five-year-old daughter *gets out* the right bottle, *opens* it, *takes* the medicine, and *puts* the bottle back. In contrast, a mother of a teenager with asthma lays out his pills for him every morning: "I'm worried he'll forget."

As youngsters get older, they can do more. Children with diabetes can finger-stick themselves at five and give their own injections by eight or nine. Those with asthma can put medications in the nebulizer, read peak flow meters, and do breathing exercises. A youngster with arthritis who needs to wear a splint can help decorate it and design the schedule, too. Adolescents with cystic fibrosis can learn to use the vibrator and perform some of their own treatments. (In that way they can sleep at a friend's house.) Teenagers can do most of the tasks involved with changing gastrostomy and central venous pressure bandages.

Congratulate Competence

Our praise can be very encouraging. We need to use it for all jobs well done, including the job of self-care. Sometimes our children may even show us that they are more on top of their illness than we are. Mary Jo's son used to take his nebulizer to preschool. Before he was three, he was telling the adults when he needed a treatment. "At first, we did not believe him, but half an hour later he was wheezing. We learned to trust him." These are golden moments for us to congratulate our children and reinforce their mastery. After all, what could be more satisfying than, for once, being smarter than Mommy and Daddy?

Be Flexible in What You Expect

Depending on their health and the family's schedule, children can participate more or less in their own treatment. Better to go with what is practical rather than try to live by rigid rules. What they need is the experience of mastery, not necessarily performing treatment tasks every day. For example, Alice's nine-year-old daughter used to draw up her own insulin shots every morning. "But it became too stressful. She was slow and everyone had to get ready. Also, my son was having seizures. Now I'll draw it up for her during the week and she'll do it on the weekends."

EXPECT OCCASIONAL NONCOMPLIANCE WITH TREATMENT

Unless a child is desperately afraid of dying, he will probably want to experiment. Are these restrictions *really* necessary? He will want to confirm these truths for himself. At the beginning of first grade, Danny related to me how his hand went into Kelly's lunch box and found a cookie. Was I sure he couldn't have that cookie? After all, nothing terrible happened. Then he promised he wouldn't go off his diet unless his hand went into his friend's lunch box again.

Also, there is only so much self-control we can expect from a child under certain situations. Sheila recalls, "Other mothers were awed at how much self-control my son had when he was nine. But it was unrealistic to expect him to go to a three-hour picnic with junk food and not try it."

And there are occasions when youngsters are just too tired or busy to do what they should do, like exercises. Many feel the way Jackie used to feel about her respiratory treatment for cystic fibrosis: "It's not anything you *want* to have time for."[19]

The question about our children's noncompliance is not, How do we avoid it? We can't. It's going to happen for one reason or another. The question is, How do we handle it in a constructive manner? Most parents will experience a mixture of indignation, fear, and even guilt when they discover that their youngster is not sticking to the program. (Believe me, I was less than sanguine when my son told me about his wandering hand.) But what do we do with our feelings?

First, don't let them take over. If we do, we will become

a slave to our indignation, fear, or guilt and respond in a destructive manner. Blaming and shaming are the most harmful responses because they devalue the child. Parents get into this when they are angry. The prototype of this response is, You are so ungrateful (in other words, bad) for doing this after the way we've sacrificed for you. Adults who say this or some variant are trying to get even with words. But this "hurting back" only reinforces noncompliance as a power struggle and distracts the youngster from the *real* reasons to stay with treatment. And, humiliation only invites a child to do some more sneaking behind the parent's back (after all, he can't afford to be honest).

There are other responses that can undermine compliance with treatment. Parents who make a point of "doing it all" communicate their lack of trust in their youngster. Usually, they take over because they are fearful that their child is not able or willing to do it himself. The mother of the teenage son with asthma who puts out his pills for him every morning says, "I'm hyper about remembering so he doesn't have to. When he forgets a dose, I'll give him a stronger one." Unfortunately, although this approach will medicate his lungs, it will not teach or inspire him to take care of himself.

Inappropriate reassurance also discourages a child from learning to care for himself. Parents usually get into the "Don't worry" routine when they feel guilty themselves. For example, one mother feels responsible that her nine-year-old daughter has diabetes. She prepares all her daughter's meals and snacks. "Sometimes she'll eat a piece of cake off my plate and then ask, 'Mom, will this do anything?' " This mother can only bring herself to say, "It won't do anything." Yet this could be an ideal time for her to talk to her daughter about the dangers of sugar. A little bit of worry will not kill the girl. Too much sugar might.

The question is, once we step outside our anger, fear, and guilt, what *do* we say? Here are some suggestions.

Always Praise Honesty

We have to stay real. None of us, and that includes adults, can stick to anything 100 percent. But it is a courageous child who can admit to skipping a pill or a shot, especially when he knows how important this is to his parents. Remember, despite our worries, his honesty will probably be far more valuable than his trying to be perfect in treatment, or anything else. We need to praise him for this at the same time that we express our disappointment about the noncompliance. That's what Sheila told her son when he came home from the three-hour picnic with junk food.

Don't Be Afraid to Show Anger

Humiliating a child is destructive, but letting him know you are angry and why can be useful. Too often, people who are angry incorrectly assume that others already know the reasons. Yet there are many adults who don't grasp the whys of another's emotional storm. Certainly, children are entitled to their moments in the dark. But it is up to us parents to make clear what made us angry about noncompliance.

It's not enough to say or imply that the child was not listening or following our wishes. This reason is inadequate because it wrongly puts the emphasis on pleasing Mom and Dad. That is not the reason to follow a treatment. Our children need to do this for themselves. We, therefore, need to share with them how scared we became and our fears of the medical consequences. Hannah recalls, "My daughter knows she is allergic to cats and gets bad asthma attacks. She needed to prove this to herself. I was really irritated because she chose to do this when she was spending a night at a friend's house and I was out of town. I was honest with her. I said,

'I did not appreciate you taking that chance because I could not have been reached for those few hours and you would have put everyone to a lot of trouble.' " This mother used her anger constructively to teach.

Side with Your Child Against the Disease

In the eyes of many children, the problem is not the illness or disability, but the treatment. The "logical" conclusion is that if they can avoid treatment, the problem will go away. This, then, becomes their rationale for noncompliance. Recently, five-year-old Jeff was running away from his mother, Karen, and his insulin injection, screaming, "You're the bad guy." This mother explained, "No, your diabetes is the bad guy and I am the good guy." Karen was happily surprised when her son corrected her and said, "No, Mom. My insulin is the good guy."

Use the Authority of Professionals

In other words, take every opportunity to tell them Dr. Jones (or Nurse Jones) says you have X wrong and that's why you need to do Y.

Children think of their parents as omnipotent and can easily interpret what we say about their condition as *our* conclusion. When they start asserting themselves by challenging us, it may be natural for them to grasp at medical restrictions as the battleground. This is why it is important to establish early on that whatever the problem and treatment is, it is *not Mom and Dad's rule.* Hopefully, the battles can be directed to other, more innocuous arenas.

If Symptoms Arise from the Child's Noncompliance, Use Them

Getting sick can be a tremendous motivator. Wheezing and fainting are direct and immediate proof that restrictions are necessary. In pointing this out, however, we need to be careful not to assume an I-told-you-so tone, which can easily turn their compliance into a power struggle. Instead, we can talk about how the symptoms felt for them, if they were scared, and how *they* can keep those uncomfortable things from happening to them again.

Donna started to get back her allergy symptoms when she was eight. After careful questioning, Sheila discovered that although her daughter was sticking to her diet, she was walking to school on a street that was being repaved. The organic fumes from the tar were affecting her. Moreover, Donna admitted that she had not wanted to tell her mother this because she would not be allowed to go to school with her friends. Sheila replied, "Yes, that's true. But look how ill you feel now. You are not going to be able to enjoy your friends, anyway."

What happens when our children do not become symptomatic? One thing we shouldn't do is slough this off with a casual, "You were lucky this time." While this may, in fact, be the case, it will not discourage them from another try. We need to take it seriously. For example, Danny did not become hyperactive after his hand put the cookie into his mouth. He also made sure to share this observation with me. What was I to say? I told him that this possibly means that his tolerance is improving and maybe one day he may not be allergic to all these foods. But right now, I said, I would hate to see him try this again, and I then went over the reasons why. (I suggest recalling past problems that *both* of you can agree on: Remember when . . .). Our pediatric allergist was then cited as the final authority on this discussion. I hope this approach will satisfy him over the next few years.

MULTIPLY THE MESSAGE

There are many ways that parents can exploit their child's world to communicate the following: You are not defective because you have an illness; you are not alone, either; and you can become competent in life, including taking care of yourself.

Reading Materials

There are numerous pamphlets and coloring books that can teach children about their illnesses. *Me and My World: All About Epilepsy,*[20] *Let Harold Do It: A Boy with Hemophilia,*[21] *So You Have Asthma Too!*[22] and *Kid's Corner: The Mini-Magazine Just for Kids with Diabetes*[23] are a few of the numerous publications made available through national organizations. And these stories generally do far more than impart facts. They stress that everyone is different, that there are other children with the same condition, that a youngster can master his treatment, and that, despite certain restrictions, there are many things he can do.

Your child may also benefit from reading pamphlets about other diseases. It's another opportunity to learn how the body works (when my daughter was four, she was fascinated by the pictures of lungs in the asthma book). Also, by learning about other conditions, your child may conclude that his lot is not so heavy, after all.

There is a wealth of children's literature that deals with illnesses and disabilities. We can read these books to help stimulate our child's empathy for others and also for the realization that he is not alone in being different. For specific bibliographies, refer to your local support group or network, such as Pilot Parent Partnerships; the local chapter of the national organization related to your child's condition; and the Association for the Care of Children's Health (3615 Wisconsin Ave. NW, Washington, DC 20016; 202-244-1801).

Play

The truism that a child's play is a child's work holds for our kids, too. Our youngster's pretending to be a baby, drawing fearsome monsters, and all the other seemingly casual games are his serious efforts to cope with life. (Adults continue to use fantasy, in the form of movies, sports, music, and so on, for the same purpose.) Professionals have long utilized a child's play for therapy—to aid his emotional adjustment. Of course, parents are not therapists. Yet we are the ones who are present when our youngsters are doing most of this activity. We may be able to support their adjustment to their condition by being sensitive to certain themes.

Play allows for the expression of emotions. At some time, most of our youngsters will feel anger, disgust, despair, you name it, about being ill or disabled. Some of them may also be afraid of death, afraid of being abandoned by us, or just overwhelmed by helplessness. They may also feel guilty and feel that they are being punished. These themes are painful and therefore most easily enacted through the props of play. Four years ago, our son spotted a fierce rubber dragon at our local swap meet. When he picked it up, he discovered that one of the claws was missing. Danny was not thrilled when Mike and I decided to bring this object home and he named this his "handicapped" dragon.

The best way to pick up our children's underlying feelings is to listen for how they treat these objects. Their attitudes and actions will give us clues. More than once Danny wanted to dispose of this monster because there was something "wrong" with it. This came at a time when he was just understanding that there was something "wrong" with him.

Parents may then have an opportunity to put in some

correction. Danny tried numerous ways to rehabilitate his dragon with paper hands, shields, and swords, depending on his mood. We made sure to praise his efforts, but also stressed that we are all different and none of us is perfect. What counts is how we live with what we have.

But while we can be sensitive to these themes, most parents will have some tunnel vision and tunnel hearing. After all, we cannot be therapists for our own children, even if we happen to have professional training. In looking back, I realize now that I could have asked Danny how the dragon *felt* about missing this claw. I could have also remarked on how important for him it was to get that claw "right" and how frustrating it must have been that he could only approximate perfection. That probably would have been closer to his experience. But I didn't. At the time, I was far too anxious for my son to stick to the treatment that delivered him from illness. I didn't *want* him to express anything negative. Fortunately, feelings don't go away. As long as we nurture our relationship with our children, we will get a second, a third, and a hundredth chance to talk over these issues.

Play also provides children with the opportunity to be big and powerful, when they feel hopelessly small. Suzanne Massie describes the elaborate use her son made of figurines when confined to bed rest.

I started reading stories of knights who did Brave Deeds Against All Odds. In a toy store one day, I discovered, to my joy, miniature knights, about three inches high, whose lances and tiny swords, sashes and ribbons all could be taken apart. They were expensive. We could not afford to buy more than one at a time. The first one, proudly mounted on a white horse, we called Sir Bobby. As his little army slowly grew, Bobby developed whole imaginary worlds around them. When, at age six, Bobby was in traction for three or four hours a day, he would spread out his knights on the sturdy wooden bed table that Bob built for him, and invent battles and jousts for his knights.[24]

Dolls, in particular, help children anticipate and master their medical trauma through reenactment. This strategy is frequently used by child-life therapists in hospitals. Dolls for injections, surgery, dressing changes stimulate children to talk about how they feel.

Play also allows children to become experts in what they cannot directly participate in. The only limit is their imagination. Baseball cards, scrapbooks of foreign countries, racetrack cars, and so forth are a few of the many ways they may travel in their minds. Board games also provide youngsters with choices when the choices in their own life have been sharply curtailed.

Certain materials lend themselves well to self-expression: art supplies (clay, drawing materials, finger paints), doctor kits, dolls, puppets, and figurines. The less stereotyped the toys are, the better. Then children can bring their own fantasies to the object instead of conforming to someone else's. In addition, the more interpersonal the activity, the better. That's because our youngsters need the opportunity to talk about their play with us. Even with art, a child can describe what is happening in his drawing—who are the bad guys, and so on. (This is in contrast to video games, in which a child follows the toy maker's fantasy and primarily relates not to a person, but to a joystick.) The field of play therapy is rich, and there are many books about it that you might like to read.

Pets

Pets have long been recognized as valuable for children. They provide companionship and unconditional love, stimulate empathy, and teach about caring for the needs of others and even about death. A youngster with special health needs can derive additional emotional benefits from his contact with an animal. In this relationship, he is able to nurture, be in charge of, and care for another living creature. This is often a change from his usual role of dependency.

Some children with an illness or disability are able to become more active through their contact with an animal. The stroking of a pet's fur may be especially meaningful to those with impaired mobility or eyesight. Mandy is wheelchair-bound from arthritis. Her family gave her a Persian cat, which she loves to cuddle and care for. Her great dream is to become a veterinarian. Kay's visually impaired son became involved with the family's dog as soon as he could crawl. "At first, he could only see her head and tail separately because of his lack of peripheral vision. Then he put them together. Now he bathes and feeds her."

Also, animals are powerful motivators and can be important components of physical and occupational therapy programs. Brushing a pet, or sometimes even the physical movements involved in everyday care of an animal, like feeding, can amplify physical and speech therapy.

Youngsters may also attribute to a pet feelings they have about themselves. Parents can listen for certain themes in the same way we would when they play. For example, according to your child, does the pet feel left out? Well cared for? Made fun of? If yes, how could he make his pet more comfortable? How can his parents help him? Your helping the pet can indirectly help your child because he will feel understood.

Children with disabilities can also use service dogs to push wheelchairs, retrieve dropped objects, turn on and off light switches, and fetch another person. The additional benefit is that a youngster must develop his assertiveness in order to train his dog to do this. Kris is wheelchair-bound from spina bifida. He wanted a service dog, but could only speak in a "soft, whiny voice." His love for a golden retriever helped him overcome this emotional limitation and learn how to take charge of the animal.[25] Also, strangers are more willing to make casual contact with impaired children who have service dogs. The theory is that the pet "breaks the ice" and somehow overcomes the usual avoidance that these kids encounter.

These many benefits hardly need to be defined in order to be appreciated. However, you may be limited as to the kind of pet you can have due to allergies, finances, time, or living circumstances. Factors to consider are your child's interest, his ability to care for the pet, the ability of a particular kind of pet to motivate and stimulate movements needed for or compatible with his particular impairments. Parents have opted for fish, guinea pigs, and other animals. For more information on this topic, contact the Delta Society, Century Building, Suite 303, 321 Burnett Avenue South, Renton, WA 98055-2569; 206-226-7357.

Find Friends with the Illness

We can tell our children that everyone is different, and that they are not alone with their disease. We can show them books to validate our assertions. But there will be few experiences more confirming than meeting a contemporary who is in the same boat. Tammy's thirteen-year-old daughter was diagnosed as having lupus after months of unexplained fever, rashes, and joint aches. "One day she said to me," recalls Tammy, " 'Mom, I want to find other friends in this city with lupus. I want to prove to myself that it's not just me.' " Her daughter subsequently developed a friendship with another teenager who had the same illness.

Other children may be a source of inspiration for our own. Denise's daughter had her asthma treatment with another girl in school. "But Erica used a mask while this girl used a mouthpiece. And sure enough, my daughter wanted to use the mouthpiece, too. I told her I'd work with her and this turned out to be a tremendous incentive." Likewise, Don's son became less fearful after he watched three boys with asthma play soccer. "Their parents were on the sidelines holding up their atomizers. The kids would run over, take a blast, and run back and play."

Sometimes our children may run across those they shouldn't emulate. Their question may then be, "How come he can get away with that and I can't?" We need to help them figure out why. Dennis Collins describes his turmoil growing up with a friend, Bud, who, as he was, was diabetic. "I could never figure out what I was doing wrong. I stuck to my diet and wound up in the hospital many times; Bud seemed to thrive on Snickers and booze."[26] The end of this story is that Bud died, and the author is now practicing law. But children will not see the long-term benefits of treatment without our help and without exposure to these kinds of articles.

Negative examples may even serve as a source of encouragement. Barry recalls, "I never associated with other hemophiliacs until I was ten. There was a kid who moved in down the street. I went to see him and I couldn't believe it. His parents only let him sleep on a mattress on the floor. All the furniture was padded and he always had to wear a helmet. I realized that I was happy, after all, being raised the way I was."

In addition to informal encounters, there are many support groups for children with specific conditions. Generally the emphasis is not on therapy, but on having fun together. What is therapeutic is *knowing* others. When Carla's son with dwarfism was six months old, she started associating with the organization Little People of America. "He grew up knowing other small people. We all had good role models."

Find a Camp

Camps for the chronically ill and disabled are not for everyone. Sometimes a youngster may be managing well without one. Mary Lou's eight-year-old son is wheelchair-bound because of cerebral palsy. She explains, "Why should I want him to go to an Easter Seal camp to play ball when he's already doing that with the neighborhood kids? And he says the same thing."

Parents sometimes fear that the association with others who are ill or disabled will undermine their child's adjustment to the mainstream. The father of a girl with asthma says, "I don't want her to think of herself as sick and that's what this camp will do to her." And the reality is that camp may expose a youngster to others who are in the more advanced stages of a disease. There will be children with cancer who are missing limbs, those with cystic fibrosis who are emaciated and hooked to portable oxygen tanks, and those with asthma who display all the visible side effects of steroids: the moon face, facial hair growth, and weight gain. Mothers and fathers may not wish their relatively healthy child to see how bad things could get "down the road." And some of these seriously ill youngsters will probably not be back the following year because they will have died.

Despite these objections, however, there are significant benefits. The camps I visited were about fun, not about sickness. The horseback riding, swimming, crafts, cookouts, and camp-outs were experiences these children might not otherwise have.

An illness or disability can foster our child's unnatural but necessary dependence on us. Camp provides the opportunity for the entire family to see they *all* can get along separately. Also, there is often some instruction in self-care. Youngsters in diabetes camp learn how to administer their own injections and check their blood and urine for sugar. At the cystic fibrosis camp I visited, there was no formal education, but the children lined up at every meal, almost as a social event, to take their enzymes. Mary, the nurse there, says, "If they get that much out of camp—take their pancrease—I will be satisfied. We teach them all year in clinic. They're here to have a good time." In asthma camp children learn how to identify when they need different medications. But regardless of whether the training is explicit or not, doing the treatment as a member of a group is a powerful reinforcer.

The settings of the camps are informal and the only opportunity these children get to see their nurses and doctors running around in bathing suits and shorts. In other words, camp and the familiarity that comes from that experience may make professionals less scary. As one oncologist said, "They get a chance to knock us out in the dunk tank."

Many of the counselors are people who have recovered or are successfully coping with the illness. Wendy, twenty-three years old, has cystic fibrosis. She is an encouraging role model for campers who think, What's the use? I'm going to die anyway. One physician with diabetes says, "It was the biggest boost for the kids that I had diabetes. At camp, they would take turns giving me the shot."

Probably the most heartening benefit is the bonding that children develop with each other. One counselor at Camp Rainbow observed, "They're always comparing notes and they support each other. If one's about to give up, the other will talk him out of it."

If you are interested in what camps are available for your child, contact the appropriate national organization.

BE READY TO DO LESS WHEN THEY CAN DO MORE

"By myself." If we are lucky, our children will insist on this when they are two or three years old and not let up. The challenge is for us to hear it and respond, especially when they are talking about their medical treatment. I say "challenge" because it is much easier for us to take charge, do all the work, and feel reassured that we are effective parents. After all, our activity means that we are fighting the disease and our youngster is "safe." One mother is fearful about her nine-year-old son with diabetes. She makes sure to inform the parents of his friends when her son stays overnight. Another mother recalls that when her daughter with asthma was six, she would ask her friends whether they had cats before the child visited. This woman is proud that her daughter has taken over this responsibility.

How do we know when we are doing too much? The answers will keep changing and we need to keep ever alert to hear our children's plea, "By myself," which can come in many varieties. Recently, I picked up Amy from a friend's house and the mother told me that Amy had complained, "My mother doesn't listen." My crime was that I had packed raisins and she evidently has started to hate raisins. My lesson was that it's time for her to start packing her own lunch, with my help.

5. Don't Make Her Friends and Don't Fight Her Enemies

With friends a man lives and thrives. Take them away, and a man is left with himself and soon he will crumple and die. A man truly needs friends, to live and be happy.

—Robert K. Massie, Jr., written at the age of ten

One of our most pervasive wishes is that our youngster know the warmth and acceptance that comes from a friend. Another is that she can somehow avoid the wounds of rejection. But it doesn't take long to figure out that wishing doesn't make it so.

Although we can do certain things to facilitate relationships, we can't make them happen. And although we can also try other strategies to help our child with painful experiences, we can't *protect* her. Many have known the frustrations that Suzanne Massie describes:

Pets and stories, knights and telescopes, pennies and stamps—all of these were fine, but they didn't quite make up for that one thing: friends. . . . I tried to enroll him in Cub Scouts, but they wouldn't accept him. We tried to send him to a day camp but the "responsibility," they said, "would be far too great for a junior counselor." Perhaps they were right. But what hurt was that nobody was willing to ask what was involved; the simple word "hemophilia" (and it could have been cystic fibrosis, epilepsy, or any chronic disease) was enough to make them say no. . . . I asked—in a quiet way, I even begged—for children to come over. Very occasionally, pushed by his parents, one would come on a sort of duty visit. When the child was with him, Bobby's face was illuminated; he was gay and happy. But soon, very soon, unaccustomed to having to play quietly for long periods, the visitor would beat a retreat, to run and play outdoors.[1]

There has been a widening of social opportunities for youngsters with special health needs since this was written. Even so, many of our kids will have a tough time with relationships for a variety of reasons. Other parents may be reluctant to have an ill or disabled child as a guest in their homes. Their fears of doing something wrong that would result in her getting sick will often override their amicable inclinations.

Also, children, and adults for that matter, form relationships by *doing* things together. Some of those with special health needs will be excluded from these activities simply because they can't do them. In junior high, Betsy's arthritis had interfered with her being able to remain upright on her bike and she had to give it up. No longer could she cruise with her classmates after school.

Aside from these practical realities, there is an inescapable cultural bias toward what's been termed "wellness" and against illness. Research suggests that this bias extends to our younger generation, too. Popular children are generally those who are perceived as more attractive. Children with physical disabilities are more likely to be rejected by their peers.[2] Only "Sesame Street" and a few other ongoing programs dare to celebrate the imperfect human being. Otherwise, our television screen is visited by a procession of plastic protagonists with every hair and everything else in place. In their quest for companionship, many of our youngsters will be charging into this unspoken wall of prejudice.

Our youngsters also have to deal with their own shame of their illness or disability. Unfair as it is, people tend to be embarrassed when they experience a decline in their competence. (The elderly and adults who are incapacitated feel this, too.) April did not want to tell any of her friends when she first found out about her lupus. Her mother, Tammy, recalls, "It was a stigma to her—she couldn't sleep over or play outside—she was too tired and didn't want anyone to know. Then one day she overheard two girls talking in the bathroom. They said she had lupus and wondered whether she was going to die. April was devastated and decided to say something."

Diseases may specifically cause shame because they disfigure (amputation for cancer), cause odors (bowel movements in cystic fibrosis), can be experienced as a lack of control (diabetes and epilepsy), and so on. Although our child's humiliation is not rational, it may be sufficiently powerful to encourage her withdrawal.

In this context, we may come to feel that our child's social skills are superfluous amenities and maybe even unnecessary burdens. Teresa felt sorry for her daughter, Betsy, who had endured arthritis from the age of eighteen months. This mother did not want to put her through the additional rigors necessary to learn about the give-and-take in relationships. As a result, Betsy knew only how to play the "baby" when her friends came to visit. But by expecting less socially, we inadvertently add to our youngster's deficiencies.

All these factors, then, may make us reluctant to thrust our youngster into social situations. Our fear, of course, is that she may be rebuffed. It may help us to remember that despite their ages, many of her peers will have the capacity for great kindness.

Many youngsters naturally show the capacity for empathy by two years of age. Toddlers will comfort a crying baby or return a lost toy. By four, almost all children believe in a rule against using force as a way to get what they want. By nine, most of them uphold the rule against using force, even when an adult says it is permissible.[3]

Some of these same youngsters are going to be able to transcend the unspoken bias against the chronically ill or disabled. One year ago, my daughter had a conversation with a friend as I was driving them home. Amy had offered this girl one of our "candy bars," which she refused, saying that she has allergies, too, to peanuts. In fact, she has no allergies but, I believe, was trying to show that Amy was not alone with the problem. My daughter then advised her not to visit her preschool because there are too many peanuts there. At that moment, they were naturally caring about each other's well-being and feelings. Older children may be even more realistic in their help. Barbara moved into a new housing development after she had a hip replacement for arthritis. This eleven-year-old girl readily became friends with the girl next door, who would remind her not to put weight on that leg.

Some children seem far less fearful of an illness than their parents are. Susan vividly remembers when her son Todd was first hospitalized for diabetes. "Several friends visited him with their parents. The boys stepped forward to have their blood drawn, too, to see what it felt like. I saw the parents cringe and back off. One even said, 'I wouldn't have that done to me.' "

Also, our youngsters may be able to transcend their fears sufficiently and thus discover how to forge meaningful relationships. Curtis is now nineteen and is about three feet tall. Despite his visible difference and numerous hospitalizations for orthopedic procedures, he has maintained a steady group of friends. His mother, Carla, says, "They are very devoted and seem to make many accommodations. The other night I noticed how they all sit on the floor when they visit in order to be at Curtis's level. When there's some event, they will come and pick him up and carry him out to the car with his wheelchair. And they are all so casual about this. After they saw the movie *Willow,* as a joke, the boys stood up and told the audience that Curtis was in it."

Our children can have friends. They may have to look harder and work harder, but there are decent kids out there. Here is how to help them.

What Parents Can Do

DON'T SKIMP ON SOCIAL SKILLS

In Chapter 3, we talked about how our children can develop competence to handle situations, such as going to a store. But there are other, more refined social skills needed to maintain a friendship. And since these are skills, this means they will best grow with practice. Toddlers rehearse how to share a doll, school-age children how to play fair at Four Square, adolescents how to be loyal to friends, and so on.

Like most skills, these require some kind of giving up or trade-off. The price of getting along with others is giving up some piece of our innate self-centeredness. Youngsters who have difficulty with this will generally have trouble joining ongoing activities. Their distorted need to feel special and different overrides their need for friendship. Instead, these children attempt to reassure themselves of their importance by trying to capture everyone's attention. As a result, they resort to breaking rules, making inappropriate noises, and performing other actions to disrupt and gain control.

A child with special health needs is at risk for this kind of maladaptive behavior. She already receives *some* special and different kinds of treatment. But she needs such treatment to only be *some*. Otherwise, the attention may feed into her natural self-centeredness. We need to be scrupulous in applying the same behavioral standards to her that we do to our other children.

Have we done that? How does your child with special health needs get along within the family? Do you feel free to say no when her requests are inappropriate or inconvenient? Do you tell her when she has disappointed you? Or do you treat her as a victim, too fragile for honesty? And how is she allowed to treat you and her brothers and sisters? How is she with friends? Does she have them, and more important, does she have *fun* with them? Does she try to resolve conflicts when they come up? Does she try to understand how others feel? What do her teachers observe?

Socialization starts early with the simple words *share, be fair,* and *take turns.* Yet effectively imparting these values is *not* simple. In *Bringing Up a Moral Child,* Michael Schulman and Eva Mekler describe parents' common mistakes with these admonitions: We merely repeat them without sufficient explanation. Our children need to hear over and over again the whys of a particular circumstance. For example:

> Suppose you take your child to a public playground and he spies an intriguing-looking toy and proceeds

to play with it or simply take it. First state the private property rule to him: "You can't just take that. It's not yours." Then give an empathy reason: "If you take it, it will make Jane [the owner] feel bad. Think how you'd feel if someone just walked over and took away your [mention his favorite toy]." Then take him with you to return the toy to its rightful owner. It's always best if he replaces the toy himself. Don't forget, though, that he does not yet know the rule, so be firm but not harsh in the way that you instruct him.[4]

The authors then discuss a third reason for living up to moral standards, which is to make a better world.

This approach can serve as a useful discipline for parents. We must come up with some good reasons for our admonitions and put them in a language that makes sense to our youngsters. But there is also a hidden benefit to teaching our child first-class social skills: When she is expected to respect others, she will also come to understand what treatment she should expect for herself.

FOSTER A HEALTHY SENSE OF DEPENDENCY

"Lean on me" is but a quaint saying for the sentimental. The ideal of independence permeates our consciousness. People are supposed to be able to do it, whatever "it" is, on their own. This notion gets started early when a youngster pushes aside his parent's hand and insists, "By myself." His self-esteem then feeds on his handling progressively more complex situations without the hovering presence of adults. Our culture and education reinforces this natural drive toward autonomy, and, paradoxically, may also pervert it. By myself, above all. And while the advantages of this value may be clear, the liabilities are not. Gradually, vulnerability comes to be confused with weakness, and therefore is shameful. And if there's one thing we all are, it's vulnerable.

This is an issue for all children, not just those with special health needs. If they have a distorted need to prove themselves independent, they will not be able to expose either their ignorance or their emotional needs. But the stakes are higher for our youngsters who are ill or disabled. If they can't ask for help, they will be even further exiled from that land called Mainstream.

The child in a wheelchair, on crutches, or who takes medications will be unable to do much away from home unless he feels good about asking others for assistance. For example, Curtis has dwarfism and has been "mainstreamed" since Public Law 94-142, the Education for All Handicapped Children Act (1975), became effective. Yet he can't do certain tasks most of us take for granted, such as carrying his own lunch tray. His mother, Carla, explains, "It doesn't seem to bother him to ask for extra help. Also, he has been aggressive about getting systems to work for him. One year, his schedule was changed so that he was going to lunch at a different time from his friends. When I asked, the school administrators refused to give him his old time back. Then Curtis went in and told them that his buddies help him and that he would feel stupid without them. He got his way. The psychologist thought he was manipulating. I thought it was great." So do I.

Early on, we need to equate our child's request for realistic help with *assertion,* not weakness. And this goes for both her emotional and physical needs. In this way, she will, we hope, feel pride, not shame.

How she asks is just as important as the asking. If she whines and we reinforce this by our response, her sense of helplessness will be fortified. If she demands and we gratify this, we are perpetuating her unrealistic sense of entitlement. Remember, she needs *just* to ask, like anyone else.

We can encourage this attitude by trying to be positive when she asks us for help. I use the word *try* because most of us will not always welcome an extra thing to do during the rush of the day. Some requests are going to be inconvenient, at the very least. In these situations, it's useful to be straightforward: "I'm glad that you asked, but right now I'm busy so let's wait a few minutes."

There may also be times when she can ask others for help, instead of having us do this for her. A year ago, my family was visiting a friend's home, and my daughter wanted to know if she could have some bologna. Mike and Amy rehearsed how she could ask this mother: "Does it have wheat or milk in it?" We can then praise our child because asking takes courage, especially if you don't know people really well.

We can also point out times when we grown-ups have looked to others for information and/or emotional support. And this has happened often enough, even with the mundane demands of !iving. For example, a friend who is a veterinarian researched the kind of minimally shedding dog we could live with. Another gave me lots of useful advice on house training, for which I was quite desperate. I told my children how lucky we were to have friends who could assist us. Let your children know you feel *good* about receiving help.

Although the drive for independence is an asset, we need to undercut the notion that the more independent we are, the better. There are numerous examples of animals that live together in mutual dependence and make their lives richer (a toddler can see this by observing ants hauling crumbs into their community hill). Healthy human beings are also dependent; this is the basis of the family. We can give examples from our own lives of how we emotionally need and support each other. Whereas parental support for children is usually obvious, parent-to-parent and child-to-parent support may not be. I think it's a real boost for youngsters to hear that their expressions of concern about us or their practical assistance has helped us.

In addition, there is a quantum difference between doing things by yourself and thinking for yourself, and then having the courage to *say* what you think. Those who have accomplished the latter are celebrated as heroes of Western civilization. Only some people, with or without their health, get to this point. A physical problem does not take this kind of independence away, either. We can mention this to our children.

PRACTICE WITH YOUR CHILD WHAT TO SAY TO FRIENDS

One mother is confused and frustrated with her teenage daughter. "I always told Emily to give a noncommittal answer about her pills. Once a friend asked what the medicine was for and she got red in the face, pointed to me, and shouted, 'Ask her!' I was taken aback and remember rattling off something about how pills supply chemicals her body does not make. I know Emily has told her social worker that she hates having epilepsy."

What's a parent to do? We want to help our child and her friends become more comfortable with the illness or disability. Ideally, we want her to say whatever should be said and she will probably need our help with this, at least initially. But we also want to avoid this mother's position of disdained mediator in which clearly no one is satisfied.

Role-playing simple explanations may aid our youngster in becoming more at ease with her peers. We need to start helping her when she is young. Carl is four and in a wheelchair. As soon as he could speak sentences, he would say

"Me no walk. I have C.P." His older brother, who is five, sometimes confirms this with "He has brain damage."

We can practice with our child *how* and *when* to say this, too. Young children may start by blurting out the name of their condition when they first meet someone. Gradually, they can learn to hold off mentioning this about themselves until after they consider this person a friend. When you talk about guidelines with your child, ask her who she considers a friend. Her feelings about the person ought to be the criteria, not necessarily the amount of time spent together.

The Association for the Care of Children's Health has a pamphlet that lists how children can describe their illnesses and disabilities. These explanations use ordinary language, relate the condition to the healthy child's experience, and are also quite detailed. Many youngsters, even those who are eight or nine, may elect to use them in an abbreviated form. For example, some of the adolescents with cystic fibrosis I spoke to simply told their friends they had a "lung problem." That was as much as they wanted to say and as much as most of their peers wanted to hear. The value of the following examples is that they can stimulate our child's and our own imagination to find our own words.

For diabetes. "I have diabetes—that means that my body doesn't use sugar the same ways yours does."

For chemotherapy with cancer. "I was really sick when I was in the hospital. The medicine they gave me for my cancer made my hair fall out. It'll grow back. I'll sure be glad when it does."

For cystic fibrosis. "I get this stuff in my lungs that makes me cough a lot—when I cough it up, I can breathe better. I have stomach problems but take pills that help me digest my food."

For cerebral palsy. "My muscles don't get the right messages to make them move the way I want them to. These metal things are braces. Some kids wear braces on their teeth."

For asthma. "I have asthma and that means my lungs give me trouble sometimes. If I get excited or if the air is dirty and full of dust, I have trouble breathing and I wheeze like this. As long as I take my medicine I am usually okay."

For hemophilia. "I have to be careful because I have hemophilia. You know when you get a cut, it bleeds a little and then dries up? Well, my blood has a hard time drying up and I bleed a lot. It's not good to lose a lot of blood, so I have to be careful."

For a heart defect. "There are a lot of parts of your heart that work to make it run, sort of like a car engine. Some of the parts of mine don't work as well as others."

For mental retardation. "School is really hard for me even when I try hard. I have brain damage and that means it's hard for me to do things as fast as you, even when I try hard."

For seizures. "Your brain tells your arms and legs how to work. Sometimes my brain gets the message wrong and my arms and legs and whole body shake. When that happens, just leave me alone. I'll be okay in a minute. It's not catching. Most of the time the medicine I take helps prevent the shaking."

For spina bifida. "I was born with part of my back still open and the doctors had to do an operation to close it. Because of that I have trouble walking and have to use special crutches. I like to do the same things you do, but I can't run."[5]

Also, it doesn't hurt for your child occasionally to mention to her friends that her illness is not catching, even when it might seem obvious. Remember, knowledge is easily submerged by fear, and sometimes the information isn't there to begin with. When eleven-year-old Pat Covelli returned to school with the diagnosis of diabetes, he was taunted by a classmate, "Why'd you come back to school? . . . You want to make us all sick? You better stay away from me."[6] Unfortunately, even Covelli did not know, then, that his disease was not contagious!

Humor can also ease the tension surrounding these discussions. Some children have a knack for this. One eight-year-old boy with diabetes describes his snacks to his friends as his "sugar recharge." Curtis sometimes explains his dwarfism by saying his mother put him in the dryer. A teenage girl on a dairy-free diet tells her friends at the pizza parlor, "Dig right in and fatten up," while she waits for her special serving. While we can't teach humor to our children, we can try to lighten up ourselves and hope they pick up this healthy habit.

Along with this role-playing, we also need to let our child know that she does not *owe* anyone an explanation. This is *her* choice, within the bounds of what's medically safe. Even those with a visible difference can make this decision. Carla recalls, "I would practice with Curtis—what if someone asks, 'Why are you so little?' We would say, 'You don't have to answer people.' Do what feels right for you at the moment."

Our child may choose to hide her condition. However, we don't want, directly or indirectly, to suggest that she should. This will reinforce her almost instinctual belief that it is shameful and she is defective. Although I don't believe that this was Emily's mother's intent in the first example, her advice to give a noncommittal answer about her pills may have contributed to her daughter's anger and humiliation.

Sadly, there is at least one obvious exception to this guideline of openness and that's when the disease represents a profound social stigma. For example, epilepsy used to be considered a form of insanity. Recently, there has been some improvement in the public's perception. However, today, children with AIDS or vulnerable to AIDS due to hemophilia are in the same boat or a worse one. We have all read about the homes of afflicted youngsters that have been vandalized or torched by neighbors and about school administrators who have sought to prevent these children from attending their schools. Says Janice, whose two sons have mild hemophilia, "They don't tell anyone and that's just fine. We have low-keyed it. Only our best friends know." I learned of another child who is now homebound because his classmates punched him in the back where they knew it would seriously injure him. This violence most likely derives from the attitudes and implicit permission of parents. If we decide in favor of secrecy, we need to explain why to our children. We need to explain the bigotry, comparing society's attitudes toward their illness with that toward minority groups. Although hiding this disease will be difficult for all, the alternatives may be worse.

IF YOUR CHILD AGREES, EXPLAIN THE CONDITION AND/OR TREATMENT TO HER FRIENDS

The unfamiliarity of a brace, syringe, or amputation can be enough to put healthy children off. The equipment or condition may become less alien if youngsters can somehow vicariously experience them. In the beautiful and instructive story *About Handicaps,* Matthew meets Joe, who has cerebral palsy. Matthew doesn't like Joe's crooked legs and copies the way he walks. The author, Susan B. Stein, explains in her commentary for parents, "Seeing Joe is proof of what Matthew fears. It can happen: a damaged child. When Matthew imitates the way Joe walks he is trying to find out what it means, and if this handicap is something he could bear—if it happened to him. It is one way of getting used to Joe."[7]

While our child's friends' comfort is not our responsibility, it may indirectly help her if we sometimes make it so. Some parents and children have allowed outsiders to penetrate their private world of illness. When four-year-old Jeff gives his permission, Karen gives him his insulin injection in front of his friends. When John's classmates visit him, they take turns using his wheelchair.

This education can also be accomplished through in-service sessions at school. Parents of younger children can talk about their child's condition—always, of course, with her consent. Brenda, who is nine, has diabetes, and knew that the kids would soon notice her special morning snacks. She asked her mother, Alice, to talk to her classmates about the illness. One of the first things Alice explained was that this condition was not contagious. She said, "It's like my wearing glasses. If I touch you, it doesn't mean that you will need to wear glasses. Brenda's pancreas is not working, so if she touches you, it does not mean yours will stop working." Then this mother explained, "When sludge is in your car, it slows it down. When Brenda does not take her insulin, her blood slows down." These metaphors do not have to be precise. Their usefulness lies in calling upon plain, everyday language to make the illness more plain and everyday.

You can enhance in-service talks if there is some way to simulate your child's condition. For example, epilepsy can be "felt" by having children lie down on the floor and close their eyes. Then you can point out how a seizure is not painful, but more like going to sleep. The difficulties in breathing that come with asthma and cystic fibrosis can be experienced by trying to blow up balloons that are securely fastened at the ends of straws or wearing a weighted life jacket. These kinds of exercises are congruent with children's natural curiosity. How many times have we seen youngsters blindfold themselves and stagger around the house in order to find out what it is like not to have the use of their eyes?

However, consider this kind of in-school education only when your child has a cooperative and truly sensitive teacher. (We will talk more about the parent-teacher relationship in Chapter 6.) I use the word *sensitive* sparingly because sometimes an adult can mouth the "right" words in talking about a child's condition and yet harbor destructive attitudes. The teacher may not necessarily be hostile; but she may be solicitous and this can cause more harm than good. One nine-year-old girl with cystic fibrosis was continually embarrassed by a teacher who would hang around her and ask questions about her health in front of friends. If the adult lacks real empathy, the result may be that our child becomes an object of pity—hardly our goal.

As a youngster gets older, she may wish to do the educating directly or have the school nurse perform this function. This can help your child grow, as this transfer of power supports her separation from us.

KEEP UP YOUR CHILD'S SOCIAL CONTACTS WHEN SHE IS OUT OF CIRCULATION

Hospitalization and homebound education mean that the illness is getting worse. Along with the physical discomfort, these arrangements also bring the loss of normalcy—all the reassuring ties and routines of a child's life. As his daughter's cystic fibrosis grew increasingly severe, Frank Deford writes, "More and more, and quite naturally as she grew older, Alex worried about being one of the girls. Going into the hospital always produced the additional concern that her friends would forget her while she was away."[8]

We need to help maintain these friendships, and thereby nurture our child's sense of belonging. This will not be easy. We will already be burdened when our child is hospitalized or homebound. Parents have used a variety of strategies, including encouraging their child's phone contacts and keeping her class up to date on her condition. Teachers have facilitated this by writing class letters. Adolescent friends with their own wheels can do the visiting. Carla describes, "Kids came every day to see Curtis in the hospital. Without that, he would have gone crazy."

Even children who are mostly at home can be made to feel a part of some larger groups. Renée is ventilator-dependent and has been on homebound teaching for a few years. Her mother, Linda, explains, "We are assigned to a new class each year and we correspond and go to class parties. She also gives talks about her illness and shows the children her equipment. The kids must ask her fifty questions. Renée brings up that she will not live long and that she almost died in the hospital."

BE FLEXIBLE ABOUT YOUR CHILD'S FRIENDSHIPS

The ideal of popularity is expressed with unflinching candor in so many advertisements. If asked, many adults would eschew such a superficial value. After all, your own opinion of yourself, not the opinions of others, is what ought to count. Yet parents may still be haunted by this misguided goal when doing the "best" for their children. You may have heard mothers and fathers advise: "Don't do this or no one will like you" or some variant. This is different from saying, "Don't do this because he won't like it in the same way *you* wouldn't like it." The former places the emphasis on other people's evaluation of you. The latter stresses empathy, or putting yourself in the other person's shoes.

It's an unfair burden to have any child seek her peers' approval in order to gain her own. Yet it is even more crucial that we dispose with this goal for our child with special health needs. Instead, we need to become flexible about the number, kind, and age of children our youngster chooses as companions. Assuming that her friends are a good influence, if she is happy, we should be happy. Rosemary, whose son has prune-belly syndrome (congenital lack of abdominal musculature), did everything she could to encourage relationships, such as inviting boys over to her house. "But he has had one or two good friends at a time, mostly girls." She concludes, "We may want our kid to have many friends, but he may be satisfied with just one."

Our child may find a pal in places we would never think of looking. Renée, who is homebound, has struck up a friendship with her nurse's twelve-year-old son Bobby. Renée's mother recalls, "One day she decided to play a gag on Bobby and asked his mother for the name of his girlfriend. Then she called him up, and in a deep voice, said 'Hello, Bobby, this is Sandy. Will you meet me tonight at Mission Ranch?' Another time Renée heard Bobby was down because he had lost a baseball game. She called him and told him a joke to get him out of his depression." Although their relationship does not fit into the preconceived notions most of us have— for example, they do not *do* activities together—clearly both are enjoying themselves.

Sometimes our child may team up with someone who is a social outcast for other reasons. One preteen with cystic fibrosis became best friends with another child whose parents were mentally ill. The latter was grateful for a stable home to visit. Friendship need not conform to any formula.

EDUCATE THE PARENTS OF YOUR CHILD'S FRIENDS

Fortunately, there has been increasing media coverage of different diseases and what it's like to have them. A quality television documentary can translate a foreign condition into an experience that everyone can relate to. "Children of Courage" (on cancer), "Alex, the Life of a Child" (on cystic fibrosis), and "Follow the Light" (on AIDS) are three of many such programs that have been aired over the past ten years. Even so, prejudices do persist. That's because an illness or disability taps into people's basic anxieties about being alive; it makes them feel vulnerable. Education can accomplish only so much. And sometimes, a few of the facts, as in AIDS, can create more fear than enlightenment. It takes a lot of exposure to override these emotional responses.

Adults may harbor negative stereotypes about the disease. The 1987 Gallup Poll about epilepsy revealed that despite the fact that over one-half the American people know or have known someone with this illness, one in three still believes that epilepsy makes other people think less of one and one's family, one in six believes that it is a form of mental illness, and one in eight believes that people with this condition should not have children.[9] These results are sobering not just because there has already been so much information made available about this condition. They also suggest that many conditions may trigger some stereotype in the minds of the uninformed. Although there have been no academic studies, I suspect that a significant number of adults think that childhood cancer is usually fatal, that youngsters with PKU must be retarded, and so on. Parents who believe this kind of misinformation may discourage their child from becoming friends with ours.

We can sometimes correct these ideas, if the parent truly wants to know the truth. Educational pamphlets, our casually mentioning the *real* practical realities of managing this illness, and even demonstrating something about treatment—such as CPT, special foods, or the syringe for insulin injections—may make the condition less strange to other adults.

Also, as already mentioned, parents may be frightened of having a child with special health needs as a guest because of the additional responsibility and risk. To my mind, this is a legitimate concern. Most mothers are going to feel an extra caution when they have another youngster in the house, anyway. If that child can get sick, they will naturally be concerned about "What if." It's up to us to allay their anxieties in order to facilitate these relationships.

We need to be patient, reassuring, and positive in talking to other parents. If we communicate by our manner or words that we are apprehensive, they are naturally going to be discouraged from taking on this responsibility. It also helps to point out the signs your child has when she is sick, the very worst that can happen, and how often or infrequently that has actually occurred. For example, Janice's two sons have a mild form of hemophilia. She says, "Other mothers are afraid that their kids could hurt mine. I am quick to tell them that I'm not afraid. Of course, I'd get upset if they were dangling from the monkey bars upside down, but otherwise you slap an ice pack on the bruise."

This reassurance is necessary, even with relatively benign conditions. Parents of my kids' friends will routinely ask, "What can they have?" I usually bring their snacks and then look in their refrigerator to see if there is anything they can eat. But every once in a while, a mother may be truly anxious about what will happen if she gives Danny or Amy the wrong thing. I say that my children know their diet pretty well and the worst that would happen will not, in any way, endanger their long-term health.

Of course, when the worst that could happen is quite

serious, we need to be on hand for that possibility. Sometimes, it helps to stay with our child when he visits. Gradually, we can be available by phone as the other parent becomes more comfortable.

If the condition is not visible, the other parents may be skeptical about whether the precautions are necessary. For example, Sheila says, "The other mothers used to question my son's need to stay away from red dye. Then, one day, one of them gave him red suckers and had to endure being with him for the rest of the afternoon. Now she's my staunch supporter."

I've experienced and heard about this problem of credibility mostly with food allergies. I suspect that the basis of this skepticism is that other parents may implicitly feel reproached for giving their kids "junk." You may be able to get around this by mentioning that you are neither a saint nor a purist about food. I've always said, "I'm sure you'd do the same thing if your child had this problem." I also let people know that our family goes to McDonald's and Wendy's like the rest of the world.

Although there will be parents who are fearful or ignorant and therefore rejecting, there will be others who are able to see and appreciate our children beyond the medical condition and inconvenience. Some will make certain accommodations without our instruction. Erica, who has asthma and a heart defect, likes a girl who lives on the same street. One day, Erica was invited to sleep over. Her mother recalls, "I got angry when I found out that the mother smoked. But I talked to her and was surprised to learn that she never does this when my daughter comes over."

Also, it is heartening how many times other parents will learn what's necessary *from* their own child. Alice, whose daughter has diabetes, was told by another mother, "It didn't cross my mind to take a special snack for Brenda until my kid asked, 'What are we going to take for her?' " John, wheel-chair-bound with C.P., was spending the night at a friend's house. The friend's mother confided, "I was a little afraid for John. But I figured what I don't know my son will tell me."

Make the most of it when others accommodate and show your child special consideration. After all, it is these experiences that will serve as the antidote to rejection and isolation for both your youngster and yourself. You can point out how Jack and his family must really like you, and so on. I know Danny and Amy really appreciate, and it makes Mike and me feel good too, when some of our neighbors buy puzzles and other inedible treats as substitutes for Halloween candy.

However, this education will demand your assertion. As one mother said in an asthma support group, "How do you ask someone, 'Do you dust and vacuum?' " There were a number of answers, but the common thread was: Be direct about why your child needs this and be ready to look with the parent for solutions. But first, you need to believe that your child and your family are worth the trouble.

FIND WAYS YOUR CHILD CAN PARTICIPATE IN GROUP ACTIVITIES

Children with special health needs and their parents have found many creative ways to join activities. John, in a wheel-chair with C.P., has been invited to roller-skating parties. His mother explains, "He goes and watches and has a blast. That's helped him feel accepted." Rosemary's son wears a total body brace twenty-three hours a day because he has no abdominal musculature. This mother says, "He wanted to do softball so I talked to the coach. Sam bats the ball and they put a runner in for him." As long as we see the goal as social contact and not the actual doing, we may surprise ourselves with the number of options available.

CREATE A QUALITY SOCIAL LIFE

Part of our child's acceptance from others and her sense of belonging may come from her stable community—if we can foster such a beast. This is no easy task. Most of us have experienced, firsthand, the consequences of our mobile society. Moving frequently undermines long-term relationships. And trying to develop these relationships in big cities is much tougher than in small towns. Yet some parents have found ways to help cultivate friends for their youngster and family.

Make your house as open as possible to other children. Some parents have equipped their homes with toys and athletic equipment—such as board games, badminton, Ping Pong, and basketball—that encourage other youngsters to play there. Carla had a swimming pool built for Curtis's orthopedic problems. "We got it for his treatment but the kids always stopped by. This was great because our son was not that mobile."

If you live in a big city, try to stay in the same neighborhood. Familiarity can erode prejudice and fear. If other families have known your child over a long period of time, some of them should be more accepting of her. This consistency will be far less traumatic on your youngster. Carla says, "We did not move and so Curtis grew up with these kids and their families. That helped him tremendously."

Religious communities can also provide this stability. Many of the parents I spoke to referred to their churches as their second family of support.

Small private schools can help your child's socialization. Parents have better control and more effective input in smaller schools. Some have told me that their child had rarely encountered teasing because everyone knows everyone else so well.

GO THE WHOLE NINE YARDS, BUT NO MORE

All these suggestions amount to quite an effort on the part of parents. For example, Carla used to take her son and his friends to sporting events so that she could deal directly with any embarrassing situations. Sheila routinely cooked her son's special treats for his whole class so that he would not feel excluded. At what point do we draw the line? Our energy and his needs.

For the first, we need to be honest with ourselves about our limitations. The cost of constantly pushing ourselves beyond them is irritability and burnout. Social needs will necessarily plummet to low priority when the family is stretched. Instead, we need to conserve ourselves for the long haul. Also, our efforts may be well beyond what he *needs* us to do. One six-year-old youngster protested after his mother invited his friend over, "That's my job." Fortunately, children do tell us."

Don't Fight Her Enemies

It is, of course, a myth that childhood is either easy or innocent. To my mind, the schoolyard playground is every bit as competitive and unforgiving as any adult's rat race. Frank Deford writes about the one incident he knows of in which his daughter was treated cruelly.

One day, when a new family moved into our neighborhood, some of the veteran kids ran over to fill the newcomers in on the territory. By the time Alex met the new kids, they had heard all about her, the little girl down on the corner that had cystic fibrosis disease. What's that? Well she coughs, but don't worry, she doesn't give you germs, but she has to take all these medicines all the time, and she's always going to the hospital, and she's skinny and you should see these weirdo funny fingers she has.

Then, when Alex dropped over, probably not looking nearly as peculiar as the new kids figured a "disease person" would look, one of them said, "Let me see your funny fingers."

And Alex ran home, crying. I was there. She fell into my arms. "They *told*, Daddy! They told the new kids about my fingers."[10]

Social ostracism is one of the most upsetting experiences for both child and parents. This kind of rejection indelibly reminds us of our youngster's vulnerability. Carla says of her son, "I find it harder to deal with than Curtis does. I just wish he could go someplace without there being a fuss." Our indignation and impotence may lead us to a variety of pitfalls, some of which are listed below.

We Tell Her It Doesn't Hurt

This is the "sticks and stones" approach to life. In our panic to take the pain away, we indirectly or directly tell our youngster that words don't hurt. One parent criticizes, "Why do you always make her opinion count for so much?" Another says, "Throw it away like a piece of garbage." Far from being helpful, this kind of advice negates the child's experience. The fact is that names *do* harm. By denying this reality, we inadvertently place the blame on our youngster for her feelings. In other words, if she were tougher, she would be able to dismiss the assault.

We Prescribe the "Right" Thing to Do

In our attempt to fix our child's social dilemma, we may be far too quick with our advice. Just as in the adult world, there may be no simple solutions. It doesn't matter if we say, "Hit him back," "Call him stupid," "Tell the teacher," or "Walk away." No matter how benign or aggressive our prescription, it's not going to work for all situations. And we may be surprised or chagrined about how these prescriptions are applied. A child who sat next to Danny in kindergarten kept goading him that his special snacks were diarrhea. My knee-jerk response had been, "Go tell him he's full of diarrhea." My son then went about repeating this gem to three other children who he felt had crossed him that day, but not to the one who made that comment. I learned.

We Take Over and Deal with the Offenders Directly

It is difficult, indeed, to witness our child being mistreated and do nothing. Sam has prune-belly syndrome, for which he wears a body brace. He also had surgery to create artificial testicles. In that way, his scrotum was able to accept his own testicles when he had a second operation at age eight. Now in junior high, he is victimized by a particular group of boys who have taken to kicking him in the groin. Because of his brace, Sam is unable to bend over to protect himself. One day this occurred in front of Rosemary, his mother. She says, "The kid yelled out, 'What difference does it make? He doesn't have real balls.' I was frustrated and kept screaming, 'He does, too.' Sam just stood there and felt terrible. You don't know what to do. I wanted to grab those kids and kill them."

While there are clearly situations in which we should

intervene, there are also others in which we should not. In our wish to protect, we can sometimes go too far, particularly with older children. Our interference may implicitly communicate that we don't think they can handle it. Carla recalls, "Once, when Curtis was about eleven, we were in the library. There were a bunch of younger children there who wouldn't leave him alone. They kept coming over and saying things like 'Why are you so small?' and 'I bet I can beat you up.' I finally told them to go away. But later, when we were in the car, Curtis was angry with me and said, 'That was none of your business. They weren't bothering me. They were bothering you.' "

Ideally, we need to separate our pain from our child's and talk over what would be most comfortable for her. Of course, this kind of restraint may be lost in the heat of the moment. If this happens, it's okay, later, to share that your anger mistakenly took charge. You can always discuss, then, what would be best next time, and unfortunately, there may be one.

How can we help our child with teasing? Despite our desire to have some control over her environment, we may be able to offer little actual protection from the emotional brutality of peers. Our child needs our support, but she doesn't need us to reinforce a "me against them" view of the world. That outlook will only add to her isolation. Yet there are some ways we can prepare her for these experiences and also help her digest them. Here are some suggestions.

HELP HER DISTINGUISH CURIOSITY FROM MEANNESS

Children will ask questions and make comments about another's difference for a variety of reasons. If our youngster is at all sensitive, it may be that anything that draws attention to her condition may feel like an assault. But it may not be. For example, it was clear that the classmate who likened Danny's snack to excrement wanted to make him feel bad. But once, my son was upset because another child asked, "Why do you always eat such important foods?" To my mind, this was a neutral to flattering inquiry. At these moments, we can put in some correction. Not all questions are designed to embarrass, even though you may feel that way. Some kids just want to find out, in the same way that you sometimes do. This distinction should reinforce a more positive outlook about others.

Life, in one of its peculiar bursts of irony, provided my son with the opportunity to feel that shoe on the other foot—how sensitive any child can be when he is different, how he can then misread another's curiosity. We had been talking about different religions at home. One day, Danny asked a classmate who is a Seventh-Day Adventist, "What things do you believe?" The child punched him in the nose.

LET HER "VENTILATE" WHEN SHE IS TEASED

Sharon's mother could not face the fact that her daughter had considerable nerve and muscle damage from polio, and since then she has had an awkward gait. Sharon remembers from childhood how peers teased her by imitating her walk. Unfortunately, her mother's denial made it impossible for her to be a source of comfort. "I would go home to my bedroom closet at night and just bawl by myself and then go prepare dinner. The reason I got so far down was that I didn't have anyone with whom to share my burden."

We can't fix many circumstances, but we can help our child by allowing her to blow off steam. We listen and avoid the three pitfalls: telling her it doesn't hurt, giving her advice about what she should do, or trying to fix it by directly rebuking those involved or their parents. As a partially disabled adult, Sharon advises parents, "Be realistic about your comfort. Don't say that Johnny won't throw a rock again when he will. But most of all, listen with your ears and your hearts so that they are not afraid to tell you what went on."

That's what Frank Deford did for Alex: "And I let her cry all she wanted. She sobbed for a long time, too, and didn't want to go back outside. I tried to tell her something philosophical, but luckily, I stopped in time, because I realized how empty that would sound. A child who is different, who has just been singled out and hurt for being different, is beyond fancy philosophy. Instead, we just hugged some more."[11]

When we are listening, we can also help our child identify her feelings and put them into words. That's a capability that everyone needs to acquire for effective living. We can ask, "How do you feel about what happened?" or say, "That must make you feel mad [or sad, or whatever] when the kids call you that."

At some point, our child may answer, "Sad? Are you for real? The kid's a jerk." In other words, our youngster may come to the sticks-and-stones approach on his own. Even Sharon, who had no parental support, recalls, "It was a real breakthrough for me when one day I finally asked myself, Is this person worth crying over?" If she can discount another's stupidity or meanness, so much the better. We just need not to discount that *for her,* and with that, her feelings, too.

EXPLAIN WHY PEOPLE TEASE

As Frank Deford wisely observed, empathy and not philosophy is what is comforting for a child's bruised emotions. In a more neutral moment, however, it may help to explain more about this social disease.

People are capable of tolerance, but they can also use the real or imagined deficiencies of others in an attempt to make themselves feel superior. This strategy is a prop and has been exploited by many throughout history. If your child is being teased, she ought to know about the prejudice directed against different minority groups. (There are books written for children about this, such as *Martin Luther King Day,* by Linda Lowery.[12]) Although this information neither compensates for nor takes away her pain, it does give her a larger perspective on the problem—mostly that it is not *hers,* but *humanity's* problem. Along these same lines, you can mention that this unfortunate drive to put others down is also directed at healthy children. Kids have been called Shorty, Skinny, Red, and so on, and these names hurt them, too.

You also can mention how children may be irrationally frightened of catching the illness or disability. In *About Handicaps,* the healthy child, Matthew, does a variety of things to reassure himself that his body won't become like Joe's. He jumps around and runs fast to make sure his legs work right. The boy dresses in boots and an army hat that he believes will protect him from anything bad happening. This kind of misguided fear also leads children to tease. That's what Pat Covelli ran into when his classmate accused, "You want to make us all sick." Here is where our educational efforts may help lessen our child's rejection.

The difficulty for many parents in dealing with teasing is *finding out* that it has happened. Recalls one father whose son lived to twenty-five with a heart defect, "Kirk didn't talk about it until it boiled over." Sometimes, a child may be ashamed of having been ridiculed and will be reluctant to mention it to her parents. But other times, mothers and fathers may inadvertently discourage this report because of their own ambivalence, particularly about boys. They may be furious about the teasing but also harbor the attitude "If you are tough enough, you can take it." For example, one mother complained that her son never told her when he was bullied. In the next breath, she said with obvious pride, "He's not the kind to tattle."

Some parents have found it helpful, especially in new social situations, to go over explicitly: "What if the kids say something about your . . ." We don't need to come up with answers and we certainly don't want to program our child for rejection. But mentioning this possibility initially may make it easier for her to talk about it later, if something does occur.

TALK ABOUT OPTIONS WHEN HE IS TEASED

Most parents feel anger about teasing, but they differ markedly on how they think their child should handle it. There are hawks: "An eye for an eye" translates to "Kick him back." And doves: "Turn the other cheek," also known as "Walk away." And everything in between. Our ideas on how our child should defend himself may, in addition, change from one time to another.

The first day of school, John, who has C.P., was goaded by one of his classmates. The child kept insisting, "Why are you in a wheelchair?" Finally, John motioned him to come closer because he wanted to tell him something. When the child leaned over, John slugged him.

This story demonstrates that aggression is as much a state of mind as body. John was not going to be intimidated. But what has also been striking for me is that all the adults who heard of this incident reacted approvingly, regardless of their personal beliefs. For example, one mother, who instructs her own son to ignore teasing, was laughing with pleasure. Her comment was, "I'll have to tell this to my husband." Most parents harbor mixed emotions when it comes to what constitutes justifiable force on the playground.

Of course, the question of righteous aggression is mired in ambivalence, to say the least. World-class thinkers, religious leaders, and political and legal systems have been struggling with this one from the beginning of recorded history. We parents are not going to come up with any absolute answers for our youngsters, either. But although we can't *tell* our child what to do about teasing, we can go over options.

Ideally, she should feel that she doesn't have to just "take it," that she has choices, and that she will be accepted at home, regardless of what transpires. She can ignore it, *if* she truly feels comfortable with this (this is what Curtis would have liked his mother to do at the library). She can tell a teacher or enlist the aid of her friends. Our child can also tackle the assault head on by asking, "What do you mean by that?" But she needs to say it in an aggressive manner, using a forceful tone of voice, looking the person directly in the eye and sticking her face in theirs. A tape recorder can be helpful in giving a child practice and feedback about how she speaks these words. Our doing this with her implicitly gives her permission to protect herself. That permission may be far more important than what actually happens.

My Name Is Not Dummy[13] deals specifically with this problem. In this unique and instructive book by Elizabeth Crary and Marina Megale, parent and child together choose different alternatives, read about the consequences, and then imagine their feelings. None of these options has a guaranteed outcome of success. For example, teachers may sometimes be sympathetic and at other times consider it "tattling" when a child reports she has been called a name. The idea in discussing and rehearsing these alternatives is not necessarily success. Rather it is to communicate that it's okay to be upset and try to do something about it. Eventually, our child may learn how to handle some of these situations to her liking.

USE YOUR INTERVENTIONS SPARINGLY

We can't take charge of most of our child's struggles. Our excessive involvement will only undermine her mastery of these situations and at the same time highlight to her peers that she is someone less able than they are. Yet sometimes we need to butt in. How do we know when? One father of an adolescent daughter wisely put it, "It's a question of what's going to make her stronger and what does she really have to face?"

Clearly, a younger child needs us not only to protect her, but also to role-model what she should and should not tolerate. In these instances, parents can explain how teasing is hurtful. Kay remembers when one of the boys she watched called her son "Four Eyes" because of his thick glasses. "I almost became unglued and I had to compose myself. I said to Thomas, 'Suppose you had big ears. Would you like to be called Dumbo?' "

When two youngsters are friends, we can also appeal to their relationship to eliminate this problem. Four-year-old Carl has a speech problem. One day Audrey, his mother, heard another child mimicking him. "I told the child, 'Jerry, it's not right to make fun of someone when they are having trouble. Why don't you teach him, instead.' And that's what happened."

But at some point we need to let her take over. Not only does this build her confidence, but it also undermines her natural but mistaken idea that *we* can fix everything. Amy was unhappy that a child teased her because she could not have sugar. "What are you going to do about it?" she demanded. Nothing, I thought. Mom's not omnipotent. Instead, I suggested she call the mother, if she was that upset. She did.

Yet we may choose to intervene at certain times, even

when our child is older. Every situation is different, depending on the nature of the teasing. A child with hemophilia who is struck is subject to more serious abuse than name-calling. But some name-calling is particularly offensive. Can our youngster handle it? Should school authorities or parents be notified, anyway, in the name of decency because this process is destructive for everyone?

We also need to consider our child's feelings about our intervention. Rosemary would love to *do* something about the way Sam's classmates treat him. "But he won't say anything. The kids trip him, but I only know this from the scrapes on his knees." On the other hand, fifteen-year-old Patty has behavioral problems secondary to epilepsy. Sometimes her father talks to the teachers when she is getting a hard time from classmates. "If nothing else, it tells her that she's supported and that means a lot."

And that's the key to helping our child with teasing. While we can't eliminate it or stop it from hurting, we can let her know that we're on her side.

6. **Make the Professional Your Partner**

Parents of children with special health needs usually have ongoing contact with professionals—doctors, nurses, teachers, social workers, psychologists, speech and physical therapists. If we are fortunate, these individuals will become our resources and help us find the best in healthcare and educational opportunities for our youngster. But first we need to learn how to maximize this inherently tough relationship.

Marie, a special-education teacher, used to feel disheartened. She couldn't seem to satisfy the parents of the children with Down's syndrome whom she taught. "They were always fighting with me for more. I never could give enough." Then Marie gave birth to a boy with Down's. "Now I can see both sides. I wish I couldn't."

Getting Along with Professionals

Even for the most mature individuals, this professional–patient/client/parent relationship is charged with conflicting expectations—for both. The most readily identifiable reason for this difficulty and the one that has grabbed media attention is professional incompetence. Experts who blunder are the ones who have been pushed into the limelight. And most of us have had some abusive experience that sticks in our memories and validates our wariness. A few experts gratuitously psychologized Mike and me instead of addressing the problem at hand; claimed expertise they proved not to have; and, of course, were unwilling to acknowledge their ignorance. Most accounts of illness and disabilities, such as *Parents Speak Out,*[1] *Borrowing Time,*[2] and *Journey,*[3] include some incident in which a doctor or teacher had profoundly and realistically failed the authors.

Yet getting along with professionals involves more than finding one who is qualified. This is because there are other, less obvious grounds for friction.

PARENTS AND PROFESSIONALS BRING DIFFERENT FEELINGS TO THE ENCOUNTER

Despite the negative press, I believe that most professionals do what they are doing because they *want* to help. Their work, then, meets at least some of their fantasies and adds to their sense of worth. However, no matter how caring they are about any particular client, their personal life and happiness are not on the line. At the end of the day, they go home.

In contrast, parents generally do not choose to have a child with special health needs, but have this thrust upon them. Unlike the doctor or nurse, we have to mourn the loss of fantasies. What would life have been like if our youngster had been healthy? And our family's happiness is on the line with every decision.

The result is that parents and professionals may shout at each other across an emotional abyss. Like Marie, there are other professionals who feel they are doing the best they can. And, privately, they may wish for a little more appreciation than they are getting. For example, a genetic counselor says, "People want an answer about whether their next child will have the same problem. We have state-of-the-art testing here, but frankly, we don't always know and they get upset with us."

Parents may feel, So what? Your best isn't good enough for me and my child. Fern Kupfer, the mother of a severely disabled son, frankly summarizes this process: "There is a certain animosity that is just *there* between parents and professionals that will *always* be there because you have these intervention programs, you can do this diagnosis, but you can't make our kids better. And when push comes to shove, that's really what we want."[4]

PARENTS AND PROFESSIONALS HAVE DIFFERENT KINDS OF KNOWLEDGE

Parents Often Lack Technical Knowledge

A meeting with an expert usually presumes that he knows more than we do. Why else would we go? Yet, this disparity may be intimidating. Even though we know better, in our sensitized state, the professional's opinion, approval, and forecast can be transformed into the voice of absolute knowledge and we may quake. I have, even with training.

Mary Lou's son John is in a wheelchair because of cerebral palsy and has been mainstreamed for two years. This seasoned mother teaches a workshop on Individual Educational Placement (IEP) for other parents. She shares her feelings in a discussion group: "There are so many things your child can't do. You live with him and already know that, but hearing four or five people say that at an IEP meeting is hard. I have good relationships with these professionals and it still turns my knees to jelly and I don't sleep the night before."

We often master technical knowledge in an effort to be on a more equal footing with professionals, to understand and evaluate their opinions, and also to ask relevant questions. This step is necessary for us to become truly competent in raising our child. However, a few parents may use information to compete with professionals and, in that way, alleviate their sense of intimidation. In the *extreme,* this behavior can be destructive. Parents can play games to reassure themselves that they are not feeling one-down. These are serious and unconscious strategies that people employ to elicit specific responses from others.

"Who Needs You?" is one attitude frightened parents may display in an effort to discount professionals. Rather than face this "necessary evil," a few will deny the usefulness of any expert advice. One father proudly told me that he hadn't taken his daughter to a physician since her birth, even though she was diagnosed with a genetic illness. "I won't depend on doctors. They do more harm than good," he said without a trace of doubt. Certainly that may be true of a few doctors, but *all*? And granted there is no ready treatment *now* for her condition, but wouldn't he want some continuing contact with professionals just in case even a palliative remedy were developed?

In another strategy, "I Know Better," parents try to feel less scared by proving the professional incompetent. Sandy is a nurse who has worked with children with epilepsy and their families for twenty years. She says, "Sometimes parents will try to take charge and end up spinning their wheels. One family got hold of a comprehensive textbook of neurology.

They looked up all the causes of seizures, including the rare degenerative diseases, and insisted their son be tested for each one. Of course, we don't automatically put people through the ordeal and expense of those tests unless there is a good reason to suspect that the problem is something other than idiopathic epilepsy.

"Another thing a few parents will do is get into having their child's blood level of medication tested. While this may give them an absolute number, it does not necessarily help in adjusting the dose. That's usually a clinical judgment and you need a doctor for that."

Knowledge may give us expertise, but it will never give us the dispassionate judgment of the experts. This is because it is *our* child we are talking about.

Professionals Often Lack Practical and Emotional Knowledge

Some of the most perceptive and unforgiving critics of professionals are professionals whose children have become patients. The experience must be an unrelenting reminder of the shortcomings of any education. Factual knowledge and clinical work do not necessarily bestow the maturity to grasp and respond to situations. A doctor may understand a disease, but not necessarily the practical and emotional consequences of it for the patient or family.

The problem is that some professionals don't know what they don't know. And the more defensive ones may not find out, either. Their role as expert has restricted their curiosity. Instead of trying to alleviate ignorance in this area, they may take on various postures to camouflage it. These are the "games" that professionals play to reassure themselves:

"I Know Best Because I Am the Expert": This is the strategy most familiar—and most offensive—to patients and their families. Sometimes that assertion, implicit or otherwise, is simply not true. A doctor or nurse may not necessarily have any idea, for example, why a child is not sleeping. A teacher may misunderstand certain disease-related behaviors as either mental deficiency or rebellion. Yet, rather than utter those difficult words "I don't know," some professionals will feel compelled to advise. From my own experiences and from talking with other parents, I have found it is not ignorance that infuriates, but the unwillingness to admit it.

"I Don't Have to Listen to You Because You Are . . . [Stereotype]": This "game" is generally not verbalized, but instead acted out in the subtle ways that some professionals treat patients and their families. Parents may be seen as denying, overprotective, rejecting, and other such terms. While this shorthand may be useful under certain circumstances, it can also serve as a detriment to communication. A social worker can employ a label as a rationale for not taking parents' words seriously. And mothers and fathers are quick to catch on when this is happening. The four mothers who wrote *Acceptance Is Only the First Battle* described a variety of ways that some professionals discounted their input:

> Each of us at one time or another has been treated as a hysterical or neurotic mother or both. We've all known hysteria, but have been driven to it by stress (financial, emotional, and physical), by the professional brushoff, by lack of information (especially current information), by conflicting diagnosis and advice, and by real fear and concern about our children's well-being. . . . We were sometimes treated as not smart enough to grasp medical terminology, so problems were explained only in layman's terms. . . . Our observations were sometimes disbelieved by professionals unless confirmed by our husbands or by another professional.[5]

PROFESSIONALS AND PARENTS HAVE DIFFERENT POWERS

Professionals' Power

Doctors, nurses, teachers, and other professionals wield a certain power simply because they often preside over our child in our absence. And while we may be able to suggest or enforce our guidelines of minimal care, we cannot create attitudes. We cannot make them like or be kind to our youngster. We must hand him over. Suzanne Massie writes,

> If Bobby were to grow up normally, that meant normal school, despite the fact that normal schools were neither equipped nor disposed to make concessions to his problem. The fact was, they did not want him at all. By law, public schools had to accept him, but it was made very clear to me that they would have preferred otherwise. . . . Yet whether the school administrators were well-meaning or not, whether they wanted to understand or not, after we had made our best efforts to bridge the gap and explain, we had to entrust Bobby to them, we had to expose him to physical injuries and psychological injuries that could wound forever. We had no choice.[6]

But there is another kind of unavoidable inequality of power. Professionals make many decisions about our child. Under certain circumstances, this arrangement may be best for everyone, provided they are both fair and competent. (For example, my pediatrician always decides which antibiotic to use for my children's frequent earaches.) But there are no obvious "right" answers for some kinds of decisions, only best bets. And our bet may make more sense to us. While we may not want to defer to a professional's judgment, we may not want to leave the relationship or the situation, either. We must, then, negotiate under circumstances in which we realistically have less influence than others.

Parents have gained the right to negotiate their child's education through Public Law 94-142, the Education for All Handicapped Children Act (1975). However, this law does not redress the imbalance of power. Go to any of the numerous IEP workshops and you will hear parents recount their "war stories." Mary Lou recalls: "They wanted my son in a physically handicapped program with four or five kids who could hardly speak. But his best asset is his socialization. I had to fight for his placement at a normal school." Another mother says, "Our school district never had a hearing-impaired child before and they found it hard to receive information from a mother."

And the law will not diminish our own dark moments of doubt when we disagree with those who are supposed to know better. Mary Lou recalls, "I did not sleep for the three months before he started kindergarten. I kept asking myself, Am I doing this for him or for me? My answer kept coming up that the teachers will have a higher expectation of him if he is in a normal school. And that's the real world, not a room with a few disabled kids."

Under these circumstances, parents can easily feel intimidated and/or victimized at these meetings. We may have our own agendas and ideas about where our child should be placed, but the professionals will, in some sense, be "running the show." Unless we bring friends, we will most likely be outnumbered, a sure trial by fire of most people's assertiveness. We will also be outeducated. The tests and terminology that have been used to evaluate our child may be unfamiliar to us. We also may not understand when we have the *right* to have input into this process and, instead, look for permission. Fern Kupfer writes, "There is anger that we parents have because we're in the know, but you're writing out the IEPs and you're making the judgments and you're the one who's determining things."[7]

The health-care professional also wields considerable power. It is true that the consumer rights movement has had some impact. Today physicians and nurses are obliged to inform and educate people about their medical treatment. However, in other ways, patients, including youngsters with special health needs and their families, have considerably less control over their medical care.

Insurance restrictions and cost-containment programs have limited the reasons people can seek medical attention that is reimbursed. Sometimes the only option for parents is a policy that excludes the medical condition and/or the child. In addition, many patients who have health plans generally have less choice about their doctors and when they can seek consultation with a specialist. The mother of a child with Down's had a strong suspicion that her daughter had milk allergies. "I wanted a referral to an allergist from my HMO, but they just flat refused. I decided to go and pay out of pocket."

Parents' Power

The term *professional parent* has been coined to describe the fact that we slowly master the relevant medical, social, and financial realities to become skilled in raising our child. We also make many decisions. This is power.

Some of our decisions will have to do with which medical advice to follow. Professionals can give us the prognosis of a particular illness. But this is a general statement based on a group average. Ultimately, what we are interested in is what our child will be able to do. Here is where the parent becomes the expert.

Only through our daily observation will we be able to

sense the limits of what to expect from our youngster. For example, a physician may advise, on general principle, that a child with asthma avoid grasses. A mother may learn, however, that her child will be able to play on the lawn with his friends if she immediately changes his clothes following this activity. I have received professional advice about how rigid I needed to be with my youngsters' diet. Some of this has worked out, some of it hasn't. But only I could have found this out through watching my children. In the final analysis, it will not be the doctor's word that makes the rule, but what *we* see when we follow his advice.

Some parents have found that well-intentioned professional advice may turn out to be impractical. Treatment for an illness is always in the context of a family's life, which often includes other children. A youngster seeing a speech therapist, a psychologist, and someone for physical rehabilitation will receive a program from each. There is only so much that parents can do. Helen Featherstone describes how she felt after a visiting nurse suggested that she brush her son's teeth three to four times a day. He was on Dilantin, one side effect of which is overgrowth of the gums.

Although I tried to sound reasonable over the phone, this new demand appalled me. . . . Jody, I thought, is blind, cerebral-palsied, and retarded. We do his physical therapy daily and work with him on sounds and communication. We feed him each meal on our laps, bathe him, dry him, put him in a body cast to sleep, launder his bed linens daily, and go through a variety of routines designed to minimize his miseries and enhance his joys and his development. (All this in addition to trying to care for and enjoy our other young children and making time for each other and our careers.) Now you tell me that I should spend fifteen minutes every day on something that Jody will hate, an activity that will not help him walk or even defecate, but one that is directed at the health of his gums. . . . What am I supposed to give up? Taking the kids to the park? Reading a bedtime story to my eldest? . . . Because there is no time in my life that hasn't been spoken for, and for every fifteen-minute activity that has been added, one has to be taken away.[8]

Most professionals won't be familiar with the sum total of our obligations and will not take it upon themselves to give us permission to quit. This is up to us. It's in our power to make the decision.

Ultimately, parents have the power not to follow advice of the health-care team and school, the power to leave them or fight them by appealing to higher authorities. Mary Lou remembers, "When John was two or three, we were inundated with programs. But nothing was fun. We decided to listen to our gut and follow just what made sense. We were told we were not dealing with reality and were written up as bad parents. I started to let him do real kid things, like pulling Tupperware out of the cabinet. It took six months for him to be able to do that, but it was a game and not therapy."

We Need to Make
the Professional Our Partner

At an IEP workshop, the leader was suggesting how parents can build their confidence for squaring off with educational professionals. "Parents do not know their rights," she said. There was a wave of nodding heads. Almost everyone shared this sense of impotence. But a bearded young man shot up from his seat. He was a special-education teacher who had just joined the local school system. He objected, "Sometimes you can go in with your rights outlined and alienate the people who are working for your kid."

That statement momentarily stopped the discussion because it unequivocally addressed our dilemma. We can't do it alone. We need an ally, not an opponent. Although it is true that we have the option to fight for our rights, this is clearly the second choice for getting what we want. People, including professional people, do not like to feel that they are being coerced. Those who do will not be giving their best. Their motions may be there, correct to the letter of the law, but not their hearts. First choice, always, will be for professionals to be working *with* us to help our child because they want to. How can we help make this happen?

SORT OUT THE SIGNIFICANT NEGATIVES

Most of us will have had at least one negative episode with a professional. I still remember with bitterness the young Ob-Gyn resident who checked me after Danny's birth. I was anxious about how his lack of oxygen at birth would affect him. This doctor, whose clean-shaven face was crunched up in a smart-alec grin, tossed out, "So what? So he won't go to Harvard." Experiences of incompetence or callousness tend to stay with parents because we are exposed and vulnerable. Ann Oster, mother of a premature infant, writes, "I am still angry five and a half years later at the professionals who were too insensitive or unskilled to give me what I needed. I am still mad at the doctor who said, when Nick was three days old, that I was in an awfully good mood for someone with such a sick baby."[9]

Even when our anger is justified, we should not allow it to poison our encounter with the next professional. If we nurse this grudge, we will surely communicate antagonism to the new doctor, or other professional. Despite their training, they also don't like being disliked, even if our attitude is not personal. Many may become less available, at least emotionally, when they sense this. Better for us to try to wipe our private slates clean and give the new person a chance.

In addition, not all negatives are equally offensive. We may not want to discount a professional for certain shortcomings. Regardless of the seriousness of our immediate concerns, she will inevitably have her off days. What counts is how far off. For example, sometimes the stress of other emergencies or personal problems may cause her to be abrupt or emotionally unresponsive. There is a big difference between this and abuse.

In addition, professionals will have different strengths and weaknesses to bring to our child. A doctor's expertise may be limited to certain areas; a nurse may be caring, but unable to answer all our questions; and so on. Their particular positives may make them worth it. The teachers at my son's first preschool were exceptionally nurturing and accommodating. As a result, his initial few hours away from home were in a supportive environment. But these professionals had been so generally accepting of children that they failed to spot that Danny had a big problem.

Also, occasionally a relatively benign remark may *feel* negative because we are exquisitely sensitive. We want to be heard and understood by the professional on our terms. Will he be on *our* side? Anything less, any inkling of his doubt, may seem like a vote of no confidence. I was one indignant mother following the first meeting with our son's new pediatric allergist. Danny had been on his special diet for six weeks and presented himself as a calm three-year-old. He gladly grabbed the nurse's hand and left the room for his blood test. The new doctor looked at us, two psychiatrist-parents, with undisguised skepticism. "He seems perfect, almost too perfect," he had said, his eyes narrowing. Later he asked, "Are you *sure* the teacher at his new preschool thinks he has a problem?" His unspoken question—It's not just you two who think this kid has trouble—screamed out in my ears. The man was wondering whether he had two neurotic parents on his hands, despite Danny's history and previous psychological evaluations.

At the time, I was angry at having our credibility questioned. But this doctor has been treating Danny with the utmost care for five years now. Of course, his opinion has changed. But, more important, so has mine. Now I see him as a professional who wanted to come to his own conclusions and not be unduly influenced by two parents who also happen to be professionals. We need to give "space" to the others who care for our child.

Sometimes, given our sensitivity, there will be *no* right thing that anyone can say. And that is no one's fault, just the situation. Helen Featherstone writes,

> I can remember flashes of irritation that seemed unjust to me even at the moment I experienced them. The epidemiologist who diagnosed Jody's toxoplasmosis interrupted his explanation of the disease to assure me that my future children would be safe. . . . I knew he was pointing out the few bright spots in a darkening sky, but I had not asked about my childbearing future. I remember thinking, I love this baby. Don't dismiss him as though someone else could replace him. . . . Another specialist terminated each consultation by telling me how beautifully I was caring for my son. His reflexive evaluation irritated me: he did not, after all, know enough about my mothering to make an informed judgment.[10]

Professionals want parents to *feel* better. After all, making people feel good is the driving force behind their choice of occupation. This force becomes that much more compelling when they can't fix the problem. In those sitations, they will naturally try words. But there may be no obvious etiquette and what comes out may be clumsy, at best. What ought to count for us are their intentions.

To sort out the negatives, we need to separate our sensitivity from the professional's limitations that truly obstruct our child's treatment or education. To do that, we need to think through what are the qualities of a good partnership.

THE GOOD PARENT-PROFESSIONAL RELATIONSHIP

Much has been written about what parents should expect from professionals and what to do when they aren't getting that. Rather than repeat this advice, I'd like to focus on the mutuality of this relationship. There are certain qualities that should be present in both parties for this partnership to work. For example, a good marriage does not come about simply by finding the right spouse. Rather, it also develops by *being* the right spouse. The same kind of thinking can be loosely applied to the parent-professional relationship. To some extent, we need to give what we expect to receive.

Both Parent and Professional Need to Trust and Feel Trusted

We naturally want to feel that we can count on the professional's good intentions—that she wants to do her best by our child. Parents readily sense when this is not the case and it is perhaps our second major complaint, next to incompetence. Jill, who adopted a girl with Down's, counsels families of the disabled. She explains, "Some doctors feel these youngsters shouldn't live and they let us know that. They don't realize how hurtful it is when they look at your baby and start out with the attitude, 'Is this child worth preserving?' "

Can I trust him? is likely to be the first question we have. However, our answer will not come from someone walking in and smiling right. Rather, we can only conclude this over time because the professional has been there for us in significant ways. The teacher who spontaneously shows an ongoing interest in our child or the doctor/nurse who consistently responds to medical problems with concern instead of annoyance will gain our confidence.

Parents, too, need to feel trusted—that their input is valued. This is more than a self-esteem issue. Mothers and fathers are the only ones to have access to certain kinds of information. A professional who discounts this is limiting his effectiveness. For example, when Loren was three he was taking phenobarbital for epilepsy. Alice recalls, "I knew the medication could cause a personality change, but my son was crazy. I couldn't control him. I called my pediatrician on several ocasions but he didn't seem to take it seriously. Finally, I brought him in and Loren lay in the hallway shrieking. I told him, 'I can't live with this. Can you?' I suppose he hears so many complaints that he had jumped to the conclusion that I was just another hysterial mother."

But little is written for parents about the professionals' point of view. Do they need to trust patients and their families? The answer, of course, is yes. Medical literature is replete with studies about the noncompliant family, the difficult patient, and so on. Teachers will talk about which parents don't seem to care about what their children are doing.

These descriptions, although far from flattering, do reflect some portion of the professional's reality. Some parents and youngsters will not say what is happening at home, reinforce what's expected at school, or be honest when they have decided not to follow through with a recommendation. The result is that the social worker, for example, learns not to trust the parent or child. The professional's effectiveness is limited and he is likely to become frustrated.

Likewise, the professional needs to feel trusted. This does not mean that the expert is *always* right or that we are obliged to follow his advice like dutiful soldiers. Rather, we need to give his opinions the same respect and careful consideration that we want him to give ours. A twelve-year-old girl had fever, weight loss, and weakness for a month. Her mother rejected the physician's advice to start antibiotics. Instead, she put her daughter on a health-food diet to "cleanse" her system. I knew this woman casually and felt compelled to mention the dangers of an untreated strep infection, which her daughter most likely had. She wouldn't hear of it. She was obviously concerned about her child, but could not entertain any other form of treatment than what she had in mind.

While this story may seem extreme, it is not unusual. I have met a number of parents who feel they are somehow "giving in" when they put their child on a medication (one mother actually told me her doctor had "won" because her child's earache had not gone away on its own after four days and the boy had to take pills). Ironically, many of these same people will feel angry and cheated when their child *only* has a virus and no medicine is indicated. Clearly, they are too ambivalent about medical help to trust their doctors.

The consumer movement has accomplished much in that it has stimulated a healthy questioning of authority in many areas. Parents demand to understand fully why their child is taking that pill or must be in that particular educational program. But the downside is that some people may be a little too willing to discount the professional's experience. The teacher who has been in the classroom for twenty years or the doctor/nurse who has treated this kind of problem for that amount of time has a fund of knowledge we don't have access to. She has a different perspective about what is normal. And I say this as a professional who must periodically abandon the comfort of my own credentials in order to become "just" a mother or a patient in order to get the most honest and informed help I can.

Parents and Professionals Need to Admit When They Are Either Wrong or Don't Know

Professional training, unfortunately, does not encourage the admission of ignorance. Rather, if one is ignorant, one is supposed to remedy this condition, and mighty soon. Ignorance is an intellectual sin. This educational approach may stimulate students to learn, but it does not prepare the professional for the real world. In the course of most careers, there will be a number of occasions when a doctor, for example, is just plain stumped. But there may be few who can admit to this, which is also too bad. Many parents have expressed renewed faith in their doctor, for example, because he could say he didn't know.

Likewise, we also need to be honest with those professionals who touch our child's life. Parents who have an overwhelming stake in needing to be right may do this at the expense of their child's health or education. I was once asked to speak to a mother whose daughter had food allergies. The mother was convinced that the first-grade teacher was picking on her daughter. "The teacher can't handle the kids so she is saying there is something wrong with Shelly." Is her daughter ever wild at home? "Oh, yes." Did you know food allergies can cause that? "Shelly is just fine in school." End of discussion.

Parents and Professionals Need to Be Able to Negotiate with One Another

There are generally two roadblocks to these negotiations. The first is when a parent has difficulty expressing his concerns. Most professionals, in contrast, are trained to do just this. Many parents' support groups discuss how mothers and fathers can deal with social workers, for example, on an equal footing. Yes, we should be able to ask for explanations, state why a certain treatment program won't easily fit into our family's schedule, and so on. However, parents may say little for fear of antagonizing the professional. Workshops on this, especially in the context of self-help groups, can be useful.

The second roadblock occurs when either professional or parent becomes hostile. Much has been said about the benefits of assertiveness versus aggressiveness. When we speak our piece without demeaning the other person, logic is supposed to prevail. That's not always what happens. Both professionals and parents are capable of becoming defensive when their opinions are questioned.

What, then, is good negotiation? From a parent's point of view, we should feel free to share what's on our mind with a professional and be certain that we have been heard. And both parents and professionals ought to feel that the relationship can survive a disagreement.

HOW PARENTS CAN FACILITATE THIS RELATIONSHIP

Later, we will talk about the specifics of the parent–health-care provider and parent-teacher relationships. However, here are some general ideas that apply to both:

You Can't Make a Bad Relationship Good

This chapter is concerned with how to make good relationships better. All these suggestions are predicated on our respect for the professional we are dealing with. If that is lacking—if we believe him to be unfair, rigid, abusive, defensive, or incompetent, no amount of work on our part is going to change this. The ideal solution is to try and find someone else.

Separate a Professional's Style from His Competence

Professionals have very different ways of relating to their patient/clients/students. Some doctors are almost Marcus Welby clones (yes, they do exist), others become your buddies; some teachers are authoritarian, others are freewheeling; and so on. We will probably run across at least one professional whose style does not suit our personality, but who is competent. Sometimes his particular expertise will be worth our adjustment. For example, my first obstetrician was an ardent patriarch who referred to all his patients as "the girls" ("How's your girlfriend?" he once asked about someone thirty years my senior). Some women may have found his manner offensive. But his passion was that his "girls" should be able to have babies. Another doctor had already advised hysterectomy for me because of a large fibroid. But the elderly patriarch was optimistic that he could successfully remove it so that I could bear children. He was the doctor for me.

Give the Relationship a Little Time

Only occasionally do first impressions "say it all." People can have strengths lurking below their surface appearance. For example, one of Danny's teachers was seen by most parents, including me, as gruff. But she was able to give us a wealth of emotional support and practical suggestions.

Our opinions of what's truly useful also may change over time. When Jane's son was five months old he was diagnosed with Wilms' tumor. "The first time I met the doctor I did not like him. He was blunt and did not make Mark's illness sound promising. Now I think the world of him because he did not try to make us feel better with false hopes."

When we start out on our journey with professionals, we may only appreciate a small piece of the "big picture." Alice was put off when her doctor informed her that her son had a seizure disorder. "I had to go to a book to find out what that meant. I became angry that he used that term. The implication was that I'm not supposed to be able to handle it if Loren had epilepsy. But later I could understand. Although he misjudged us, many people do not easily accept that label."

Talk to Her as if She's on Your Side

We can't *make* a professional care about our child and it is usually fruitless to work with one who is not motivated. However, for the professional who is, a parent's unwarranted antagonism is deflating. Her education does not erase her human need to feel good about her work and the people she works with. In the end, her discouragement will be our defeat, too.

Parents are prone to becoming hostile when we hear something we don't like. This is the "kill the messenger" approach to upsetting news. A teacher may get only arguments when she tries to give parents feedback about their child's behavior problem. The result of this defensiveness is that her efforts are not reinforced at home, the child must then go through additional discipline to conform to school standards, and the professional is dissuaded from giving any additional updates.

We also get angry about unfortunate events that still may be beyond the professional's control. For example, doctors may be blamed for the known side effect of a necessary medication. Despite patient's rights and education, many of us, in our heart of hearts, will wish that a doctor could sometimes be more powerful than she is. And for good reason. A little more power on her part might eliminate a little more suffering for our child. But our unjustified anger toward professionals about the inherent risks of one therapy is going to make many of them think twice before recommending the next.

If we truly believe in the professional's good faith and competence, it will be much more to our child's advantage for us to talk about how we *all* can handle whatever the problem is. In this way, the professional will feel supported in her tasks and we will feel reassured that she is being totally honest about our child's condition and his options.

Reinforce the Positive

Although it is not our duty to nurture the professionals' ego, it doesn't hurt to let them know when some advice has worked out for the better. Often, their initial fantasies of their impact during training are far in excess of the reality (a doctor friend once lamented to me that he went into medicine to save life and limb and he had yet to do either). However, most professionals still retain some need to feel effective. Mentioning when this does, in fact, occur with our child's care or education should only fuel their motivation and continued interest.

ROLE-MODEL FOR YOUR CHILD
HOW TO MAKE THE PROFESSIONAL HIS PARTNER

Our implicit attitudes about how to relate to professionals will be communicated to our child whether we wish it to be or not. Each time we mention or respond to some occurrence involving these people, our voice will most likely be tinged with some judgmental emotion—approval, admiration, disgust, disappointment. And this may occur, even when our words are relatively neutral: She gave you *more* homework today, or He put you on *more* medicine.

A professional's competence, responsiveness to our needs, and honesty are the criteria that most parents will use to evaluate him. Another, less obvious factor is our prevailing attitude toward "authority figures." How do we generally feel about those we perceive in control?

Based on our childhood background, some of us may be prone to placate, challenge, and so on. Also, a variety of national events from the Vietnam War and Watergate to the newsmaking misrepresentations of big business has spawned a cultural skepticism toward those who have power. Sometimes our particular bent toward authority may have little to do with the individual with whom we are dealing. For the benefit of our children, we need to become familiar with our own tendencies in this matter. The parent who is overwhelmingly suspicious will probably antagonize some professionals who sincerely want to help. A parent who is uncritically trusting may inadvertently settle for ineffective help.

Once we become aware of our own implicit attitudes, we can better control them. Even professionals we respect can't possibly satisfy us all the time, and recognizing this does not mean that we will avoid frustration. But we also don't necessarily have to share this feeling with our child. Or, if we choose to, we can do it in a manner that teaches him something about the relationship.

The question, then, is what do we *deliberately* want to communicate to our child about relating to the professional? Our youngster will, first, need to feel trust in order to get any benefit. If we inadvertently and unnecessarily undermine the teacher or nurse, our child will be less likely to follow treatment or do what's required in school. Therefore, we need to support their authority so that our child can place his confidence in them without experiencing any conflict of loyalty. ("Mrs. Lane helps many children with diabetes figure out what to eat. I think she can help you.") In addition, we can exploit this authority to help our child accept what's necessary. ("Mrs. Lane wants you to follow this diet. Not just me and Dad.")

Along with our support of authorities, we also need to communicate the right to *question* them. The mother of a twenty-five-year-old daughter with epilepsy recalls in a group discussion, "I never questioned the doctor and always sent her out of the room. Now she's going to someone who has overmedicated her and she doesn't know enough to ask. I did not prepare her to be an adult with epilepsy."

But communicating the right to question authority is an issue that goes far beyond being an informed patient. Many injustices have been committed by groups because people blindly followed their leaders. One antidote to uncritical obedience is to nurture, early on, our child's right to ask. Our home, the medical office, and the classroom are good places to start. These arenas are our youngster's first brush with those in control.

Another way we can teach the right to question authority is to share our own experiences with them. We've all had disagreements with "authorities" in schools, stores, at work, and so on. We can use these to communicate to our children that we have options other than passive acceptance of some ruling. This process becomes even more relevant when it takes place with our child's teacher or doctor. It is important, however, to explain these situations in a manner that does not undercut our child's relationship with these individuals.

There may be times when we are disappointed in a professional. In these situations, we don't have to pretend they are perfect. We just need to be mindful of how we express this. One mother was upset that her child continued to have breakthrough seizures, despite trying different medications. She was questioning her pediatrician's judgment and wondering whether she should be going to a neurologist instead. Her child was also losing confidence. Whatever she chose to say, she needed to acknowledge everyone's frustration without denigrating the doctor. If she had, she would most likely be sowing the seeds for her youngster's noncompliance with the next professional—who might, in fact, recommend an effective treatment. ("I am disappointed that your seizures go on and on. Dr. Barns may be good with earaches, but I think we should try a nerve doctor for your seizures. Most doctors are not expert about all parts of the body.")

There will be times when we just plain disagree with a professional. We may need to support her authority while still letting our child know that there are other views on the matter. For example, Jason and his classmates were watching a school play. The boy whispered to his friend that the production "sucked." The friend then reported his comment to the teacher. Jason was publicly rebuked for his criticism. Although his mother was not thrilled about the language, she let her son know that he had a right to his opinion, especially since he did not broadcast it.

Unfortunately, there may also be circumstances in which a professional has acted outrageously. When this happens, we do need to undermine *that* person's authority, emphasizing that that individual is the exception, not the rule. Loren, who has epilepsy, had a harrowing experience with his first-grade teacher. Alice, his mother, had explained his condition to the teacher at the beginning of the school year. "I said that he was in good control but if he had a seizure, his left leg would extend and she could just walk him to the nurse's office. She said, 'Fine,' but gave me no other feedback. Later, I told my husband I did not know what to expect from her."

Alice found out. "After Loren had his first seizure, she ran around like a chicken without a head and made his classmates move to the other side of the room. The nurse had to get him in a wheelchair, even though he could walk on his own. Of course, all the other six-year-olds must have thought he had something terribly wrong with him."

She wanted to correct any misunderstandings resulting from this incident by giving a talk about epilepsy for her son's classmates. This teacher refused without any explanation.

"But the crushing blow came when she made him wear a sign with his name on it in the playground. This was supposed to let the aides and everyone else know that he wasn't allowed on the monkey bars."

Loren eventually had surgery for his seizures. "I sent him back to school even though the term was almost finished and his teacher had been devastating. I didn't want him to get the message that he was in such bad shape he couldn't go back."

Alice eventually explained to her son, "Mrs. Jackson did not understand you and we sure wouldn't want her or anyone like her to teach you again." While we should never take undermining these authorities lightly, there are situations in which anything less would be unfair to our child.

We have talked about general principles in making professionals our partners. Here are some specifics.

Partners in Health-Care

There are a variety of factors that negatively impinge on the doctor/nurse/therapist–patient relationship. As already mentioned, parents have a host of realistic questions and concerns when dealing with these professionals. Is this person going to prove competent? When the answer is obviously no, the experience can be unsettling. Diane took her eleven-year-old son, who has hemophilia, to her health-plan providers because he was in a crisis. "The nurse thought the treatment was just an injection. That discouraged me because I assumed that doctors and nurses would know. Even my son said, 'Let's get out of here.' "

But competence can sometimes be a difficult call, even for parents with medical training. That's because a doctor's advice may be based on years of experience in treating children such as ours, not necessarily on the facts cited in textbooks and journal articles. Also, a doctor may be competent in some, but not all, areas. How are we to judge? If we are not correct in our evaluation, we may seriously shortchange our youngster. Is it any wonder that some parents arm themselves with the latest technical knowledge with the intention of quizzing their health-care professional?

We also wonder, What will this professional's attitude be toward my child? The sobering fact is that there are some who harbor destructive stereotypes about certain conditions. The most destructive is that those with the illness or disability are hopeless. For example, Peter had his first seizure when he was nineteen. "The first doctor treated me like I was a cripple and told me to get a job with no stress. I'd still like to know where that exists. I had to go to six or seven [doctors] to find one who was matter-of-fact and would listen to me." He is now forty, the father of two, and a magazine editor. The mother of a son with autism advises, "Some doctors mislabeled my son as mentally retarded and didn't even want to look at him. Find ones that are genuinely willing to treat your child."

Another question is: What will the health-care professional's attitude be toward me? We naturally want to be accepted as an intelligent contributor to our child's care. The nurse/doctor who either discounts us ("another hysterical parent") or is guilt-provoking ("What did you do this time?") will discourage our participation.

In addition to these questions, there are the practical realities of the medical encounter that make it a stressful experience and one to dread. Many of us will ponder the logistics and outcome of an appointment days ahead of time. How will we get there? The difficulties of traveling to a strange hospital in a big city may be considerable, especially with an ill child. What treatment will the professional advise? How will I feel about it? How will my child feel about it? Even sitting in a waiting room is a stress: it's always longer than we'd planned for and we just *wait* to be called. Once we make it into the examining room, the medical evaluation process is one of both physical and emotional exposure. No matter how diligent we've been, we may worry, Will I be found lacking by these authorities? Despite all these concerns, we need to maintain a relatively calm and confident exterior for our child. Our encouragement will be that much more important if he is scheduled for a painful procedure. It is easy to see why parents may hate going to doctors. But this should usually be a separate issue from hating the doctor.

We need to sort through our feelings. Some of us may rarely be made happy from these experiences. The question is: Why do we feel bad? Has the professional failed to meet his obligations of being competent or having a constructive attitude toward working with our child and us? Or are we really reacting to the painful reality of our child's illness? Martha was distraught when she learned about her four-year-old daughter's leukemia. She says of her pediatrician, "I knew he became emotionally involved because his eyes would fill up, but I was never going to break down in front of him. I realized later that I was mad at him for finding this illness."

If we are basically satisfied with our health-care providers, here are some suggestions on how to enhance this relationship.

USE HEALTH-CARE PROFESSIONALS
ACCORDING TO THEIR STRENGTHS

We need rapport with the professionals with whom we have ongoing contact. When the physician who diagnosed April as having lupus gave her mother some papers and said, "Go home and read it," this mother decided that there would not be enough give-and-take in the relationship. She says, "What I like about our new doctor is that he's not up on a pedestal. He listens to us and is learning, too." We need this kind of put-our-heads-together mutuality to figure out the nitty-gritty questions that come up in living with a chronic illness.

On the other hand, specialists that we and our child see on a limited basis may not be particularly involved with the totality of his life and that may not matter. Martha remembers, "We took Heather to an oncologist for her chemotherapy spinal injections. I'd try to ask him about what kinds of activities she could do and whether she'd be able to go to kindergarten. I realized that my pediatrician was the one to answer these questions."

Also, some excellent pediatricians may not be particularly attuned to the social dilemmas that come up with chronic illness. Their focus understandably tends to be on the medical management and not, for example, on how one should deal with a live-in mother-in-law who criticizes a parent's handling of the condition. Yet the latter is undeniably important, too. Ideas on how to handle relatives, friends, and your child's peers may best be answered by support groups, nurses, and social workers.

BE AS SPECIFIC AS POSSIBLE ABOUT YOUR CONCERNS

These questions may have to deal with the diagnosis, your child's expected growth and development with the condition, the use of past, current or future medications, tests, referrals to specialists, and so on. Some of these may be short-term concerns and others will be long-term. And some of the answers may only come with time and experience in living with the condition, from support groups and from doctors and other health-care professionals. But we have to start asking to begin to discover what the parameters are and to whom we should address our concerns.

Use all the help you can get in formulating questions for doctors and other health-care professionals. This ought to be at least a two person process. I brainstorm with my husband in order to define more precisely what we should be worried about. Support groups can also give you the benefit of other parents' experiences. It may be useful to call and discuss questions, before a doctor's visit, with his nurse. In that way, there will be sufficient time put aside in the appointment for answers. The nurse will be able to inform the doctor of your concerns, some of which may require digging (for example, "Does a new brand of vitamin fulfill my children's greater calcium needs because of their dairy-free diet?"). Sometimes, the nurse will be able to answer questions for you.

Make a list of the questions before you visit. If you haven't already called them in, you can say to the doctor, "I have two things I want to ask. When should I ask them?" Remember, it is easy to forget the information you hear because of the intensity of these moments. I sometimes make myself write down answers. This allows me to double-check my comprehension and makes it easier to tell my husband what happened.

MAKE SURE YOU AGREE WITH
THE BASICS OF YOUR CHILD'S TREATMENT

There are certain areas in which parents and health-care professionals need to reach a meeting of the minds. These include: when an office visit is necessary, what constitutes an emergency and how the parent should handle it, and how to modify treatment within certain limits to fit a child's lifestyle. Serious disagreement about these issues will make it difficult to work as partners.

KEEP RECORDS

Your Observations
These are especially important, both for your doctor and for you. Long before it becomes obvious, there are certain subtle

or individual behaviors your child may exhibit that indicate his condition is changing. For example, mothers used to ask me how I knew when Danny was reacting to food and not just being a wild kid. He's an active child, anyway. (Generally, these parents were not being nosy, but were worried about their own children.) Although by that time I had read a number of books about food allergies, what I said was based on my observations. Danny behaves in a way that's unmistakable, once you know what to look for. Likewise, other parents who have children with asthma and diabetes have told me about their children's characteristic signs. These observations will help us monitor our child's health, as well as the effect of any new treatment.

Other People's Observations

As well as we know our children, we will not be able to predict how they will fare with their condition away from home. We need feedback from other people—parents and teachers. Information about irritability, drowsiness, and so on when your child is with others may help you and your doctor consider the effectiveness or side effects of treatment.

Other Professionals' Observations and Treatments

The health-care "system" is generally not that, but a collection of unintegrated services and professionals whom the parent has contacted. Parents become the "case managers."

Although you may assume otherwise, professionals will not necessarily communicate with each other. The physical therapist may not be aware of the neurologist's thinking and vice versa. You need to make sure that everyone is up to date about your child's health.

You can coordinate your youngster's care by requesting that letters be sent or phone calls be made. But sometimes the information does not make it to its destination in a timely fashion. I have found it most effective to ask the professional for a copy of the medical records or summary letter, which I can then file and also give to another.

TRY TO FACILITATE YOUR CHILD'S RELATIONSHIP WITH HIS DOCTOR, NURSE, OR THERAPIST

This will not only make him feel more a part of treatment, but also prepare him for becoming an informed adult patient. For medical appointments, books on doctor visits and doctor kits are the first steps in helping the young child get used to physicians and nurses. As he gets older, he can take a more active part during the appointment. To help him, go over *his* questions before the visit and role-play with him how he can ask them. During the time with the professional, try to word the discussion so that it also includes him, even as a listener. (For example, "The teacher says he's better adjusted" can be put: "The teacher has said that he is getting along better with his classmates. What do you think, Johnny?") Also, let your child answer any of the professional's questions that he can. You can always add other relevant information.

TRY TO MAXIMIZE RELATIONSHIPS WITH HEALTH-CARE PROFESSIONALS IN THE HOSPITAL

There are many excellent pamphlets on how to help your child with the stresses of hospitalization. The key strategy here is to maintain what's familiar as much as possible. Class letters, favorite toys, family audio- and videotapes fall into this category. Also, parents need to try to make what's new— that is, the hospital experience—less strange. Playing "hospital" at home and preadmission visits are two ways. But we still must negotiate with the myriad of professionals who touch our child's life.

If your youngster has repeated admissions, have a care plan and history written out to take to the hospital. In this way, all professionals will be fully informed without your worrying about forgetting relevant details. If several doctors are involved in your child's care and the stay will be more than several days, you may want to request a "care conference" with these professionals. This will help assure that there is a coordinated effort in your child's treatment and that all are informed of his condition and previous reactions.

Parents find themselves negotiating with professionals over a variety of issues, many of which involve asking them to change routines. And hospitals can have notoriously rigid routines. When Jane's infant son had kidney surgery, she recalls, "They wouldn't budge and did things by the book. I think they ought to let a child sleep and not check him every fifteen minutes." Susan Duffy says, "Every time Keough went in, they'd slap a mister on her trach. This made her suctioning a lot less, but it tied her physically to one spot. We never did that at home." Sherry had to keep after the nurses to give her two-year-old daughter pain medicine for her third-degree burns. "She was in isolation. They'd leave her alone for long periods and not come back. I was particularly concerned that she have her medicine before physical therapy so that she could handle it better. They would sometimes skip this, saying that she already had a pacifier. I told the nurse that just because she can't talk doesn't mean she can't feel."

There is no easy way to tackle these issues. Some routines may be rigid and seem almost ruthless, yet still be in the best interests of your child (for example, the doctors may feel an every-fifteen-minute check following surgery is necessary to troubleshoot a complication). But other schedules may be for the convenience of the staff (it is easier for nurses to suction a child less often). Although routines may seem unfair, they may also be necessary. Effectively taking care of many ill children's needs requires a certain order and predictability. Some incidents may seem plain lackadaisical or even cruel, as in neglecting to give pain medications to Sherry's child.

How are we to judge which schedules and decisions are genuinely necessary and which should be optional? First, we need information. Find one or two professionals whom you trust. They should be people who are flexible and communicate in some way that they are concerned about patients' physical *and* emotional comfort. Direct your question to the professional who can most likely answer it. Doctors may be the only ones able to answer certain questions; nurses and social workers can answer others. If you are wondering about a routine, ask the professional involved the reasons for it. Can you think of another option that would not be disruptive? For example, one mother was told that she would not be able to bring in a cot to stay overnight with her child. She slept upright in a chair. And most important, make sure you understand the answers you are getting.

Use positive strategies in working with professionals. This is different from being seductive or flattering, the "honey" approach to catching bees. In most relationships, our acknowledgment of what's right will encourage the other to repeat that behavior. And, whether or not it's fair, patients and their families who talk *only* about what's wrong can easily be categorized as "difficult" or "complainers." Once that happens, it becomes hard for professionals to neutrally hear and respond to their requests.

One positive strategy, then, is to deliberately state something that is going well before mentioning what is not ("Jack likes his new room with his bed next to the window. He likes to look out. But it gets a little stuffy. Is there any way to open the window?"). Another is to attribute good intentions to what has gone awry ("I know you didn't want to skip Jack's sleeping medicine, but . . ." as opposed to "What's the matter with you people? Can't you remember to give him his medicine?"). If the professional you are dealing with proves unreceptive, try another.

These suggestions are first-line strategies for relative inconveniences. There are transgressions in which nothing less than a parent's complaint or threat to a higher authority will rectify the wrongdoing. (I would put Sherry's situation in that category.)

One of the latest trends in pediatric hospitals is to have on-site volunteer and staff parents whose children have been inpatients at that facility. In this way, families can talk with others who have been through the experience and get another perspective about their concerns. These helping parents can serve as the families' advocates within the system, link them to services, and suggest options. The additional contact between professional and parents should help reduce suspiciousness on both sides.

Partners in Education

Most children with illnesses and disabilities have normal intelligence and do not qualify for special education. Yet, most will probably need special considerations from their teachers and school nurses. (I shall use the word *teacher* here for convenience. However, what follows applies generally to school nurses, too.)

First, our child may be at greater risk for academic failure than his healthy classmates. Fatigue, minor learning disabilities, and frequent absences may interfere with instruction. Many absences will be short-term, which means he will not qualify for homebound teaching. We will need to have ongoing contact with his teacher to monitor how our youngster is doing.

Second, whatever our child's medical regimen (medication, special diet, limited exercise), he will probably need to follow it during the school day. What are his alternatives in how he carries out his treatment? We will want to minimize his self-consciousness and maximize his compliance. We will have to work out these "hows" with each teacher, individually.

Third, our child's social adjustment may be affected by his current health. What can his teacher do to encourage his participation and relatedness?

This is a tall order for any educator, but nonetheless desirable if our child has a chronic illness or disability. But although we want and need this good communication with teachers, most of us will have a variety of fears in dealing with them. These include:

Telling the teacher about the illness will cause her to treat our child differently. Pity: One mother says, "My son had to have a special snack each day. His teacher would announce to the class, 'Only John can eat because he is sick.'" Insensitivity: Another parent reports, "My daughter could only eat her snack on the playground, next to the wall where the punished kids were sent." Overly alarmed: "When I told her my son had hemophilia, she thought he was going to bleed to death in front of her." Expecting the worst: "I told her my son had food allergies and right away she said, 'He must be hyper.'"

The teacher will not sufficiently understand the illness. "He looks normal but has a rare metabolic defect in fat metabolism. She never grasped how life-threatening it is and did not follow many of my requests."

The teacher may not keep information confidential. "There was a fight between Ryan and another boy. The teacher told the boy's parents that Ryan had diabetes and a behavior problem, even though the fight was not only Ryan's fault. I was furious."

———

All these fears present real possibilities and, in fact, were taken from parents' experiences. Some parents are so concerned about the teacher's biases, that they say nothing. Martha's daughter was successfully treated for leukemia. "I never told her kindergarten teacher because I was afraid she would be singled out as sick."

But silence is not an option for most of us. Our child will need her teacher's help in order to negotiate the academic, medical, and social demands of school. And to be fair, many of these professionals, armed with an accurate understanding of a student's needs, have made heartening accommodations. Barbara has juvenile arthritis and needed to do what's called "proning" once a day. This procedure requires that she lie flat on her abdomen strapped to a table. The twelve-year-old girl started doing this in the nurse's office during lunch hour. But her teacher was concerned that she was missing out on socializing with her friends. This professional located the right-size table, placed it in her classroom, and told the girl that she could prone during history, since that was mostly lecture. Now her friends take turns strapping her in.

Our child needs his teacher on his side, if possible. Here are some suggestions on how to make her your partner.

SELECT YOUR CHILD'S TEACHER, IF POSSIBLE

In some schools, parents have the option of deciding with the principal which teacher is best for their child. Certain irrationally fearful professionals may have a tendency to segregate an ill child. This was probably the reason behind the teacher's cruel handling of Loren's epilepsy. But others may be much more flexible and almost transform a "problem" into an asset. One teacher gives turns to each student to push a wheelchair-bound child. This becomes a social event for the youngster who is handicapped and an exciting privilege for his classmates.

TELL THE TEACHER AND SCHOOL NURSE ABOUT YOUR CHILD'S ILLNESS

Sometimes parents will choose to wait and see what happens before bringing undue attention to their child. Their rationale is: Why say more than is necessary? There may be risks in informing teachers, as described on page 214; but there are also risks in keeping them ignorant. The most obvious risk is that the teacher will be unprepared for any medical crisis. A child who is having a seizure, a bleed from hemophilia, or an asthmatic attack will get better treatment if the teacher is aware of the condition.

Another risk is that the teacher who is uninformed may inadvertently react negatively. One mother recalls, "I started making my kids muffins from millet when they were first diagnosed with wheat allergies. My daughter gave one to her teacher. The woman just about gagged and asked, 'Is your mother trying to poison you?' I realized, then, that I had to talk to her about their diets."

In addition, teachers, like many of us, are prone to categorize individuals, especially when dealing with large numbers. First impressions, even when false, can have staying power. Carmen says, "I used to think I'd let things develop, but then I learned that it can be hard to change someone's mind. Ben's first-grade teacher actually told him that he was retarded. She wouldn't budge in her judgment, even after I let her know he had learning problems from food allergies."

EDUCATE THE TEACHER AND SCHOOL NURSE ABOUT THE ILLNESS

Chronic illnesses are relatively rare and most teachers will not have direct experience with them. As a result, they are likely to feel uncomfortable and there is bound to be at least some misunderstandings. Eleanor's daughter attended a religious elementary school ten years ago. "They always confused food allergies with her not liking the lunch," she recalls. Their enlightenment should make them more at ease with your youngster's condition and also pave the way for quality management while he's at school.

The first step, then, is to provide pamphlets about the condition, if available. Fortunately, many national organizations are now publishing teachers' guides to cancer, hemophilia, diabetes, and so on. This material specifically addresses the concerns in the classroom. Doctors' notes will serve the same function.

But written material will do little good unless we talk to the teacher about the specific needs of our child.

TELL THE TEACHER AND SCHOOL NURSE ABOUT YOUR CHILD'S SPECIFIC NEEDS

How we tell the professional is at least as important as *what* we say. We may have a different impact on this individual depending on whether we are calm or anxious. We may believe that communicating a certain parental anxiety will alert her that our child's problem is serious. But we can overdo this to everyone's detriment. Denise, whose daughter has asthma and a congenital heart defect, found out the hard way. "I was concerned that Erica be properly watched and told the nurse her history—that she had been hospitalized twenty-five times in two years and once had a cardiac arrest. I could see from her bulging eyes that I was scaring her to death. Now if my daughter just twitches she calls me and the doctor, too. I've had to try and undo some of this by reassuring her."

Remember, many professionals will be anxious about caring for your child. When confronted, Loren's teacher had shrieked to Alice, "I can't handle him in the classroom. Suppose he falls and breaks his head?" even though falling was not a part of his seizure. More often than not, our task will be to calm down the professional and communicate that, yes, she will be able to handle him. To do this, it is best to stick to a matter-of-fact presentation of his problem, without going into emotional details. At least initially, it won't be useful for you to share your own trepidations.

It helps to deemphasize this facet of him. Sandy, who runs an epilepsy support group, counsels, "Always start with something positive about your child—such as, he plays basketball or likes the art class. Then casually mention what you want to say about the illness—such as, his medicine has been changed and could you watch for breakthrough seizures. Then end with something positive. In this way, the teacher comes to know your child as more than the epileptic." This advice can be useful for all conditions.

Once we have cultivated our matter-of-fact manner, what then should we tell the teacher? Everything that relates to any problem that *might* come up in school. And we may not be able to tell her all of this in the first meeting. There may be many facts to absorb and they may keep changing, too. Rather, we should aim to impart this over a period of time, starting with the essentials. I would suggest the following information:

How the Condition Might Affect Your Youngster in the Classroom

The teacher should know, specifically, if your child with arthritis can't open a milk container or if your child with cystic fibrosis will be coughing up mucus. This is especially important for children with invisible limitations involving concentration, behavior, or energy. Don recalls, "My son's teacher once said, 'I don't know why he isn't performing better. He's gifted.' I told her he is often up all night in the shower trying to breathe. But I send him to school anyway rather than have him home watching TV."

What Treatment Regimen He Needs to Follow During the Schoolday

In essence, parents can propose, "How can we, parent and teacher, arrange his treatments so as to minimize his exposure?" Simple accommodations may mean a lot. The child with diabetes who is allowed to go to the bathroom without raising his hand or one who can take his medication at lunchtime in the privacy of the nurse's office will be spared unnecessary discomfort.

Parents can also ask, "How can we arrange his medical regimen to maximize his participation?" The child with asthma who can keep score at a soccer game or with diabetes who can eat her own snacks at a class party will feel less left out.

What Are the Signs that the Condition Is Out of Control and How Should the Teacher Handle This?

Give the teacher a written procedure of what to do and whom to call, and bring in any necessary medications, snacks, and so on. Let her know if these crises are to be expected or are relatively rare. Give her an accurate appraisal of your child's competence in both detecting and dealing with the crises. Some teachers may not trust a youngster to know what's going on with her body. One mother was furious when she was called to pick up her preschooler who was having an asthmatic attack. "We've never been the kind to say 'Oh, honey.' Her attacks are just business and she takes care of them. She'll tell adults when she's wheezing. I found out that there was a substitute that day and she didn't believe her."

Let the Teacher Know You Will Inform Her of Any
Changes
Of course, this is essential for the child whose health is either deteriorating or under increased medical supervision. But even if your youngster's condition is stable, it can be reassuring to mention that to his teacher every so often.

HELP THE TEACHER SET LIMITS, IF NEEDED

Although we want a teacher to accommodate to our child's needs, we don't want her to be either permissive or solicitous. This will only discourage our youngster from doing her best (or her most normal), confuse her about her realistic place in the world, and draw additional attention to her differentness. Don's two teenage sons have asthma. "I know the older one can get a wise mouth when he's tired and usually feels like he should be entertaining his classmates. I told his teacher, 'Set limits with him. He doesn't have to be a cartoon man.' She immediately asked, 'What about his illness?' I told her to separate the two. 'He can't help his wheezing, but he can help what he says.'"

HELP THE TEACHER AND SCHOOL OUT, IF POSSIBLE

Volunteer work can be an effective way to cultivate a relationship with your child's teacher, aside from discussing her medical condition. Teachers generally need the help and are grateful. You need the extra contact to get the teacher's spontaneous feedback that you might not get otherwise. Also, being in the classroom, even if it's only a few hours every other week, will give you a chance to observe your child and draw your own conclusions. One mother advises, "Be politically active in whatever situation you are in. Get to know everyone involved with your kid. Be positive and supportive with them, but don't be afraid to get angry, too."

7. Don't Write His Ticket to the Future

The Trouble with Adolescence

Adolescence has a bad reputation, even among parents trained in mental health. "We survived" is the most many professionals will publicly admit to. The reason for this reticence is that they, along with everyone else, can offer no solid advice on how to make this period serene.

It's a time when a youngster is generally compelled to make his mark showing how he is separate from, and maybe superior to, his parents, a process known as establishing one's identity. Suddenly, what the kid next door says may carry more import than our seasoned words.

Because of our adolescent's movement away from us, he may barely hear our advice about the major issues he is confronting: sexual development, drugs and alcohol, career. And if he chooses to ignore our wishes, we quickly realize that we can't force him to do what we want. Instead, we are reduced to appealing to his reason, which occasionally may seem a tenuous state at best.

At the same time, we must reconstruct a sense of ourselves apart from child rearing. Both mothers and fathers need to fill the emptying nest with new activity. And although both parents and teens may recognize that this separation is for the better, we still may be tugged, and sometimes wrenched, by our ambivalence. Seeing the present as truly passing is a formidable vista at any age.

Despite the immense impact of many medical conditions on their lives and outlooks, our adolescents will be more adolescents than anything else. Regardless, their day-to-day needs, perceptions, and identity will usually be locked into where they are in life.

The first time I met Jackie at cystic fibrosis camp she was dressed in a tie-back halter and shorts. She could have been any teenager, except that at that moment she was hunched over the edge of a canvas cot while a respiratory therapist, a bearded young man in hospital greens, pounded methodically across her back. "This is my first year as a counselor," she informed me, and Mary [the nurse] is gonna introduce me to my kids. She says I'm gonna have to be more responsible and I tell her to cut loose." Someone turned on a radio and thumping music invaded the infirmary. Her shoulders began to shimmy to the rhythm, her fine blond hair bouncing across her shoulders. "Last night was graduation. We didn't sleep and I haven't had a treatment since yesterday." The therapist lurched after her undulating back with his stethoscope. This is a girl who earlier wrote, "I wanted to be your average obnoxious teenager."[1] Although she was not obnoxious, she was of her age.

To the confusion of adults, many chronically ill youngsters

have expressed just this. Ellen Ruben recalls, "Adults expected me to live like a textbook diabetic, but I was more concerned with living like a teenager."[2] Ryan White, who had hemophilia and AIDS, wanted a driver's license and car.[3] In other words, they want to be what they are. We can't escape their adolescence.

Getting Ready

While some parents speak of this period in their child's life as a cataclysmic event, it is generally a gradual transition. And almost everything that goes on before will be preparatory. What your child brings to the adolescent issues will depend on what strengths he has previously nurtured. Even so, we still may be confused about our role in this process. Says a mother of a daughter with epilepsy, "When do I stop being the concerned parent and let her begin to be that independent person?" Here are some suggestions on how to prepare for the teenage years.

START LETTING GO

Cut the cord. Pull back. Back off. Despite the words, it isn't simple, however you say it, whether your child is healthy or ill. For years, our hovering presence has replenished our peace of mind. And those of us who have been intensely involved with caretaking have become accustomed to his necessarily prolonged dependence. Our child's physical safety may have been at risk. "He is so vulnerable," says Carla, whose son has had multiple orthopedic procedures because of his dwarfism. "I still don't know what he'll do if he has a flat tire in the desert." And we may also have been wary of his emotional fragility. Gary's daughter has social adjustment problems from a rare form of epilepsy. This father says, "For years, I would intercede to make things okay. If she had a fight with her friends I would talk to the parents. I didn't want them to cut her off."

As difficult as this is, these parents and others have managed to move away from their youngsters' side. What helped them was a firm belief in the need and inevitability of this transition. Yet the actual step—to get up one morning and *not* do—is not at all a philosophical experience. It's a gut wrencher for many. Be prepared.

One mother of a nineteen-year-old college student confesses in a discussion group, "Leaving him on the sidewalk while I drove off to work was the hardest thing." Her son has cerebral palsy and had to cross five lanes of Phoenix traffic in a wheelchair to catch the bus to school. His first day, the bus didn't have a ramp so he had to wait for a second bus. The ramp of the next bus jammed and he had to wait for a third. "He was an hour and a half late and scared. But he's finishing his first year now. He tells me, 'Mom, I've got it licked if I can just get on the bus. The driver is always there to help me off.'" Hopefully, we can muster the strength to allow this to happen. And it does take strength.

Start Early
Allow your youngster to do the early teen activities as much as possible. Slumber parties, football games, and junkets to the fast-food franchises all serve to prepare him for being more independent. These early excursions also give us a chance to reexamine the reality of our fears. Carla explains, "We let Curtis go to the movies even though I was worried about him being teased, and to rock concerts even though the crowds scared me."

Make Freedom Explicitly Contingent on Responsible Action

This contingency is not just for your child's safety, but also for your sanity. It is a reality that some youngsters will be more vulnerable away from home. We have the right to reassurance. We've earned it. One mother says about her son with brittle diabetes, "I always made it clear to him that I'd be upset if he were late and didn't call. I wasn't going to live like that. He knows to get in touch if he wants to use the car again."

Let your child prove to you that she can handle whatever she wants, in small steps. One mother is reluctant to let her eighteen-year-old daughter drive. The girl is functioning relatively well with autism. In hopes of dissuading her, the woman set up a series of roadblocks. "I told her we couldn't afford another car and she took money out of her savings. Then I told her she had to learn how to drive both a stick shift and an automatic and sure enough she did this and got her license, too. Now I'm going to say something about the insurance money, but I know she'll get it from somewhere. I think she's going to drive, but frankly I'd rather she take the bus."

Consider Extra "Freedoms"

Some parents, in an effort to help nurture their youngster's autonomy, will allow for certain privileges not awarded to their other children. For example, one father gave a car to his sixteen-year-old son with juvenile arthritis. "He needed the mobility. My other kids had to wait till college."

This may seem unfair, and yet still be our choice. And our other youngsters may protest. Although we need to explain our decision, we should not justify it; that would only feed their sense of being cheated. The father of the sixteen-year-old told his other kids: "I know this is not fair, but I can't help it. It's the best we can do."

Let Your Child Make as Many Decisions About His Life as Possible

Daily decision making is an ability that should be encouraged early on in childhood. Only over time can our youngster acquire the confidence to make choices, the knowledge to decide wisely, and the strength to live with mistakes. As a teenager, what shirts to buy, when to go to bed, what to say to teachers ought to be his call, not ours. If we try to make it ours, we may prevent him from seeing that he can do this on his own.

Hilda remembers doing too many things for her daughter with epilepsy. By the time she was a young adult, Polly refused to go shopping by herself for clothes. "She said that she was afraid of having a seizure in the store, even though she was in good control. I used to nag her about this because she's a medical secretary and needs a wardrobe. But one day I told her that I gave up. I couldn't *make* her do it. The next week Polly called me to say that she had bought her first dress on her own. It was a milestone."

Expect Your Child to Assume More Responsibility for His Medical Treatment

Tell him more. As mentioned in Chapter 4, an adolescent is capable of understanding his condition beyond what he can touch and feel. He can begin to make the abstract connections between what's wrong with his body, what he experiences (his symptoms), and his treatment. This knowledge may not necessarily direct his behavior because of emotional issues, which we'll deal with later in this chapter. However, the more realistic the input he gets, the more it may eventually override these issues.

We can start by filling in his information gaps or finding professionals who can. Our child's questions may have become too sophisticated for you to answer. How well does he understand his medication, its side effects, and what it is accomplishing? A teenage girl with arthritis was concerned about how her medicine might affect her fertility; her doctor answered these questions. What about the course of your child's illness? One young man with diabetes was so afraid of going blind that he had never looked into the actual statistics, which were far more hopeful than his fantasies. Does your child understand the reasons for all the preventive measures he is taking? One fourteen-year-old girl with cystic fibrosis did not grasp the need to maintain her weight and let it drop below what was healthy. Does your child know what, if any, heredity is associated with the illness?

Have him take over more of the daily medical treatment. Handing over the reins demands parental self-restraint. We may need to keep our fear to ourselves so that our youngster will have the chance to deal with his, on his own. Doris Lund describes how her son insisted on managing his leukemia.

> Eric kept the bottle on the kitchen table. No one had to remind him to take his pills. He was, as he had wanted to be, in charge. A day or so after he brought the methotrexate home from the pharmacy, I happened to notice the box, in which the drug had been packaged, in the kitchen wastebasket. Out of curiosity, I fished it out and began to read the little folder which was stuffed inside. It was hard to read, the tiniest type, but it described the many possible side effects of the drug. I read the list and my heart began to pound. This was a rough game we were in.[4]

What medical management can you hand over to your teenager? Although there are no absolute guidelines, there are obvious examples of when parents are overdoing their part. Who's weighing out the food for a special diet? One mother saw that her rationing her son's protein was inappropriate but, nonetheless, could not stop herself. "I feel guilty that I haven't controlled what he eats, but I don't have that control now." Who takes out the pills in your house? The mother described in Chapter 4 felt compelled to lay out her son's asthma medication every morning.

Have him handle at least some of the treatment questions that come up. At some point, you need to do more than tell him what to do, and this will depend on his emotional maturity and how complex his treatment is. A teenager needs to do the deciding. For example, the adolescent with diabetes should think through on his own how to adjust his insulin to accommodate his new after-school sport schedule. What he plans may be in conflict with your suggestions. Assuming this is not life-threatening, the experience should be instructive. Hilda's eighteen-year-old daughter refused to take her allergy shots. "She's had a miserable spring but at least she knows now why she needs the shots."

Many of us may be able to sense when our activity in this area is more to reassure ourselves than to meet a realistic need of our teenager. Without invitation, do we find ourselves irresistibly launched into assisting him? We can learn by comparing notes with other parents in support groups. What are our child's peers capable of doing now? Remember, his control of his medical management does not have to be all-or-none. What we do depends on his emotional maturity and the practical demands of treatment. For example, Jackie's parents always had to perform her CPT therapy, but she always took care of her enzyme medication.

Let his *relationship with the doctor come first.* We need to retire as the mediator between our youngster and his physician or nurse. For example, instead of asking him about his blood sugar and then calling the professional, we can help him schedule an appointment *for him* to talk about it. Even better is to have him eventually make these appointments himself.

USE THE ILLNESS TO TEACH RESISTANCE TO PEER PRESSURE

There's a potential upside to being different, especially if our child's condition is not life-threatening or severely debilitating. He may become more at ease with the idea of not having to be like everyone else. And whereas this experience will probably not erase his pull toward conformity during adolescence, it may help fortify him against going all the way, whatever that might entail.

Illness or disability might teach our child that it is *right* that he should take care of his own physical needs first before considering the reactions of others. As parents, we have the opportunity to expand and elaborate on this lesson. It will also be *right* to take care of his emotional needs and follow his own ideas, that is, to *choose* being different, under certain circumstances. Long before he becomes a teenager, he will encounter many instances in which we will hope our youngster will not acquiesce to the power of the group—for example, not ganging up on another who is vulnerable or not breaking school rules because his friends are.

Point to the strength your child has demonstrated in caring for himself to talk about these other values. We can say, It is not easy being different, but at a school party you are able to "pass" on cake that your friends are eating. This takes courage. It also takes courage not to call someone names just because your friends are doing it. We need to decide if something is wrong for us, regardless of what others are doing. This is true even if you don't have diabetes.

The ability to resist peer pressure is an advantage at any age. During the teenage years, this capability may allow our youngster to rebel wisely. It may mean the difference between his experimenting with drugs and becoming a habitual user. Wendy, a twenty-five-year-old woman with cystic fibrosis, recalls, "I tried smoking marijuana just to fit in. I don't think there's anything my parents could have done. I was determined to do this, but I was careful not to go overboard."

ENCOURAGE HIS TRUST IN OTHER ADULTS

Part of any teenager's emotional journey away from his parents will naturally involve his seeking relationships with other adults. Our youngster with special health needs will need these also, to supplement what we realistically can't give him. For example, we may not have the knowledge or the emotional stamina to answer his questions. As a teenager, Wendy was determined to find out more about the consequences of her cystic fibrosis. "I wanted to know everything—about getting married, about whether sex would be normal, and could I have children. I wanted the facts, not consolation. Only my doctor could tell me without feeling sorry for me."

A youngster may see his parents already so upset by his condition that he can't bring himself to share his grimmest fears and moods. When Christine's son, Lenny, was fourteen, he was hospitalized for cancer. She remembers, "He confided more in the staff than he did in us. Even today, he does not say much except about the checkups." Lenny confirms this: "My parents were already freaked out. I didn't want to make it harder."

Remember, there is no shame in this. We have not failed our child because he no longer comes to us. We are simply too invested to be his dispassionate confidant. The fact that our teenager is able to use other adults to comfort and guide him should be a sign that we have done something *right*.

We should give our implicit and/or explicit permission for these relationships. Otherwise, our teenager may feel guilty that he is abandoning us by not meeting *our* needs as parents. Our consent can be conveyed in many ways. Our own lives will be the most powerful lesson for our youngster. We can mention how our confiding in close friends and/or relatives has been helpful for us. This communicates that it's okay to need comfort and ask for it outside the immediate family.

Camps, meetings, and support groups (see Chapter 8) often have adult members with the illness. These individuals are generally present because they *want* to be role models. Angela, a nurse who is in remission from rheumatoid arthritis, joined an adolescent support group. She explained, "I never had this kind of group when I was sick. A lot of these kids are at the same age I was when I got it and I think I can help." This woman's optimistic attitude and level of functioning (she works full-time, dates, exercises) is sure to be an encouraging example for many.

We can let our teenager know how glad we are that he has found someone with whom he can talk. When some question comes up, we can always "pass" on the answer, if appropriate, and suggest he ask that person.

There may be circumstances when we need formally to seek out a professional adult relationship for our teenager (a psychiatrist, minister, social worker, psychologist, and so on). Is he putting his life at risk by abusing medical treatment, drugs, or by engaging in other potentially dangerous activities? Or has he had prolonged and disturbing moods (becoming withdrawn, pessimistic, or excessively irritable)? Detecting these criteria in our own youngster may not be simple. Parental love can blind us. Many mothers and fathers have been initially shocked to learn about their adolescent's drug addiction, only to realize later that this was the reason for weekends in bed, unaccounted time away from home, falling grades, and evasive answers to questions. The best we can do is keep our ears and minds open and not turn away from what disturbs us.

HELP YOUR TEENAGER FOSTER A SENSE OF USEFULNESS

In Chapter 3, we talked about how chores nurture a young child's sense of usefulness. He, too, can contribute. Our teenager will continue to have this need, whether he recognizes it or not (by this age, the work ethic can get a bad rap). He may be less conflicted about exercising some of his usefulness outside the home. Jobs can fuel our adolescent's budding independence, in addition to giving him a small dose of the Real World. Rosemary's thirteen-year-old son is in a body brace. He gets up at 4:00 A.M every morning to deliver newspapers on his bicycle. "He wanted to do this and feels so good about earning the money. Also, he stutters and this job requires that he talk to people to collect the payment."

Employment may help an adolescent make career choices not only about what is realistic, but also about what he likes. Curtis had always been advised to go into computers because of his dwarfism. His mother recalls, "He took a job at American Express, but hated sitting in front of a computer terminal six hours a day." Instead, he found he preferred working in a metal scrap yard one summer because "everyone talked, even though the job was miserable."

Adolescents who are unable to hold a job have found emotional rewards in volunteer work. Betsy is wheelchair-bound from arthritis and no longer physically able to continue her college studies. Her mother takes her two evenings a week to donate her clerical abilities at the local hospital. Betsy says, "Without this, I'd be in a shell. At least now I'm getting out and not just watching the soaps."

We can encourage our teenager by pointing out that the value of work is not only in money, but in the satisfaction you get and in what you give. There are wonderful examples in everyone's town of parks, museums, programs for the elderly, the ill, and so on, that have been made possible through people's unpaid efforts. Our youngster, too, can feel proud to help make that kind of contribution.

Teen Issues of Those with Special Health Needs

Superimposed on the expected adolescent concerns are those about how the illness will affect our youngster's future. Heidi, who travels the country talking to groups about Williams syndrome, is repeatedly asked by others with this genetic condition: Will I be able to live away from home? Lead a normal life? Get married? Have children? These questions will probably occur to most of our teenagers. They will be searching for the answers, sometimes without us. Here are some suggestions.

EXPECT *SOME* SADNESS

Teenagers with special health needs may be unhappy for any number of reasons. Although these reasons may not be new, their adolescent perspective is. Some will go through a renewed awareness of how their condition limits them. (Newfound freedoms ironically may serve to highlight old dependencies.) Wendy remembers fighting with her mother daily about her respiratory treatment. "She banged my back whether I wanted her to or not. I couldn't visit friends until she was done. Although I am grateful now for her attitude, I told her many times that I hated her."

Those with more severe limitations may be quite disheartened by their inescapable dependency. Sandra Gaskell, who is wheelchair-bound, writes,

> I miss just simply being able to walk out the door, shouting to my mum "Ta-ra, I'm just going to town, won't be long." . . . First I have to find someone that can drive me by car to my destination (knowing of course that he can lift me). Then I have to take a female with me to help me to the toilet. I make sure there is enough money in my purse for a taxi in case I can't get a lift back. The indignities of being handicapped get to be a bit much for me. . . . After being in a chair three years it would be a lie to say I wouldn't prefer to walk.[5]

A teenager may also feel stigmatized, in a new way, about how he is different from his peers. Wendy, who has cystic fibrosis, recalls trying to keep up with her friends. "I can accept my limitations now, but I couldn't then. It was maddening to be told I couldn't go on a hike, for example. I tried everything I could not to stick out like a sore thumb."

With the discovery of the opposite sex may come concerns about how the condition may detract from our child's appeal, even when the difference is invisible. In junior high, Angela developed the typical moon face from high doses of cortisone for rheumatoid arthritis. Some of her classmates called her "Fat Face." She did not date during high school, even after her remission had begun and this side effect disappeared. "I had a bad body image and became real shy. It wasn't until after I went to college in another state that I felt more positive about myself."

Teenagers with potentially fatal illnesses are generally aware of this aspect, regardless of what parents choose to reveal. Life no longer innocently stretches ahead for them. Lenny says that he always knows his cancer could come back, and that has changed the way he feels. A young woman with cystic fibrosis says, "It's depressing to know that at eighteen there are more years behind me than I can look forward to." And some of those well into their twenties and thirties continue searching for how to live under this shadow. Barry, married and a father of two, has hemophilia and wonders whether he will get AIDS from previous transfusions. "If that happens to me, I've promised myself—I'm not going to get down on myself. It's out of my control."

Many of us will be alarmed by our youngster's sadness and our helplessness. We can't take this feeling away and we can't fix the situation that creates it, either. Some parents have a relationship with their child that allows for the sharing of these emotions. Angela says, "My mother is my best friend. She always listened and that made the difference." April has lupus and so does her mother. "I always talk to her because she can really understand what I'm going through." Here the ingredient is listening without necessarily advising.

But our child may not want *us* to listen. In these instances, what's crucial is what he does with his feelings. Can he talk about them with others? Wendy recalls, "I had a strong relationship with my doctor instead of my mom and dad." Is he pointed in the direction of going on instead of giving up? Going on means that he doesn't withdraw, but continues to live life as best he can. For example, despite her sadness, wheelchair-bound Sandra Gaskell dares to go to town without her family. If our answers to these questions are no, if our teenager appears more hopeless than anything else, then we may want to talk with him about professional consultation.

EXPECT *SOME* REBELLION AGAINST TREATMENT

Frustrated parents will sometimes see adolescence as synonymous with rebellion, that indignant outcry against authority. What's so special (so good, so perfect) about *your* rules? they are asked. Some may worry whether their youngster is headed toward big and unfixable trouble with drugs, school failure, and so on.

In addition, parents of an adolescent with special health needs may fear his rebelling against treatment. And we have reason. In extreme cases, his rebellion can prove life-threatening in the future, even if not immediately. The revolt may occur in a youngster who has faithfully followed his medical regimen up till now. His resulting denial of illness can assume a variety of forms:

"I Can Conquer Anything"

Along with an adolescent's increased capacity for abstract thinking also comes his sense of invincibility. The latter can be quite unrealistic and override logic. Our youngster may intellectually grasp the physiology of his condition; but this information does not necessarily trickle down to his feelings and behavior. Instead, he may believe that although these facts are true, they don't apply to him. He's "from Missouri" and wants more than a little showing. Barry recalls going through a period of denial that lasted until he was thirty. "I never admitted I was a hemophiliac in high school or college. There wasn't anything I didn't try, except maybe boxing. I learned I couldn't play tackle or go snowshoeing."

"My Life Is Only Now"

A teenager is aware of the implications of the life cycle—that is, that we all grow older. Yet he may be living as if there were only the present. The future is but a tissue-thin abstraction.

Ellen Ruben recalls feeling, Why bother? as a teenager with diabetes: "Staying in control to avoid serious complications in ten or twenty years was an impossible concept for me to understand. Especially since, at the moment, I felt strong and healthy. . . . I began sneaking food. I stopped testing my urine and fooled around with my insulin, skipping injections occasionally just to prove that I really didn't need it."[6]

"I'll Be Okay If I Can Fool the Doctor (Nurse, Parent)"

A teenager may feel anger about his restrictions and hopeless about being able to follow them. In response, he resorts to subterfuge. In the childlike part of his mind, he confuses the motions of following the "rules" with the desired goal of maintaining health. Denise Bradley recalls her struggle to control her diabetes. She writes, "I knew I could not diet, so I just played along by letting her [my nurse] think I was trying."

For many, insight alone proves pathetically inadequate to stop self-destructive behavior. Bradley recalls, "And what about my diabetes? Indeed, my obsession with eating was affecting other areas of my life. For example, urine testing—at which I had once been faithful—was now something I despised. . . . I took fewer tests now because the color of the tape always turned from yellow to dark green, which indicated a high level of sugar in my urine. Angrily I would curse the results, knowing that the Tes-Tape® did not lie."[7]

The resulting guilt about noncompliance and deceiving others can sow the seeds for further transgressions. "For me, though," says Bradley, "learning how to drive had a more subtle and dangerous meaning. Acquiring wheels was freedom from the watchful eyes of others and made it easier to hide my lack of self-control. I did all the things comedians joke about. I would drive to fast-food places and order enough food for three adults, ordering it to go so it appeared that I was buying it for a group of people."[8]

"I'm Just Like the Other Kids"

A teenager's growing need for peer acceptance may cause him to suppress any evidence of illness or disability. In Chapter 4, Jackie described how she forced herself not to cough in school from her cystic fibrosis. Sheila's fourteen-year-old son is determined to Trick-or-Treat on Halloween with his friends, despite his food allergies. This mother says, "We can't stop him. We just live through it."

What are we to do? Although education is important, it may not stop a teenager's fight with treatment. The emotional issues may have far more sway with his teenage behavior. We feel the imprint of these issues in living with our adolescent. At times he may act as if he is invincible, live in the present, both resent and feel despair over restrictions, and want to be like his friends.

This is not markedly different from the way younger children feel, but they trust us more and we have more control over their actions. With our adolescent, we often struggle with where and how to draw the line, but we may not be effectively able to do either, at least directly. Instead, we must watch and hope that he will stumble onto the path of reason. This can be frustrating. One mother says, "I have to sit on my hands to keep up my child psychology and not start child abuse." Here are some suggestions:

Stress His Independence by Suggesting, not Telling

Out of fear, parents may begin dictating what their teenager should do. If he is already bucking the program, more stringent demands, no matter how much in his self-interest, may only escalate his noncompliance. In utter desperation, parents sometimes fall back on scare tactics—such as warning the youngster with diabetes that he'll lose his legs.

The difficulty with this strategy is that it stimulates the youngster to struggle with his parents about who will win instead of focusing him on what he needs to do for himself (see Chapter 4). We can help refocus him on the real issue by always emphasizing that it's his *choice*. Treat him as if he is the "master of his own fate"—which he is, anyway.

Sheila's fourteen-year-old son who has milk and wheat allergies is now experimenting with junk food when he goes out with his friends. "When he comes home screaming I can only isolate him and medicate him. I tell him, 'This is your decision to break the rules and these are the consequences.'"

Stress How Treatment Makes Him More Normal

As we have seen earlier, many people, not just children and teenagers, can view the treatment rather than the illness as the culprit. This is especially true for conditions with "silent" (relatively painless) symptoms. We need to remind our youngsters how their medications and other treatments allow them to be *more* like their friends. The clever parent can even exploit her teenager's anxieties about normality.

One mother advises her daughter with epilepsy, "Take your medicine or you will flop around on the floor and your date will bring you home." And don't forget vanity as a great motivator. If his medical treatment somehow results in improved appearance, *use this*. Sheila says, "My daughter figured out for herself to take her thyroid medication and follow her diet. If she goes off, she retains fluid. Her doctor even told her that if she breaks these rules she won't be pretty. Hopefully, someday she will find a better reason."

Use the Principle of Logical Consequences

Making a youngster responsible for the results of his noncompliant behavior provides a far more powerful feedback than mere words. For example, the teenager with epilepsy can't drive when he doesn't take his medication. One family demands that their sons with hemophilia pay the deductible for transfusions when the mishap was brought on by their own imprudence. Another adolescent gets asthma from drinking milk. His mother simply reminds him, "If you sneak, you will miss out on your track meet."

Cultivate Your Patience

Our teenager's denial is mostly out of our hands. The issues that give rise to noncompliance can be worked through only by him, not by us. They—and all youngsters, for that matter—need to come to terms with their dreams versus reality. What is heartening is that most adolescents with special health needs do. Sarah Halley told the group at the 1986 American Juvenile Arthritis Organization's annual meeting that for most of her teenage years she was convinced her disease would go away if she could stick it out to adulthood. She remembers going to great lengths to hide her condition, such as wearing long skirts to cover her knees. "I refused to accept any limitations until I was literally immobilized. I did a lot of damage because I did not take care of myself. Also, I was exhausted from years of suppressing any expression of pain or anger." At age twenty, this young woman looked squarely at X rays of her eroded knees. "It finally got to me seeing my destroyed joints—not the years of pain nor the pleading from my mother. I finally realized that I was no longer ju-

venile and I still had the disease. It was not going to go away."[9]
No one could have told her that until she was ready to see
it for herself.

Not all denial is undesirable—only what clearly undermines
a youngster's health. What some might judge as "not facing"
an illness can also be seen as an asset, a fierce determination
to "conquer" it. Todd instructed his Scout leader on how to
inject him with insulin in case of emergency. He was not
going to let his newly diagnosed diabetes interfere with his
twelve-mile hike down the Grand Canyon with his troop.
Jerry's son suffered through many life-threatening episodes
of asthma as a child. "After these harrowing experiences, he
seemed to have to prove that he had finally licked the problem. In high school, he became a soccer player and helped
win the state championship."

DON'T SKIMP ON SEX EDUCATION

This issue easily gets safely tucked away, out of our habitual
line of vision, with statements such as "She isn't interested"
or "That's not for him." In fact, many parents, not just those
of the chronically ill and disabled, may tend to minimize their
youngster's sexuality.

Our denial of their sexuality is a way to hold on to our
child. No matter how earnestly we may embrace the idea of
his autonomy, our heart may sometimes recoil from this prospect. Raising children both generates and consumes a lot of
our passions for many years, an experience that carves us into
who we are and molds meaning into our lives. Is it any wonder
that we are tempted to turn away from the physical expression
of our youngster's eventual departure?

We may be at a loss about *how* to talk about this topic.
Our personal beliefs may be at odds with sexual mores. For

example, if we review the facts about birth control, are we condoning premarital intercourse?

However, parents of adolescents with special health needs have additional worries that may serve to feed this denial. Our youngster's sexual activity may be potentially dangerous. Pregnancy may be ill advised for the woman with cystic fibrosis or a cardiac condition. We may have concerns about what an intimate relationship would do to her emotionally. Will she be rejected?

In addition, there is a cultural bias that stereotypes those with disabilities and chronic illness as asexual beings. Harilyn Rousso, a therapist with cerebral palsy, writes,

> I have found that people with cerebral palsy often show a surprising lack of curiosity and knowledge about the sexual aspects of their lives. Too often, societal attitudes, family attitudes, and self-doubts have conspired to prevent this curiosity from developing. Since cerebral palsy is a lifelong disability beginning in infancy, an important aspect of this conspiracy is the fact that the individual has been socialized from childhood onward into the disabled role, which is, in essence, an asexual role.[10]

Rousso's obervations hold for many medical conditions, especially when a young adult has an illness that deforms, an invisible disease that carries a negative connotation (such as epilepsy), or one that is simply not accepted by his parents.

A few years back, in a documentary called *The Skin Horse,* people with disabilities were interviewed about their sexual relationships. The following day, an acquaintance of mine spontaneously commented, "How disgusting." Of course, the point of the program was that many "normal" people have trouble dealing with this, as did this woman.

Why the prejudice? The cultural aversion may have as its basis an irrational and profound terror. "Normal" people generally do not wish to see themselves as having too much in common with those who have conditions they fear, such as a handicap. (Perhaps the underlying process is that if I see one thing similar, I will see other things, too, and I may somehow move magically closer to acquiring that condition. I must therefore see myself as different.) This avoidance is mostly unconscious, defies logic, and is therefore hard to put into words. The same irrationality is probably responsible for the public's denial of sexuality in the elderly. Which mortal doesn't fear growing old? This group, too, must not be considered "normal."

But a family's and a society's denial will not negate our youngster's sexuality. Biology has a long history of triumphing over attitudes. However, our denial may, in fact, do significant harm. At the very least, our silence communicates pessimism about our adolescent's sexual potential. Without a word from us, he will learn that dating, sex, marriage, and children will not be for him.

Our silence will also not protect our teenage daughter, in particular, if we are worried about her being spurned or manipulated. Ignorance only sets the stage for victimization. Added to whatever physical problems she has, she will also be handicapped in her understanding of social cues and consequences of behavior.

We need to approach our youngster's education about sex with the same deliberateness that we employ with his medical condition. And we should start early. When he is a young child, we can teach him about public and private behaviors, use anatomically correct words, point out examples in the animal world (the proverbial pregnant cat), and answer his questions. His curiosity will be not just about where babies come from, but also about secondary sex traits. We should be honest about the facts, but not overload with too many, as in talking about his illness or disability.

Remember, too, that this early learning has as much to do with sex roles as sex. Do we have different standards of behavior for our sons and daughters? Who sets the table? Who gets reprimanded for hitting? In the extreme, if we feel that women are weak and here to suffer while men are powerful and here to exploit, that's what we will communicate. The daughter with special health needs will have her helplessness reinforced, and the son will be discouraged from talking about his fears. Sexual prejudice can be expressed in many ways. Years before her son with diabetes reached puberty, a mother warned him of the dire consequences "if he ever got a girl in trouble." Obviously, the sexual revolution passed by this woman.

What we say to our teenager will, of course, depend on our beliefs, which may differ from the prevailing teenage lifestyle. There is no one answer on how to bridge this gap. However, we still need to say *something*. And we can take solace from the fact that this task is not any different from the general one that we parents have. Long before our child reaches adolescence, we try to instill personal values, which may differ from what our child observes in life and that other significant arena, television.

Whatever we decide, it should follow what we would say to our other, healthy adolescents. Most of them will have equal hormones, if not equal opportunity. And this message needs to be more than a list of dos and donts. As in everything else, our adolescent needs to develop his own reasoning more than he needs to follow our rules.

Michael Schulman and Eva Meckler, authors of the book *Bringing Up a Moral Child,* point out that teenagers need to be sensitized to the moral issues of sexual intimacy—that it is an experience of *sharing,* not of *taking.*[11] Does a person treat his partner considerately or is he exploitive? Both girls and boys can be guilty of exploiting, even though they may express these attitudes differently. And this is relevant whether the teenager is at the kissing stage or having intercourse. If we teach him to treat others well, he will expect that for himself and this should help protect him from being abused.

No matter how pessimistic we may *feel* about our adolescent's future relationships, often we are not in a position to *know.* Harilyn Rousso writes,

> One of the most amazing discoveries when I first started going out was that it was not so hard, that there was nothing out there that was beyond me. I could be accepted, appreciated, even desired, disability and all—not by all people, but by enough people. While this discovery was a great source of joy, it also made me sad and angry because I had missed out unnecessarily on a great deal of time and opportunities for socializing, for social and sexual expression. I say unnecessarily because it was only a *myth,* the myth of asexuality, or lack of sexual entitlement, which held me back.[12]

LISTEN TO YOUR CHILD ABOUT PEER RELATIONSHIPS AND DATING

Peers

In Chapter 5, we talked about how to help our children form friendships. However, we will have little opportunity to orchestrate these relationships in our child's teenage years, nor should we try. But we can be his sounding board, when he chooses us.

"Just listening" is not easy. Most parents have an emotional knee-jerk reaction when they hear about their youngster's pain. I struggle with this all the time. We grab for the old favorites, such as "If I were you . . ." and the frail encouragements, such as "Don't be silly, it will work out." Even at the time, these words may ring false; at least they serve to help *us* feel better.

Instead of giving advice, we can ask questions to help our teenager understand his point of view: Why do you feel that way? What do you think you can do about it? and so on. What's important here is the process of his thinking this through with us or another adult, not necessarily finding a *solution*. Sometimes there is none, just best bets for the issues he faces.

One question will be whom to tell, if anyone, about his condition. While his secrecy may be isolating, his sharing may make him feel intolerably vulnerable. Some teenagers choose to hide their illness and manage to find other plausible reasons for their absences, crutches, or chronic cough. Others do wish to present this part of themselves to their friends. When they do this will be on their schedule, not ours. Lenny moved to a new school after his cancer treatments and the nurse became his best friend. "These kids are just not like me," he told his mother. However, after his first year, he was pleased when he eventually did decide to reveal what had happened. "My friends have been encouraging."

Like other teenagers, those with chronic illnesses or disabilities may blossom as adults, especially once they begin to see more of the world through their own eyes. Their ideas of what they can comfortably share with others are bound to change. For example, Cheri Register has had chronic liver disease since she was nineteen. She advises, in *Living with Chronic Illness,* "If you want your friendships to be thorough, genuine, and firm, then you must trust your friends with the knowledge of this experience that is formative of your personality, your habits, your outlook on life. Rather than anticipating their reactions, which is tantamount to controlling them, you must trust your friends to decide for themselves how fully they want to be involved in your fate."[13] But, remember, this is a woman who has lived with her illness into mid-life and has gained the maturity to take this risk and also allow others this leeway.

Another question our teenager will have is how he wants others to treat him. One common fear is that he will be either patronized or pitied by his friends, both of which happen often enough. We can help our youngster put into words what attitudes and actions make him uncomfortable. Armed with this awareness, he will have the option of trying to shape these relationships. Wendy is only twenty-five, yet she has the courage to be specific with her close friends about how she wants them to handle her cystic fibrosis. "I tell them about my illness right off, but I don't dwell on it and I don't want them to, either. I let them know *not* to ask, 'Are you okay?' when I am coughing. I also ask them not to look at me when I am bringing up mucus. This embarrasses me. And, please, never tell me I look tired when I'm getting run down." Far from alienating, this kind of education can be a relief. Many are at a loss as to how to treat those who are ill or disabled. (See Chapter 8.)

Dating

Relationships with the opposite sex present another area in which our teenager will struggle with the questions of what to tell and how he wants to be treated. Some with special health needs may perceive themselves as "defective goods." One young woman with epilepsy keeps her illness a secret because, "No one of decent quality would be interested." Added to this self-deprecation is the reality that some dates will be rejecting. Dorothy remembers how her boyfriend promptly dropped her once he learned of her juvenile arthritis. "He was into tennis and downhill skiing and wanted someone who could be athletic with him." Sharon was ostracized by her high school classmates because of her impaired walk from childhood polio. "Any fellow who dated me in that small town was raked over the coals."

Despite the difficulties, teenagers with special health needs do date. While we can't directly help our youngster with the *how,* we can sometimes help them think through the related issues or find another adult who can. For example, he will need to develop his own sense of when he wants to tell a date about his condition. The relationship should be serious enough for this intimacy, yet not so far along that the other person feels duped.

Our youngster may go through a painful learning process about what kinds of reactions he both wants and can tolerate from those of the opposite sex. Wendy first went out with one boyfriend for six years. "He could not talk about my C.F. and would not visit me in the hospital. Many years later, he told me he could not handle it." She then had a relationship with a respiratory therapist. "He helped me accept my disease, but his attitude would change when I was admitted to the hospital. He wanted someone more perfect." Now she has a friend who is able to be with her when she is ill, too.

Also, as in many things, a positive attitude doesn't hurt. For example, some teenagers have cultivated a fuller sense of themselves beyond their illness or disability. Jackie says, "In Colorado, I never told anyone I had C.F. It was always allergies. I felt if boys knew about it, they would not want to date me. But here I have blond hair, blue eyes, and I also have C.F." These young people may come to view themselves as not so odd for being different. Angela tells her friends about her arthritis, even though she's been in remisssion for years. "I usually find everyone has something. I had one serious boyfriend I told and found out he was on anti-depressants."

SUPPORT HIM IN HIS MOVE AWAY FROM HOME

Most of our adolescents will want and be able to go out on their own. Much to the surprise of her parents, at eighteen, Wendy decided to leave Iowa for the Southwest. "I wanted to be in a climate where I could exercise all year and also be near doctors who were expert about C.F." She now maintains her own apartment and is the medical secretary for seven specialists. When our youngster moves out, we can help with some of the practical arrangements, such as locating a manageable place to live and local medical care, along with giving our blessings.

Even young adults who are too impaired to live by themselves may take advantage of various supervised living arrangements. In these instances, we need to start early to make this option happen in our community. Jill says about her four-year-old with Down's, "I want to avoid putting Laura in a situation where she is my companion in old age. I now am working for programs that, with some luck, will be in place when that time arrives. I would like to see her in a group home with a circle of friends her own age, and not too far from me." We need expert legal advice to arrange our finances advantageously for our young adult. There may be many more options already available than we would imagine. These options have been admirably covered in a book, *Disability and the Family: A Guide to Decisions for Adulthood.*[14]

HELP YOUR CHILD RESEARCH HIS VOCATIONAL AND/OR HIGHER EDUCATIONAL AND CAREER CHOICE

A vocation is more than a way to bring home the bread. It is our conduit to friends, our reservoir of our future dreams—

in short, a mighty big piece of our identity. Yet our young-ster's preparation and choice of occupation can easily be re-duced to an exercise of hit-or-miss.

Students today are able to graduate from high school without the ability to make a living. Getting a diploma has little to do with later being able to get a job. And most vocational programs are not geared toward those who have special needs due to an illness. In addition, those who give our adolescent career counseling will not necessarily be tuned in to what he can and can't do. There is no test that will tell us all we need to know, either. And, often, what at first glance appears to be a professional's well-thought-out advice may, in fact, be tainted with unrealistic prejudice. "Spare him," "Don't set him up for failure," and so on are the clichés repeated by school administrators, physicians, and counse-lors. (Remember Peter's doctor? After diagnosing his epi-lepsy, he recommended, "Get a job with no stress.")

As a result, our youngster may bounce between conflict-ing counsel that has little to do with what his future could hold. Yet these can be weighty words for the adolescent. Wendy recalls, "The doctors discouraged me from going to a four-year college because the demands would make me sick. My brothers wanted me to go and my parents left it up to me. My dream was to be a respiratory therapist. At least I work in a medical office."

We and our teenager will need to be aggressive and de-liberate in finding solutions that *may* work for him. *May* be-cause we probably won't be able to predict, and neither will his doctors, what will be his health, his medical insurance needs, and all the other variables that affect whether he makes it.

Vocational education begins when your child is a toddler, not in ninth grade when he first meets the counselor. Most younger children will fantasize about what they want to be when they grow up in terms of who they meet, see on television, or read about. Carla recalls, "Curtis did a lot of unreal thinking, typical of his age, such as, he wanted to be a fireman." These daydreams need not be bounded by our child's limitations. We don't need to correct him. What's important is that he does dream. Children's life experiences can then feed into their sense of reality.

Early on, we can foster this education by talking about how Mom and Dad work and what that means for us. In other words, we can stimulate the work ethic. What do we communicate about our occupation? Do we feel we are making a contribution? We don't have to pretend that our job is always great, only that we value it.

When we go out into the community, we can talk about the different jobs that make a supermarket, a bank, a library function. And our discussion can include the reasons people take different jobs—wages, creative satisfaction, social contact, and so on.

As he gets older, a child's limitations will most likely make themselves apparent without many words from us. Chuck is an eleven-year-old with hemophilia. His mother says, "He loves football and we take him to the games. Once he said, 'I wish I could do that.' I didn't answer and he added, 'Maybe I could be an umpire. Maybe I could do that without hurting myself.'" The process of blending hope with what's possible takes time and this youngster is just beginning.

But by late adolescence, your child needs a somewhat realistic assessment of what's possible. There will be no formula because our children will have different abilities and limitations, even with the same illness. For example, Jackie is now in college, majoring in journalism. "I will need to find a company that has good insurance and extended leaves of absence in which I can work at home. As I get older, I will have to be in the hospital more often."

We can also help our teenager better research his options with organizations such as the Higher Education and the Handicapped Resource Center,[15] the National Information Center for Children and Youth with Handicaps,[16] and the national organization related to his condition. Other invaluable sources are adults with the condition whom our youngster can meet through support groups and annual meetings.

As an adult, our youngster may have to deal with prejudice at a job or university. For example, a small business employer may have preconceived ideas about why he should not hire someone with a chronic illness, including concerns about days missed and high utilization of health services. And even young adults in educational settings may run across those who harbor destructive stereotypes. Peter was one of a few applicants who were recommended for a West Coast graduate school. "But four out of five of my references dropped me. I later learned that they believed my epilepsy would keep me from ever holding a job so why should I take up any space? This was twenty years ago, but still, they were college professors. Now I advise others with epilepsy to lie. Perhaps this is unethical, but I have been denied enough promotions to take this route."

Although there are laws against discrimination under specific circumstances, they may not protect our youngster in *his* circumstances. The booklet *Employment Issues for Hemophilia* explicitly advises, "It may *not* be in your best interest to disclose [the illness] for either or both of the following reasons: (1) if the employer is not held accountable to federal or state 'rights to employment' laws, and you believe that the employer will discriminate against you because of your hemophilia; (2) if you believe that your hemophilia in 'no way' interferes with your completing the required day-to-day duties."[17] In other words, less may be better if you're not protected by law and if your silence won't hurt you or someone else.

Even if our youngster is legally protected against discrimination, the problem of "Go prove it" remains. Fighting an injustice does not always give you your due, nor does it make up for the time and energy lost. There is no good answer. We hope our youngster will have sufficient emotional reserves to meet this situation with his best bets and without blaming himself. Like Peter, he will learn that while it is not fair, it is also not his fault.

MARRIAGE AND CHILDREN—IT HAPPENS

Having a family is undeniably difficult for those with special health needs. But they do it. They and their mates necessarily must hammer out questions of caretaking, sex roles, and the prospect of future disability and even death. *Living with Chronic Illness*[18] and *Borrowing Time*[19] are two books that give realistic accounts of how some adults have faced these dilemmas. These books are affirming, despite the fact that the pictures these authors paint are in no way rosy. People cope. And they do more than that, too.

Cheri Register, author of *Living with Chronic Illness,* adopted two girls and is now raising them as a single parent, even though she has a cystic liver. Pat Covelli, who wrote *Borrowing Time,* says: "We finally decided that we wanted to share our lives with children: our entire lives. We know, more than most, that sharing also includes the possibility of great pain in the future. . . . I will pass down, among other traits, diabetes. That fact will haunt me for the rest of my life. . . . A person cannot pass down anything more valuable than love, and I will love my child forever."[20]

Although these people and others we meet may seem courageous, many of them would strenuously object to being considered either extraheroic or special. They do what they have to do and what they can do. And that path is open to our youngster, too.

8. Stay in the Mainstream

The Problem of Isolation

WE AVOID PEOPLE

Living with chronic illness can dig a deep yet invisible gulf between us parents and the rest of the world. Especially during a medical crisis, our output of care, energy, and worry may deplete us for other people. Given our preoccupation, what can we possibly bring to the daily patter of normal existence? What could I say to a group of mothers who proudly mimicked their toddlers' first words while I quietly cringed at the diagnosis, autism, which was tossed out about my son?

Other people's concerns, in light of ours, may seem spawned from another emotional universe. Parents may feel what Suzanne Massie described: "Hemophilia had wiped out any interest or ability I might have had for superficial relationships. It sharpened my need for knowing the essentials and made me impatient for social trivialities."[1]

Oddly, as much as we may dismiss these trivialities, we may long for them, too. I wanted to fret like other mothers about how my son was getting along with his playmates. Instead, I wondered whether he would ever have any.

Even if we get the opportunity to voice our most private fears, do we want to? Certainly not all the time. One mother/social worker I had confided in responded with, "What an interesting *case* he is." And even when we choose to say nothing, there will be some who, regardless of how genuine their interest may be, take it as their God-given right to ask questions. As Annie said in a discussion group, "For the rest of my life, I'm expected to explain. I'm sick of it." Her five-year-old daughter was found to be hypothyroid, and then hearing and visually impaired. She's been explaining for years. Even the stares that one gets while walking down the street can be enough to send the most hardy, the most thick-skinned of us into hiding. We may decide to spare ourselves and withdraw from what feels like an intrusive and yet indifferent world.

PEOPLE AVOID US

This gulf is also dug by others who can't bear witness to our pain. Many parents have described a falling off of long-term friendships when their child became ill or disabled. "They couldn't handle it. They were in the child rearing years, like us, and it was apparently too much for them." Still, the hurt remains.

Kim and her mother, Laura, who used to live in my small town, told me one of the most disheartening examples of this. Kim, then eighteen, had been away at a Massachusetts college when she was found to have a brain tumor. She had emergency surgery and, over the following two months, was hospitalized three thousand miles away from home. When I spoke to Laura over the phone later, she described how family friends wrote to her daughter regularly while she was out of state. "However, once we got her back, they were terrified. We'd see these people in the shopping mall, they'd see Kim in a wheelchair, and we'd watch them scurry off in the opposite direction. Yet we're the same, except that we've had to deal with our own vulnerability." One day I was browsing through our one-lane shopping mall when I saw a woman pushing a toothpick-thin teenage girl in a wheelchair. I knew instantly who they must be and went over to identify myself. How appreciative this mother was that I actually walked over and acknowledged them. How great must have been their disappointment that this action was even worthy of mention, no less appreciation.

Kim died within the next six months. When I last talked to Laura, two years later, she said, "I'm still angry. We lived in that town for seventeen years. I had four close women friends. Our kids grew up together. In the two and a half years that Kim was sick, two of them came to visit only at Christmas and two never came. Stuff like that is hard to pass off."

We Can't Afford Isolation

NOT FOR US

As irrelevant as it may feel, we need that *superficial* layer to our lives—that casual contact with others that concerns itself with recipes and the weather. We desperately need to exist in some world, other than our own desperation. In addition to our child's condition, life seems to be packaged with enough other unanswerable questions that will continue to nag at our serenity. Often, we can only research the givens, make our decision, and then go about distracting ourselves.

The *superficial* reprieves us, and, for those who know how to exploit it, restores sanity. Marion, a woman I knew who was dying from Parkinson's, taught me that long before I had children. For five years, I witnessed her steady deterioration. As her voice faded to inaudibility and her boardlike body went from wheelchair to bed, I stumbled about for those "right" words. Finding none, I talked about the minor details of my existence that either amused or frustrated me. One day, I blurted out that I wished I could say *something*—referring to the relentless rampage of her illness. In between her heaving gags, she let me know that there was nothing anyone could say, but that she enjoyed my visits. I realized, later, that she didn't seek to be more immersed in the "real" issues of her life; rather, she wanted to escape them, if only vicariously through those minor details of a friend's life.

There are many ways we can cultivate this surface existence that blends into the normality around us. We can take pleasure in the narrowly defined contacts we have with people, the ones that don't know too much about our troubles— a storekeeper, a waitress, a mailman. Those we see regularly may welcome some conversation outside the strict domain of their function. And this adds another tiny, but at least removed, dimension to our lives and that of our children. The man who photocopies my manuscripts and the woman who owns the health-food store where we shop are some of the "strangers" I have come to enjoy.

Hobbies are great getaways, too. In the midst of unending uncertainty about their daughter, Gary and his wife each decided to pursue an interest. "My wife sings in a church group and she guards that time jealously. Once a week I carve ducks with a colleague." They also make sure to take time for each other. "We learned the hard way—the problem is going to be there, anyway. If putting in an effort would have made the difference, we would have stopped it a long time ago." And we can also recharge ourselves by going out with the "girls" or "boys." Coffee klatches got a bad name in the 1970s—a sure sign of spiritual degeneration. Yet I have found that when I am feeling up-a-tree, sitting around a friend's kitchen table can be the best medicine.

But there is a more serious side to our reaching out. Our child's illness can curl us inward so that only our frightening unknowns loom before us. We can come to feel singled out, as if that elusive state—the life without trauma—was meant for someone else. For me, there is nothing shameful about misery loving company, or at least seeking it. We need to see our battles as in the company of others. We are not alone. (Understand that this is an offensive message when it comes from someone else, in the form of, You're not the only one with problems.) Yet this view can bestow a small comfort when it germinates within our being. How many of us are thrust into lifelong struggles of one sort or another? Just looking at the estimated statistics in the general population for alcoholism (10 percent), divorce (almost 50 percent of marriages), and child molestation (25 percent for girls and 10 percent for boys) and personally knowing those who have weathered these assaults is a sobering slap in the face. Life without trauma is mostly a fantasy.

Also, although this is not meant as a Pollyanna promotion, some parents achieve a larger view: They accept how things have worked out and cull some small good, despite the illness, from the experience. (This message—At least you have something to be grateful about—is also offensive coming from someone else.) For many diseases, there is no decipherable brighter side. Yet some mothers and fathers do discover a positive thread to the fabric of their struggles.

In Chapter 2, we learned how Kathy McGlynn turned herself into an epilepsy expert. For eight years, she combed libraries and consulted with out-of-town physicians to find a reason for her son's behavior problems. "In a way, I am glad it was so bad because I knew something had to be wrong. What do parents do when there's just a little problem and you think it's your fault or your kid's?" I understand her feelings. I say the same thing whenever anyone consoles me about our food allergies.

Other parents have expressed the "bittersweet benefits"—that even though they would never wish this on their child, they and their youngsters are fuller human beings because of it. Carla says of her son who is a dwarf, "He copes with the little problems. My daughters get upset if they have a pimple, but he already knows that life isn't what it's cracked up to be." Mary Lou recalls, "We lost everything financially with the hospitalizations, but we kept our family and friends. We found a value that we believed in and tested it. Money isn't the end-all." She adds about her son with cerebral palsy, "I learned patience as I watched John try small tasks and not give up." Linda remembers when her daughter saw a wheelchair-bound woman trying to leave the restaurant. "No one went to help her and right away, Renée said, 'Daddy, go over and open that door.' Another woman who was watching came over and said how sensitive Renée is to other people. And she is."

Our child's illness or disability expels us from conventional expectations about life. We may feel so much more finely for others who have taken this journey, for whatever reason, if we reach out to them.

NOT FOR OUR FAMILY

Our own family cannot afford to be isolated either. We must teach our children how to live in the world without apology. And we can teach only by showing. Mary S. Akley, the mother of a disabled child, writes, "Autism is a very traumatic but effective cure for caring too much about what other people think about you. It is perhaps the ultimate liberator."[2]

Once we shed our apologies, we can advocate—and I'm not talking here about political groups. Supporting our youngster in her world begins with us, the individual parent. We need the belief in our value, the attitude that we have a right to mediate for her.

We can use the circumstances of our daily lives to show our youngster how to assert herself without fear. Advocacy happens when we are faced with a storekeeper who ignores our child's requests because she is in a wheelchair, a swimming coach who refuses to allow her on the team because she has epilepsy, or even a mother who is panicked about her visiting her house.

How we talk about these encounters will have profound impact on our youngster—and may stimulate either his isolation or his socialization. Show him the advocacy of persuasion, that fighting is not always necessary, that there are people out there who are sympathetic and sometimes even more than that. Eleanor's daughter, Marcy, has food allergies. They used to live in a close-knit midwestern neighborhood. At 3:00 P.M every summer, the ice-cream man's bell rang and the kids would swarm around his truck. "My daughter couldn't have this and felt left out. I started to talk with the other parents and found out they didn't want their kids having ice cream every day, either. We all agreed on once a week— Marcy could tolerate that—and we had the driver change his schedule."

Our youngster *needs* to feel that the world is not entirely hostile to her. And, frankly, that's no snow job; it isn't. Make sure to talk about times people have willingly accommodated, to offset her negative experiences.

A couple of years ago, McDonald's had been flooding the

television networks with ads for their "Happy Meals," including the prizes. We couldn't eat this "Happy Meal," although we spent more money buying their salads and juices. Of course, this upset my kids, who saw their friends getting the Ghostbusters, Berenstain Bears, and other gewgaws. Our local franchise was supportive, but could not sell me the prizes separately because that "went against the rules." I eventually called the regional manager, in front of my children, to appeal this decision. I left two messages with his secretary, mentioning the company's commitment to children with chronic illness. Two days later, we heard this man's voice on our answering machine: He would make some arrangement. My kids just about danced a jig.

McDonald's made a card for my children so that they could get the prize with their salads. Since then, we have opted for the "Happy Meal" minus the bun and cookies so that Danny and Amy now have an almost total fast-food experience. However, I hope what they take from this is that people may be willing to accommodate to their needs.

Through our example, our youngster may learn to reach out to others, an asset that could serve her well into middle age. Nancy Woodrow writes in the "Reader's Exchange" of the *AJAO Newsletter:*

> I am a forty-one-year-old "kid" with polyarticular JRA [juvenile rheumatoid arthritis]. . . . I recently cleaned out my garage and spare bedroom to make room for a companion who will help me with the extra household chores I must do when I am not busy at my job as an accountant. I found many mementos from my twenties and thirties, which were good years for me. . . . My true loves are traveling and camping. In my twenties, I was able to do everything from ascending the pyramids in Mexico and tending sheep in

Australia to climbing a mountain (with the help of many kind people).

Despite all this I still had JRA and at thirty had to retire from my job as elementary school teacher. I fought back. I returned to graduate school to get a master's degree in accounting and changed careers. I continued to fight on a physical level as well. After several joint operations, I learned to solo sail in a catamaran and I traveled three times to Alaska via plane, dog sled, and raft.[3]

This woman goes on to describe the many different things she has done with disabled adolescents through the activity program and Girl Scout troop she helped form. She advises parents, "If you allow them to develop independence, [your children] will live happy, fulfilling lives."

And she is still reaching out to others. She ends her letter: "After two hip replacements last year and an acute flare-up in my heels and hands, I realize that I am not going to be as active as I was, and I will probably find it more of a challenge just to continue working. This part of my life I face with a little trepidation, and I would love to have the advice, counsel, and even friendship of those of you who have walked this path before me."[4]

How to Fight Isolation

FRIENDS AND RELATIVES

Friends

The addictive greeting, "How are you?" or "How is your child?" can be painfully ambiguous for parents whose children have special health needs. How do we, who may be writhing from either the knowns or unknowns, respond to this conditioned response of meeting someone? As Suzanne Massie so succinctly put it, "I got sick of being asked that all-purpose meaningless formula . . . that sets up barriers of false interest between us. There is only one answer: I am fine. Any other answer is unacceptable. Imagine the startled surprise if I had answered, 'I am in despair.' "[5]

Most of the time, this "How are you?" is, of course, a social form. But in the context of a child's illness or disability, this harmless greeting can become intrusive, especially when people try to make it into an expression of authentic concern they don't feel.

Cheri Register describes the social consequences of her cystic liver disease in *Living with Chronic Illness*.[6] She points out a variety of commonly inflicted clichés that families of youngsters with special health needs are also bound to run across. Substitute a child's name and you may have heard this sentence before. Sometimes people imbue the question with extra meaning, as in "How aaaare you?" or "How are you feeling?" Even more annoying are the other variations: "You're looking good so you must be feeling better" or "You should take care of yourself."

Although these social forms may be offensive, this is not most people's intention. Most people will want to acknowledge the problem in some way. But what should they ask to be helpful or show concern without being intrusive? Many stumble, as I did with Marion, for the "right" words. There is no obvious etiquette, as Register observes in her book.

But lack of social form is not the only difficulty in these situations. An illness or disability is emotionally charged for everyone, not just us and our child. People's fear of our misfortune also makes it hard for them to be genuinely compassionate. Sometimes, they may feel irrationally guilty about another's bad luck. (There, but for the grace of God, go I. But why should I?) Or, maybe they feel more vulnerable. (This could happen to my child, too.) These usually unconscious emotions can be sufficiently upsetting so that otherwise reasonable people can come out with thoughtless comments, comments that through their pity, lecturing tone, and so on, assert how they are different and therefore immune to the problem. And although they may feel that their intentions are good, good intentions are highly overrated, especially when people are basically ministering to their own fears and not to our situation.

Harold Kushner, in *When Bad Things Happen to Good People*, gives a moving account of the origin of "Job Comforters"—an expression that has come to describe people who intend to help, but are mostly directed by their own needs, not those of the victim. They, therefore, make matters worse: "Under the impact of his multiple tragedies, Job was trying desperately to hold on to his self-respect, his sense of himself as a good person. The last thing in the world he needed was to be told that he was doing something wrong. Whether the criticisms were about the way he was grieving or about what he had done to deserve such a fate, their effect was that of rubbing salt in an open wound."[7]

What follows, then, is how some people may offend us. And while many have been kind to me and to other parents, a callous remark, like some errant thorn, can embed itself in the memory. Perhaps this list of various ways in which people can offend will help some of us identify these experiences and put them into perspective.

Pity. Whatever the words or actions, the message is that there is something terribly wrong and you are supposed to feel helpless. Marie gave birth to a Down's child with a heart defect and received three sympathy cards. Her husband was told by a friend, "I would have gone to the hospital but I didn't want to gawk."

Those who pity may escalate their attempts to elicit our helplessness when our behavior does not immediately and obediently conform to this expectation. For example, after you tell someone you are handling it, their "Still, it *must* be terrible" is truly terrible.

Callous remarks. Most of us have our monster stories, which we take out and parade when we are feeling particularly disgusted with The World. After a "Phil Donahue Show" about surgery for epilepsy, Alice's relatives called to find out why her son didn't have some of his brain removed. Alice says to a parent group, "Why not take out his whole brain, if they are so eager!" In another group, Pam describes how a so-called friend referred to her own child's misbehavior by saying, "You just wait. We're going to start calling you David [Pam's son]." David has developmental delays, including some behavior problems, secondary to a calcium metabolism defect. Pam says, "And she had to tell me this, too."

Those who make these callous remarks may be callous enough to make them in front of our kids. This can really hurt. One play-group mother, who was evidently indulging in a moment of superiority, wagged her head knowingly at me and said in front of my son, "And it's really *something* to raise a child like Danny." Fortunately, the comment was ambiguous enough that I was not concerned for his feelings. But that's not always the case. With grosser comments, we are faced with either shrugging it off and hoping our child does not get the drift or drawing attention to it by directly responding. Of course, what we decide to do will depend on many variables: what we feel our child understands, our personality, what we feel the other person could understand if we explained, our relationship with her or him, and so on.

However, with those with whom we have ongoing contact, we need to give them some inhibiting message (dealt with later in this chapter).

Pseudo-empathic remarks. There are few comments more abrasive than when someone tells you he *knows* how you feel, when he knows nothing. Even for those who have experienced some similar misfortune, it is still presumptuous to believe that one totally grasps another's inner life. Worse than that is when he says he knows how you feel and it's not so bad after all . . . because. Like many other remarks, this one discounts feelings, *our* feelings, because the other person cannot tolerate them. They are too upsetting for him.

Unrealistic comfort. Offering comfort is as basic to humanity as assault. Yet comfort can turn into a kind of an assault when the person offering it is ministering to his own fears, not ours. How many parents have been foolishly reassured that their child's diabetes, or whatever, will go away. One mother, whose four-year-old son is autistic, announced in a group, "I'm going to vomit over the next person who tells me that Einstein didn't talk till he was five." This assurance attacks our freedom to talk about reality and what may be troubling us, and is in no way a comfort.

On the other hand, what a relief when friends and relatives restrain themselves. Jill's daughter was being tested for AIDS because she received a blood transfusion at birth. "I was so grateful that none of them said it would be okay."

Criticism. Sometimes this criticism comes camouflaged as unsolicited advice: "Have you tried so-and-so?" They only want to be *helpful,* so how can we get mad? Says Dorothy, who has had juvenile arthritis since her late teens, "It's annoying that, almost weekly, friends will tell me, 'I have the greatest idea on how to get rid of it'—as if I haven't looked into all the possibilities myself."

Either directly or more subtly, people can make comments to suggest how the situation is our fault or we are not performing the best that we could or should. When Martha's four-year-old daughter with leukemia was not responding to chemotherapy, members of her church told her she wasn't praying hard enough. There was my park friend, mentioned in the Prologue, who assured me that she would handle it differently if her daugher had my child's problem. On a pseudo-scientific level, how many so-called informed folks reduce the cancer, arthritis, or whatever of others to "He must have too much stress in his life."

The implicit assertion here is that they know, they have the secret, of how to avoid our misfortune. That's why their message is offensive. Their "helpfulness" serves to reassure themselves that this thing won't happen to them.

Idealization. People also put distance between themselves and misfortune by employing an opposite strategy, which is to idealize the victim. All of us have trouble acknowledging the ruthless randomness of life, accepting that tragedy is not reserved just for the heroic. Tragedy can happen to anyone.

How many parents have been told, "God must have chosen you because you're so good," or, "I don't know how you do it, I never could." Of course, they could "do it." What choice do any of us have, really? Run away? Kill ourselves? If we don't seize these options, then we dig in and deal with it as best we can. (A few friends have even told me they could never do what I do—the special diet for my children—although my lot is a relatively easy one. Yet if food were to make the difference between their child's emotional withdrawal and his normal social adjustment, I'm sure they would embrace the remedy, as I have).

Although these words are meant as compliments, they unfortunately elevate the youngster with special health needs and his family to an unreachable pedestal, unreachable by them or by anyone else. This idealization makes it difficult for us to express anything negative, such as wanting to throw in the towel, every now and then. This sentiment would surely disappoint our audience, "The World," who have come to explain our burden by virtue of our special strength. Since they are not that strong, the less-than-logical conclusion is that it can't happen to them.

Relatives

Our parents, sisters, and brothers can absorb irrational guilt from our misfortune. Our blood ties infuse it with new meaning and make it personal for them, too. Some relatives will openly blame themselves, especially if the condition is genetic or has some hereditary component. At first, Janice's mother had not been able to handle the fact that her grandson had hemophilia. Janice says, "She felt real bad for not having told me that it runs in our family and then it happened."

And this guilt would not be so noxious if it just sat there. But when our relatives, unable to tolerate it, transform it into something else—such as finding the condition to be someone else's fault—they eliminate themselves as a potential source of comfort. The thinking here is: If they find themselves not guilty, then they are not obliged to get involved. Becky told her mother when she found out her three sons' retardation was due to fragile X. "Right away, she said, 'I always knew your father was strange.' But what hurt was my mother's attitude, not where this might have come from. She was raised in the deep South, where if you had a genetic disease you were some kind of mutant."

Guilt can also be transformed into denial, which isolates us from our relatives. Tammy's mother cannot deal with her granddaughter's lupus and repeatedly protests, "But April looks so well," no matter what condition the girl is in. Alice says, "To this day, my mother-in-law will not use the terms *epilepsy* or *seizure disorder*. When she does talk about Loren, it's always, 'Does he still have one of those things?' " In fact, the first reaction of this grandmother to the diagnosis had been "He did not get it from our side of the family."

In addition to guilt, our relatives, particularly our parents, may go through the same gamut of emotions and behavior that we do—the anger, overindulgence, and everything else described in Chapters 1 through 3.

Take the Initiative: Educate Your Friends and Relatives

Susan Duffy says, "We've always been open about Keough. You do your best to get them into the fold. If they don't get with the program, then the hell with them."

But what is our program? What is it we want to communicate to friends and family about how we want them to treat us and our child? The answer will be different for all of us, and we will probably find out what we want mostly through our contact with others. For example, I learned that I don't want people insisting in front of Danny and Amy how burdensome, tasteless, or limiting our diet is. I don't want them to carry on with, "You mean you can't have this, too?" In fact, I don't wany *any* remarks that will either undercut my kids' compliance with what they have to do anyway or give them new reasons to feel sorry for themselves.

Here are some suggestions on how to educate your friends and relatives:

Tell them what they should not say. Whether we mention our child's condition or not, some will want to say something.

But their words may be damaging, especially in front of our youngster; this is especially so when we have regular contact with them—relatives, baby-sitter, play-group mother. We don't have to merely listen.

Let people know what's hurtful, in private, with tact. The formula I generally use, which works well for unsolicited advice and pity, is: "I know you want to be helpful or you are really concerned, but . . ." and then explain how their comments are not helpful. There may be some who don't grasp your message, or others who turn defensive ("That's not how I meant it"), but only the most obtuse won't drop it after you bring it to their attention. And if they can't knock it off, you can decide, as Susan did, the hell with them.

We can also handle some comments in front of our children by directly correcting their misconceptions. For example, when a friend remarks about how few places we must be able to eat with our allergies, I list all our usual haunts, adding a benign, "It works out fine."

We can take a comment that implies pity and turn it into a compliment for our child. "You mean he has to go to Dr. So-and-So every week for shots?" "Yes," you may answer, "our child is very brave [responsible, etc.]."

When all else fails, don't forget the non sequitur. Who says we have to make sense? And just because someone makes a comment, we are not obligated to respond to it. Instead, we can blatantly change the topic. Our food is awful? Nice weather (great fishing, shopping etc.) these days.

Tell them what they should not ask. There may be any number of other questions we would prefer not to answer: How much does his treatment cost? Do you feel guilty because he got the illness from you? How long do you think he'll live? Like Wendy, who has cystic fibrosis (Chapter 7), we can be explicit with people about what *not* to ask.

An alternative is to develop a repertoire of euphemisms that will satisfy most, yet spare us the pain of going into detail. One mother of a dying child describes her son as going through "an unstable period" each time he's admitted to the hospital.

Tell them how they can help. Most want to help, but the "how" in many situations may not be obvious. Can they take care of your other children while you take your ill one to the doctor? Do interference with a meddling relative because you're about to "lose it"? Bake a casserole? Assigning tasks to friends and relatives who wish to pitch in is in no way a burden. It relieves them of the search for a way to be useful.

Talk with them about topics other than the illness. If we are fortunate, we will seek comfort with friends. We drop our canned statements prepared for the rest of the world and reveal some of the turmoil within us and our family. But even with our most hardy confidants, we will also need to dilute this process with the discourse of daily living. This can be accomplished by asking questions about *their* lives. In fact, like Marion, we, too, can delight in this distraction.

Injecting this normality will keep us from assuming a too-dependent role. We do not want to deplete these relationships. After a while, many may come to resent the vicarious burdens—and also feel guilty about feeling this way. And most friends will not announce when they are "burning out" on our problems. But if they are impatient or avoiding us, that may be what's happening and it's time to lighten up.

For our guilty *relatives, especially our parents: normalize.* Many of our relatives can be supportive in our struggles; others cannot. Some of those who are unable to give emotionally may be feeling guilty. This can poison their relationship with us and our youngster. Guilty grandparents, in particular, may be defensive or denying, which usually leads to their withdrawal.

In these instances, we may want to encourage their involvement by trying to get them off this irrational hook. Many times, we can't accomplish this directly. Telling relatives not to blame themselves is not enough. We can indirectly help them by keeping up the normal and expected grandparent (aunt, uncle, etc.) functions. Send those photos and artwork through the mail so that they can feel related. Describe the usual kid stuff, along with what's happening with your child's illness.

Guilty grandparents may also overindulge our youngster, which leads to conflict. Audrey's mother asks about her four-year-old wheelchair-bound son with cerebral palsy: "How's the poor baby?" Audrey replies, "He's not a baby. He doesn't wear diapers." When Carmen's son with food allergies visits her parents, they give him a stash of all the forbidden foods. In these situations, we need to be straightforward about what harm they are doing (use the "I know you only mean well, but . . ." formula). In this way, we can redirect their need to indulge our child into something more constructive.

STRANGERS

All the difficulties described for friends and relatives go even more so for strangers. These folks have no vested interest in getting along with us and therefore feel less accountable for their words and behavior. Whatever our response, it should, ideally, allow us to feel better (usually, less helpless) and also role-model for our child.

Stares
This silent act of aggression can easily lay shame on the youngster with a visible illness. Some parents choose to tackle these encounters head on, rather than shrugging them off.

Audrey was in a department store when her son had to go to the bathroom. "Two ladies stared at us when we passed. Maybe I was having a bad day, I don't know, but the more I thought about it, the more I felt that they needed to be taught a lesson. I went back to them and said, 'I noticed you were staring. Don't you know that is rude?' They both fumbled and one finally came out with, 'We were admiring how cute your child is.' " Even if this mother was having a bad day, she did a good thing. She showed her son that he doesn't have to put up with this public form of humiliation.

Some youngsters, by the time they reach adolescence, will develop their own strategies. Recently, Carla's family visited Disneyland. There were lots of looks, because of Curtis's dwarfism. "Actually, he handled it. My daughters cried." Their solution? The four of them stared back. And Curtis offered to show some passersby his behind, too.

Comments and Questions

For reasons unknown, another's problem sometimes grants strangers carte blanche for comment. Those with obesity only need walk down the street to be barraged with advice and judgment. Some youngsters with special health needs and their families have similar experiences. Annie, the mother of a hypothyroid girl with hearing and visual impairment, says at a support group, "I'm so sick of people asking how old my daughter is and whether she is retarded. She wasn't talking by twenty-two months and I was lying about her age in the grocery store. Some days, I want to shout, 'You know what: I don't want to tell you.' "

And we don't have to. We can use some of the strategies described for friends, or we can ignore them, or we can ask them what they think and then agree with whatever they say. And if we don't feel obliged to maintain the pretense of a friendly conversation, we can always ask them what makes our life their business.

HAVING OTHER CHILDREN

Parents of youngsters with special health needs have sometimes found that having other children normalizes their lives, despite their already significant stresses. Some want their youngster to have a brother or sister to relate to and for them to have more of a family focus. Others want to temper their concerns. "I was dwelling too much on the What-ifs. Then I became too busy for that," says Carla. And still others want to reassure themselves that they can have a healthy baby.

Whatever the motivations, many of the parents I spoke to have been pleased. One frequent comment, which I found to be true in my family, is that a healthy youngster helps you see the health in the one who is ill. Carla had two girls after Curtis. "I remember seeing my daughter doing something, and I thought to myself, 'Why not Curtis?'"

But this is in no way a recommendation, only a report. People make this decision from the gut, not from the head. However, if you are thinking about having other children, you are not crazy, and you are in good company.

SUPPORT GROUPS, NETWORKS, AND NATIONAL MEETINGS

Support Groups

These groups have different strengths, depending on their form. One kind is typically started and run by a doctor or nurse associated with the local hospital. Often, these are the local chapters of national organizations, such as the National Hemophilia Foundation. These organizations offer ongoing education to parents about new treatments, insurance, and so on. The professional can provide a kind of personal hot line for questions and insider interpretations of procedures at one's medical center. A potential disadvantage is that this person's presence may inhibit parents' discussions about parent-professional conflict and advocacy.

Another kind of group is formed and run only by parents. These tend to be less structured and allow for more discussion about feelings. However, they lack the professional perspective, which may be a significant lack, depending on the issue. Members will often invite different professional speakers to keep them up-to-date on more technical issues related to the condition.

Not all groups are disease-specific, especially in smaller communities where there are not enough numbers. The four mothers who wrote *Acceptance Is Only the First Battle* formed a support group in Missoula, Montana. Two of the women have a child with Down's syndrome, one has a child with cerebral palsy, and one has a child with a rare form of epilepsy. Did they have enough in common? They write,

> We have discussed everything under the sun, it seems—from how to get a disinterested youngster to want to crawl (a dirty ashtray set two or three feet beyond reach worked like a charm for my daughter), to handling a nonhandicapped sibling's craving for attention, to methods of dealing with slow or recalcitrant insurance companies, to where one can find a liquor store in Salt Lake City if one's child is there for surgery. No subject has been too large or too trivial for attention. We have found in most instances that if something is bothering one of us, it is also bothering the rest of us or has in the past. Sometimes we've even found solutions.[8]

Regardless of the form of the support group, families get lots of different kinds of help.

Talk about how you feel. Many times, our spouse may be slogging through the same emotional swamp as we are and be unable to comfort us. And many friends may be unable to listen to our uncensored thoughts: Have we ever hated our kid for the pain he's caused us? Our husband for escaping the chaos at home for the seeming sanity of work? Our wife for giving all she's got to this illness or disability? Our neighbor for having a normal child and being happy?

One can't readily share this with just anyone. We need to talk to others who have been there, generally in a support group or a parent network. Comments such as "I could let it out" or "I could cut through the amenities and deal with the basics" describe this process. We need the release that comes with disclosure.

Sometimes we fear, as one mother announced in a hemophilia group, "At the rate he is using the clotting factor we will be out of insurance by the time he's twelve." Or we will confirm another's experience, as one father said, "That happens to us all the time. I'm sick of people asking if I or my wife gave my son the diabetes." Or we feel safe enough to expose our shame. One mother despaired about her daughter with hyperactivity, "I always thought we'd have a close relationship. But, if I'm really honest, I have to say I can't stand being around her."

Learn more about the illness. All of the groups I visited, regardless of form, had a strong educational focus. And this is far from an academic endeavor. The issues were pivotal for people's lives and future planning. For example, the hemophilia group had many updates on AIDS, the epilepsy group on newer medications, the cystic fibrosis group on in utero testing. We can't make informed decisions without this information and one place to get it is in a group.

Get help from other parents. Other parents may be our best resource for answering certain questions. These usually involve the little things, the tips, that ultimately set the tone for how we hope our child will handle her illness.

The parent who pulls out special home-from-the-hospital toys for her youngster or the one who makes a special diet snack of peanut butter faces with raisin eyes has learned this not from a doctor or a book, but from another parent. Other information, such as competent baby-sitters, willing preschools, and likely insurance companies are the kind of gems we can learn here.

Members also help each other practically. Many parents will visit the hospital and stay with someone else's child to give the mother and father some rest.

Advocacy. Support groups can help us with individual advocacy. For example, Annie's kindergartner is supposed to get one hour of special education a day, according to her IEP. The girl has hypothyroidism, along with hearing and visual impairments. But the teacher is frequently sick, and the principal will neither fire her nor hire reliable substitutes. This mother has learned of professionals who could help her through her parent group.

On a more formal level, parents banding together have altered procedures of their local institutions, such as schools and hospitals. One mother who volunteers says, "I believe in being active in the hospital. I can't change my child's illness [heart defect and asthma] but I can change the comfort of his surroundings. I can't lessen other parents' pain, but I can listen to them and it helps me not to drown in my own." On the national level, parents' efforts have made and changed laws.

As beneficial as these groups may be, some parents may have initial reservations. During an interview, Kathy

McGlynn, one of the founding mothers of the Missoula, Montana, group, recalls,

> I felt like I did not belong because my kid was doing just fine on the medication. But I went anyway and realized that we had problems in common—like I've been through the mill with this kid and I have these feelings, too. Originally, I thought I'd go for six months, but it took me two years to unwind. Then I decided that I wanted to give something back. As it happens, my son has developed new difficulties and the group is still helping me.

However, other parents may find that support groups are not for them. Sometimes, their child's condition is much more or less severe than others in the group. One mother, who has a son with a mild form of hemophilia, says, "I feel out of place here because my problems, if you want to call them that, are so small." Another who started her epilepsy support group now has a teenage daughter with intractable seizures. "I've been about everywhere to get my kid better. There's no place left to try. I'm in a different spot from the young mothers coming in with kids who are newly diagnosed."

Going to a group may tell us more than we want to know or are ready for. The father of a newborn son with Down's syndrome and heart defect recalls, "I was approached just after my son was born and I was sure that the last thing I would ever want was to join a club because my son had this illness."

Our needs will change over time and so will our need for this kind of support. Jane went to an oncology group when her infant son was diagnosed as having a kidney tumor. "It was someplace where I didn't have to keep up a front. I could just go and get mad." But now, following surgery and chemotherapy, her son is in remission, and perhaps cured. "It's hard for me to go to a meeting. When someone who has just learned about their child's cancer joins the group, it brings back all the bad memories. I was coming home bummed out and it took me a few weeks to realize that this was no longer doing me any good. A number of moms dropped out, like me, when their children were doing well. They wanted to put this behind them."

Networks and National Meetings
Networks and meetings allow families to learn about the latest in medical breakthroughs, parenting, and advocacy issues on a national level. Some meetings will also have sessions specifically for young adults. Here they can meet others with the same condition and talk about dating, sexuality, and careers.

These contacts are particularly invaluable for the family whose child has a rare condition. "The parents usually know more than the doctors, because they've never seen a case before," says Rosemary, whose son has prune-belly syndrome. Medical breakthroughs for these diseases will not be well publicized and knowing someone across the country may be the best way to find out. Adelle's son has an immunodeficiency disease and recently learned of a new experimental treatment through her parent network.

Learning about how other children and their families function through these networks can be reassuring. Adelle says, "There's a thirteen-year-old boy in Michigan with my son's problem. I call the mother about once a month and compare mouth sores. My son always spits out blood when he brushes his teeth. It was good to find out that this happens and they can live with it."

Parents can also be reassured to find out the level of functioning of older children with the same rare illness. Kay recalls, "When Ted was first born with albinism, we met a five-year-old girl who had the same condition. It was helpful, even though they were years apart. The girl was the same age as my daughter, and I could see that they were doing the same things."

In addition, these national telephone networks serve as an emotional support for parents. Becky is the contact person for fragile X in her state. "I get two or three calls a week. Some parents even consider suicide because they don't know how they can handle it."

GETTING AWAY

Most parents need to get away as a couple and as a family. Although the truth of this is almost universally recognized, the logistics of both can be a considerable challenge for parents of children with special health needs.

As a Couple

A limiting factor in taking time off is usually our guilt caused by either leaving our child or using government-funded services. What Susan Duffy says about overcoming this feeling could apply to many of us. "It's easy to put your life on hold. But we had to make a provision for ourselves. We had to survive in the short term." The obvious can elude us when we are miserable. We need to maintain our own emotional health to be there for the long haul.

Another limiting factor is finding competent help. Some communities have government-funded respite services that are available to those in financial straits. Support groups sometimes generate lists of baby-sitters in their area, including interested nursing and special-education students. Parents can use the brochures put out by their national organization to educate their care giver. A few support groups have formed their own baby-sitting co-op. Some of these programs have been elaborate, including workshops on how to care for the different youngsters.

And some, like Susan and her husband, went into the community and recruited. She recalls, "Once we saw that our daughter's trach was not coming out soon, we had to do something about our sleep deprivation. We set it up so that we could have one good night of sleep a week. Keough went to her godmother. Then we beat the bushes for a competent baby-sitter. We trained three who could care for her so that there was a cadre of people in town who could help us. Then we took off one weekend a month. We should have done this sooner."

As a Family
Time away from daily pressures is good for all families, including ours. Some parents have been quite inventive in how they carry out this normal activity. Susan located a portable suction machine that could stay charged for a day and a half. "Keough needed to be suctioned about ten times a day and four times during the night. We took this machine everywhere—to restaurants, movies, and even on camping trips with Keough."

Sometimes just a small trip can do the job. Renée can no longer travel far from medical centers because of the increasing likelihood of an emergency. Her mother says, "We go to the local resorts here where someone else pulls down the bed and we have a change of scene."

Despite the severe medical conditions, both families have managed getaways. Our solutions will all be different, but they are probably out there. We should be able to find them, as long as we are committed to the normality in our lives.

Notes

CHAPTER 1: DON'T ASK "WHAT DID I DO WRONG?"

1. Frank Deford, *Alex: The Life of a Child* (New York: The Viking Press, 1983): 22–23.
2. Robert and Suzanne Massie, *Journey* (New York: Warner Books, 1976): 82.
3. Susan Duffy et al., *Acceptance Is Only the First Battle* (Missoula: University of Montana Affiliated Program, January 1985).
4. Ann and H. Rutherford Turnbull, eds., *Parents Speak Out: Views from the Other Side of the Two-Way Mirror* (Columbus, Ohio: Charles E. Merrill, 1978): 203–204.
5. Grant Oyler, "Go Toward the Light," *Reader's Digest,* November 1988, p. 250.
6. Helen Featherstone, *A Difference in the Family: Life with a Disabled Child* (New York: Penguin, 1981): 42–43.
7. Joseph Wambaugh, *The Onion Field* (New York: Dell, 1973).
8. Eugenia Gerdes et al., "Perceptions of Rape Victims' Assail-

ants: Effects of Physical Attraction, Acquaintance, and Subject Gender," *Sex Roles* 19 (1988): 141–53.

9. William McWhirter and Debbie Kirk, "What Causes Childhood Leukemia? Some Beliefs of Parents of Affected Children," *Medical Journal of Australia* 145 (October 6, 1986): 314–17.

10. Margaret Stanzler, "Taking the Guilt out of Parenting," *Exceptional Parent,* October 1982, pp. 51–53.

11. Harold S. Kushner, *When Bad Things Happen to Good People* (New York: Avon Books, 1983): 108–109.

CHAPTER 2: IDENTIFY THE PROBLEM AND LEARN HOW TO LIVE WITH IT

1. Susan Duffy et al., *Acceptance Is Only the First Battle* (Missoula: University of Montana Affiliated Program, January 1985): 3–7.

2. Ann and H. Rutherford Turnbull, eds., *Parents Speak Out: Views from the Other Side of the Two-Way Mirror* (Columbus, Ohio: Charles E. Merrill, 1978): 144.

3. Robert and Suzanne Massie, *Journey* (New York: Warner Books, 1976): 156.

4. Ibid.: 158.

5. Jackie Cottrell, article on cystic fibrosis, *Seventeen,* forthcoming.

6. Cheri Register, *Living with Chronic Illness: Days of Patience and Passion* (New York: Free Press/Macmillan, 1987): 29.

7. Cottrell, *Seventeen.*

8. Pat Covelli, *Borrowing Time: Growing Up with Juvenile Diabetes* (New York: Thomas Y. Crowell, 1979): 28.

9. Massie and Massie, *Journey:* 69.

10. Frank Deford, *Alex: the Life of a Child* (New York: The Viking Press, 1983): 71.

11. Julia Ellifrier, "Life with My Sister," *Exceptional Parent,* December 1984, p. 16.

12. Ibid.

CHAPTER 3: DON'T FEEL SORRY

1. Mae Gamble, "Helping Our Children Accept Themselves," *Exceptional Parent,* June 1984, pp. 49–50.

2. Jackie Cottrell, article on cystic fibrosis, *Seventeen,* forthcoming.

3. Susan B. Kleinberg, *Educating the Chronically Ill Child* (Rockville, Md.: Aspen, 1982): 208.

4. Robert K. Massie, Jr., "The Constant Shadow: Reflections on the Life of a Chronically Ill Child," in N. Hobbs and J. M. Perrin, eds., *Issues in the Care of Children with Chronic Illness: A Sourcebook on Problems, Services, and Policies* (San Francisco: Jossey-Bass, 1985): 14.

5. Harilyn Rousso, "Fostering Healthy Self-Esteem," *Exceptional Parent,* December 1984, pp. 9–10.

6. Harold S. Kushner, *When Bad Things Happen to Good People* (New York: Avon Books, 1981): 128.

7. Robert and Suzanne Massie, *Journey* (New York: Warner Books, 1976): 130.

8. Ellen Ruben, "A Former Teen Speaks Out," *Diabetes Forecast* 39, no. 4 (June 1986): 33.

9. Helen Reisner, ed., *Children with Epilepsy: A Parent's Guide* (Kensington, Md.: Woodbine House, 1987): 203.

10. Elizabeth Kornfield, *Dreams Come True* (Boise, Idaho: Rocky Mountain Children's Press, 1986).

11. "Growing Up with Juvenile Arthritis—Perspectives as Adults," 1986 American Juvenile Arthritis Organization Conference videotape (1314 Spring Street NW, Atlanta, GA 30309; 404-872-7100).

CHAPTER 4: TEACH HIM HOW TO CARE FOR HIMSELF

1. Jackie Cottrell, article on cystic fibrosis, *Seventeen,* forthcoming.

2. Pat Covelli, *Borrowing Time: Growing Up with Juvenile Diabetes* (New York: Thomas Y. Crowell, 1979): 32.

3. Mae Gamble, "Helping Our Children Accept Themselves," *Exceptional Parent,* June 1984, p. 50.

4. Frank Deford, *Alex: The Life of a Child* (New York: The Viking Press, 1983): 36–37.

5. Sara Arneson and June Triplett, "How Children Cope with Disfiguring Changes in Their Appearance," *American Journal of Maternal Child Nursing,* November–December 1978, pp. 366–70.

6. Denise Bradley, *What Does It Feel Like to Have Diabetes? A*

Diary of Events in the Life of a Diabetic (Springfield, Ill.: Charles C. Thomas, 1988): 39.

7. Robert and Suzanne Massie, *Journey* (New York: Warner Books, 1976): 132.

8. Jackie Cottrell, *Seventeen*.

9. Helen Reisner, ed., *Children with Epilepsy: A Parent's Guide* (Kensington, Md.: Woodbine House, 1987): 63–64.

10. Earl Grollman, *Explaining Death to Children* (Boston: Beacon Press, 1969): 11–13.

11. Myra Bluebond-Langner, *The Private Worlds of Dying Children* (Princeton, N.J.: Princeton University Press, 1978): 234–35.

12. Associated Press, "Five-Year-Old AIDS Victim Tells Class of His Bad Blood," *Courier* (Prescott, Ariz.), April 26, 1988, p. 2A.

13. Gregory K. Fritz, M.D., Judith William, Ph.D., and Michael Amylon, M.D., "After Treatment Ends: PsychoSocial Sequelae in Pediatric Cancer Survivors," *American Journal of Orthopsychiatry* 58, no. 4 (October 1988): 552–61.

14. Bradley, *What Does It Feel Like:* 167.

15. Covelli, *Borrowing Time:* 75.

16. Massie and Massie, *Journey:* 260.

17. Bradley, *What Does It Feel Like:* 23.

18. Ellen Ruben, "A Former Teen Speaks Out," *Diabetes Forecast* 39, no. 4 (June 1986): 32–33.

19. Jackie Cottrell, *Seventeen*.

20. *Me and My World: All About Epilepsy,* Epilepsy Foundation of America, 1981.

21. *Let Harold Do It: A Boy with Hemophilia* (Berkeley, Calif.: Cutter Laboratories, January 1979).

22. Nancy Sander, *So You Have Asthma Too!* (Glaxo Inc., May 1988; Five Moore Drive, Research Triangle Park, NC 27709).

23. *Kid's Corner: The Mini Magazine Just for Kids with Diabetes,* a publication of the American Diabetes Association (1660 Duke St., Alexandria, VA 22314).

24. Massie and Massie, *Journey:* 129.

25. Bruce Henderson, "A Dog for Kris," *Reader's Digest,* July 1986, pp. 127–31.

26. Dennis Collins: "Snickers and Booze," *Diabetes Forecast* 39, no. 4 (June 1986): 14.

CHAPTER 5: DON'T MAKE HER FRIENDS AND DON'T FIGHT HER ENEMIES

1. Robert and Suzanne Massie, *Journey* (New York: Warner Books, 1976): 134–35.
2. S. A. Richardson, N. Goodman, A. H. Hastorf, S. A. Dornbusch, "Cultural Uniformity in Reaction to Physical Disabilities," *American Sociological Review* 26 (1961): 241–47.
3. Michael Schulman and Eva Mekler, *Bringing Up a Moral Child* (Reading, Mass.: Addison-Wesley, 1985): 81.
4. Ibid.: 90.
5. *Your Child with Special Needs at Home and in the Community* (Association for the Care of Children's Health, 3615 Wisconsin Ave. NW, Washington, DC 20016; 202-244-1801): 11–12.
6. Pat Covelli, *Borrowing Time: Growing Up with Juvenile Diabetes* (New York: Thomas Y. Crowell, 1979): 30.
7. Sandra B. Stein, *About Handicaps* (New York: Walker, 1974): 10.
8. Frank Deford, *Alex: The Life of a Child* (New York: The Viking Press, 1983): 79.
9. J. La Martina, "Uncovering Public Misconceptions About Epilepsy," *Journal of Epilepsy* 2, no. 1 (1989): 45–48.
10. Deford, *Alex:* 66.
11. Ibid.
12. Linda Lowery, *Martin Luther King Day* (New York: Scholastic, 1987).
13. Elizabeth Crary and Marina Megale, *My Name Is Not Dummy* (Seattle: Parenting Press, 1983).

CHAPTER 6: MAKE THE PROFESSIONAL YOUR PARTNER

1. Ann and H. Rutherford Turnbull, eds., *Parents Speak Out: Views from the Other Side of the Two-Way Mirror* (Columbus, Ohio: Charles E. Merrill, 1978).
2. Pat Covelli, *Borrowing Time: Growing Up with Juvenile Diabetes* (New York: Thomas Y. Crowell, 1979).
3. Robert and Suzanne Massie, *Journey* (New York: Warner Books, 1976): 82.
4. *Equals in This Partnership: Parents of Disabled and At-Risk Infants and Toddlers Speak to Professionals* (Washington, D.C.:

National Center for Clinical Infant Programs, 1986): 22. (Copies available from the National Maternal and Child Health Clearinghouse, 38th and R St. NW, Washington, DC 20057; 201-625-8410.)

5. Susan Duffy et al., *Acceptance Is Only the First Battle* (Missoula: University of Montana Affiliated Program, January 1985): 25.
6. Massie and Massie, *Journey:* 85.
7. *Equals in This Partnership:* 23.
8. Helen Featherstone, *A Difference in the Family: Life with a Disabled Child* (New York: Penguin, 1981): 77–78.
9. *Equals in This Partnership:* 29.
10. Featherstone, *A Difference in the Family:* 38.

CHAPTER 7: DON'T WRITE HIS TICKET TO THE FUTURE

1. Jackie Cottrell, article on cystic fibrosis, *Seventeen,* forthcoming.
2. Ellen Ruben, "A Former Teen Speaks Out," *Diabetes Forecast* 39, no. 4 (June 1986): 33.
3. Jack Friedman, "The Quiet Victories of Ryan White," *People,* May 30, 1988, p. 91.
4. Doris Lund, *Eric* (New York: J.B. Lippincott, 1974): 62.
5. Helen Exley, ed., *What It's Like to Be Me* (New York: Friendship Press, 1984): 74.
6. Ruben, "A Former Teen": 33.
7. Denise Bradley, *What Does It Feel Like to Have Diabetes? A Diary of Events in the Life of a Diabetic* (Springfield, Ill.: Charles C. Thomas, 1988): 40.
8. Ibid.: 42.
9. Sarah Halley, "Developing Strategies to Deal with Long-Term Illness," 1986 American Juvenile Arthritis Organization Conference videotape (1314 Spring Street NW, Atlanta, GA 30309; 404-872-7100).
10. Harilyn Rousso, "Disabled People Are Sexual, Too," *Exceptional Parent,* December 1981, p. 21.
11. Michael Schulman and Eva Mekler, *Bringing Up a Moral Child* (Reading, Mass.: Addison-Wesley, 1985): 28.
12. Harilyn Rousso, "Disabled People": 22.
13. Cheri Register, *Living with Chronic Illness: Days of Patience and Passion* (New York: Free Press/Macmillan, 1987): 84.
14. H. R. Turnbull et al., *Disability and the Family: A Guide to*

Decisions for Adulthood (Baltimore: Paul H. Brooks, 1988).

15. Higher Education and the Handicapped Resource Center, the National Clearinghouse on Postsecondary Education for Handicapped Individuals (One Dupont Circle, Suite 800, Washington, DC 20036-1193).

16. National Information Center for Children and Youth with Handicaps (Box 1492, Washington, DC 20036).

17. Edward Carrai and David Linney, *Employment Issues for Hemophilia* (New York: The National Hemophilia Foundation, 1983).

18. Cheri Register, *Living with Chronic Illness.*

19. Pat Covelli, *Borrowing Time: Growing Up with Juvenile Diabetes* (New York: Thomas Y. Crowell, 1979).

20. Ibid.: 127.

CHAPTER 8: STAY IN THE MAINSTREAM

1. Robert and Suzanne Massie, *Journey* (New York: Warner Books, 1976): 147.

2. Ann and H. Rutherford Turnbull, eds., *Parents Speak Out: Views from the Other Side of the Two-Way Mirror* (Columbus, Ohio: Charles E. Merrill, 1978): 39.

3. *AJAO Newsletter* (Atlanta, GA.: American Juvenile Arthritis Organization, Fall 1987): 3.

4. Ibid.

5. Massie and Massie, *Journey:* 145.

6. Cheri Register, *Living with Chronic Illness: Days of Patience and Passion* (New York: Free Press/Macmillan, 1987): 48.

7. Harold S. Kushner, *When Bad Things Happen to Good People* (New York: Avon Books, 1981): 89.

8. Susan Duffy et al., *Acceptance Is Only the First Battle* (Missoula: University of Montana Affiliated Program, January 1985): 3.

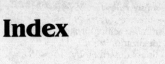

Index

Grateful acknowledgment is made for permission to reprint excerpts from the following copyrighted works:

Alex: The Life of a Child by Frank Deford. Copyright © 1983 by Frank Deford. Reprinted by permission of Viking Penguin, a division of Penguin Books USA Inc.

Journey by Robert and Suzanne Massie. Copyright © 1973, 1975 by Robert Massie, Suzanne Massie, and Robert Massie, Jr. Reprinted by permission of Alfred A. Knopf, Inc.

A Difference in the Family by Helen Featherstone. Copyright © Basic Books, Inc., 1980. By permission of Harper & Row, Publishers, Inc.

When Bad Things Happen to Good People by Harold S. Kushner. Copyright © 1981 by Harold S. Kushner. Reprinted by permission of Schocken Books, published by Pantheon Books, a division of Random House, Inc.

Article by Jackie Cottrell. By permission of *Seventeen* Magazine. Copyright © 1988 by Triangle Communications Inc. All rights reserved.

"Helping Our Children Accept Themselves" by Mae Gamble, *Exceptional Parent Magazine,* June 1984. Reprinted by permission of *Exceptional Parent Magazine,* 1170 Commonwealth Avenue, Boston, MA 02134.

"Fostering Healthy Self-Esteem" and "Disabled People Are Sexual, Too" by Harilyn Rousso, *Exceptional Parent Magazine,* December 1984 and December 1981. Reprinted by permission of *Exceptional Parent Magazine.*

"A Former Teen Speaks Out" by Ellen Ruben, *Diabetes Forecast,* June 1986. By permission of the publishers.

What Does It Feel Like to Have Diabetes? by Denise Bradley. By permission of Charles C Thomas, Publisher, Springfield, Illinois.

Children with Epilepsy: Parents' Guide by Helen Reisner. Reprinted by permission of Woodbine House.

Your Child with Special Needs at Home and in the Community, Copyright 1989 Association for the Care of Children's Health.

What's It Like to Be Me by Helen Exley, by permission of Friendship Press.

Letter from Nancy Woodrow, *American Juvenile Arthritis Newsletter,* Fall 1987. By permission of American Juvenile Arthritis Organization, a member of the Arthritis Foundation.